In defence of councillors

MANCHESTER
1824

Manchester University Press

In defence of councillors

Colin Copus

Manchester University Press

Published by Manchester University Press
Altrincham Street, Manchester M1 7JA
www.manchesteruniversitypress.co.uk

British Library Cataloguing-in-Publication Data
A catalogue record for this book is available from the British Library

Library of Congress Cataloging-in-Publication Data applied for

ISBN 978 0 7190 8832 2 hardback
ISBN 978 1 5261 6255 7 paperback

First published 2016
Paperback published 2022

Typeset by Out of House Publishing

Contents

Preface to the paperback edition

Since 'In Defence of Councillors' was published in 2016 the roles, responsibilities, tasks, functions and pressures experienced by councillors have continued to develop, change and intensify. In that five year period some 28 councils have been abolished and merged to be replaced by eight councils, with a loss of 1,133 councillors and a net loss, taking into account councillors on the new councils, of 420 councillors since the book was published. That figure however, does not include any loss of councillors in the same period as a result of reviews undertaken by the Local Government Boundary Commission for England. Moreover, the Secretary of State's announcement in 2021 that a further 20 councils would be abolished and replaced by four new unitary councils by 2023 could see a loss of anything up to 600 councillors. It won't stop there.

Yet, while we are consistently losing councillors, and with them the space and opportunity for citizens to take part in local self-government and the governance of their communities, the remaining councillors experience greater demands on their time from their councils, their communities and individual citizens seeking help with their cases and grievances, which in turn will have a considerable effect on the private, social and work-life of the councillor. Councillor workload does not reduce as councillors are 'disappeared'.

In addition, the complex networks of public, semi-public, private and third sector bodies, agencies and organisations with which councillors are spending more and more time interacting, continue to develop, become more complex and spend public money, make public policy or commercial decisions that affect the development of communities for decades to come, but do so without a single vote being cast or any direct lines of accountability to the public. Councillors, as our local elected officials, are the only ones with the electoral legitimacy to seek to influence and shape networks and the direction of travel of their participants' strategies and polices. Indeed, councillors are the only ones with the moral and political leverage to seek to hold to account these networks and their participants and demand information, explanation and justification for their actions and inaction.

In 2016, when 'In defence of Councillors' was published few of us would have heard of Zoom or Teams unless we were talking about fast cars or football. But today's Zoom-laden world has provided another challenge to councillors and one which they have meet with considerable skill and adaptability during the Covid-19 national lock-down. Remote meetings not only placed a strain on councillors and on democratic services officers to maintain local democracy, continue with open debate and decision-making and enable public attendance at council meetings, but it also provided ways in which those councillors who might find it difficult to attend a council meeting – those in full-time employment, younger people, and those with family or caring responsibilities - could take part more easily in council business. Remote meetings also provided new opportunities for public engagement, public participation and public and media observation of the work of the councillor.

Yet, it has not all been good news. The infamous Handforth Parish Council zoom meeting has led some to erroneously suggest that we are being buried under a Tsunami of angry, vicious, ill-tempered and badly behaved councillors, which in reality is far, far from the case. Handforth has also lead to renewed calls for a change in the law so that councillors, in England, can be removed from office – if only temporarily – if their behaviour slips below that of a Saint.

We are being lead down a path of treating councillors as naughty children requiring sanction and punishment, rather than asking some simple questions: Why do councillors get angry or lose their temper? Why do they get frustrated? What delays and obstructions are they experiencing from their councils? Are we giving them enough information, advice, support or resources to carry out their work as local politicians? Do we respond quickly and sufficiently enough to their questions and enquiries? Why do some councillors see council officers as obfuscating or concealing details, knowledge or intelligence that would be of use to them? What is it councillors want or need to carry out their representative responsibilities? Why hasn't what they agreed been done, or done in the way they requested? Why haven't things been explained to councillors? Why would a councillor feel misled, denied information and advice, or obstructed and ignored? That some councillors can feel this way indicates the undermining for their status that has occurred over time. Addressing these questions and others like them would be far more valuable to local democracy than kicking councillors off the council. But these questions are not asked as we would ask of almost anyone else, - to understand their behaviour – rather the response is let's just punish councillors by removing them from office. The only people who should be allowed to remove councillors from office are those that elected them in the first place: the voters.

Another part of the image of bad behaviour is that of bullying. Bullying is a term far too easily attributed to the behaviour of councillors, especially as what may appear as bullying to those in the council may be to the electorate an example of an assiduous, hardworking and determined councillor who is fighting their case for them. In these situations one's bully is another's knight in shining armour. When a councillor has a particularly problematic piece of case work around an issue that is damaging an individual or family's well-being, a slow response from the council may elicit a passionate and determined response on behalf of the resident; phone calls, multiple emails, perhaps even expressing anger at the delay.

The councillor occupies a role that is open to accusations of bullying and possible disciplinary procedures for doing their job as they are elected to do.

There is a wide-spread fundamental misunderstanding of the role and work of the councillor – so, as the book does – let's defend them. As elected representatives and local politicians councillors have the right to ask questions, seek explanations and justifications from the political and managerial administration of the council (and external organisations) and to do so in a forthright and robust fashion, should the need arise. They have the right to a timely, informative and accurate response to the issues they raise and to the questions they ask. They have the right to be taken seriously and yes to be addressed with respect and politeness, not from a faux deference but from a genuine respect for, and understanding of, their office and from a cognisance that they are elected by, speak on behalf of, and represent, local residents. By answering the questions above and adopting a different attitude to councillors we renew the respect and the status of local government, local democracy and our municipal institutions – but it all starts with understanding councillors, not denigrating, diminishing and demonising them.

It is easily observable since the publication of 'In Defence of Councillors' that councillors still have an image problem with the public, the media and the government – and with some in local government itself who have too readily accepted a negative image of the councillor. The centre's attitude towards councillors is based on as much a misunderstanding of their work as it is on wishing there were fewer of the pesky blighters to get in the way of what the centre wants to do and how it wants it done. Nowhere is the disdain for councillors more stark or clear than in the recent remote meeting debacle with the Secretary of State insisting that a change in the law was necessary to allow remote meetings to continue beyond the 6th May 2021 (but not being prepared to do it) and then for the courts to judge in his favour. That a cabinet minister and the courts had to decide whether or not councils could meet in specific ways is indicative of our centralised system, lack of trust in local government and disdain for councillors. Equally, little consideration seems to have been given to the health risks to councillors in a pandemic or to the extremely short period of time needed to find suitably 'social distanced' venues for council meetings.

Within our shrinking councillor population there is to be found all human vices and virtues – in that way they are truly representative of the wider population. But the reality of the life of the councillor is that of the elected representative closet to the citizens and communities represented being embedded within and being a part of those communities, where they very often work, will live, socialise and have their network of contacts through local organisations, clubs and societies. They do not spend the best part of the week in London as do our MPs. Councillors are easy to find, accessible, visible, contactable – councillors know the 6.30am phone call, the Christmas Day knock on the door from a constituent with a problem, the late night emails and phone calls. Councillors will know the impossibility of just popping to the shops, the pub, a restaurant or the school playground, without being approached by a member of the public wishing to talk to them about a case work problem, or why the busses don't come down a certain street, or why they can't get an appointment with the GP – the councillor is the representative they can approach and who they expect to sort out the problem – whether the issue is anything to do with the council or not.

Much of what we know about the time councillors spend on council work underestimates the hours they commit to being a councillor because of the difficulties in assessing how much time is taken up by the sort of interactions above. We know that the culling of councillors – which seems to be a long-term policy of the centre – will mean increasing workloads for those that remain. Our system of remuneration for councillors is inadequate and unlike MPs many councillors have a reluctance to increase the allowances they receive – despite the recommendations of independent remuneration panels – in a form of local self-denying ordinance. When councillors do bite the bullet and increase allowances the resultant press and public outrage shows we want to get our local democracy on the cheap. Accusations of 'living the life of Riley off the rates' abounds, despite the rates having been abolished over 30 years ago. But, the consequence of a system which doesn't' recognise the input councillors make to local government and local democracy means many can be out of pocket, suffer career damage or loss of pay at work, lose their jobs or have to give them up to continue with council work.

With the pressures and tensions councillors experience, the nature of our centralised system, the lack of freedom, powers and autonomy they have to govern our localities and the effect on their private lives of council membership, we can reasonably ask: why would anyone do this? But, they do and we should be grateful they do for without councillors, there would be no local self-government at all. So, let's stop knocking, mocking and belittling our councillors and start defending them – read the book to find out in more detail how and why.

Preface

It has long been my aim to write a book that celebrated all those who put themselves through the agonies and ecstasies of election to the office of councillor. The purpose for doing so was partly to redress the balance between a decaying public image of the office and its holders, partly to give deserved public recognition to those that make often incalculable personal sacrifices to become and stay councillors, and partly to acknowledge the contribution councillors make not just to the governance of their communities but also to the governance of the country. But my main aim was to produce a work that reflects my long-held passion for local government, democracy and representation, a passion I know is shared by councillors everywhere.

The office of councillor is probably one of the most misunderstood, criticised and maligned of political positions; indeed many in government, the media and among the public would like to see fewer councillors. Yet, the office of councillor is one of the most fundamental political offices in any democracy, on which rest the (supposedly) higher offices of state. It is also an office which enables communities to govern themselves, as far as the centre will tolerate, and, even in highly centralised systems, it can provide the localities with a line of defence against any central power. But it is also a position from which councillors can co-operate with and work alongside any government for the betterment of their communities. It is an office that makes demands on its holders, not just politically, but personally, on their careers, families, friends, neighbours and on their personal and private time – but, as this book shows, councillors give willingly of this time and do so knowing the personal costs it may entail.

Local government, particularly in England, is seen by central government as a mechanism for implanting its own policies and bringing about the social, economic, political and technological changes it wishes to introduce. In England, the centre also sees local government and councillors as somehow imperfectly formed, not quite right yet, in need of constant tinkering or wholesale overhaul. Thus, government will inquire, investigate, report, restructure and change the powers, functions, responsibilities, tasks, duties and expectations of local government and the office of councillor. The centre will be tempted to continue with this process of reform and reshaping until it feels as though it has finally got local government and councillors right – or until the right to continually tinker or radically reform the office no longer rests with the centre. So, change and adapting to change is a constant part of what councillors need to do. And it is not just centrally inspired change with which they must cope. Other forces impact on local government and on the roles of the councillor; globalisation, urbanisation, Europeanisation, economic downturn, community assertiveness, political cynicism and the often cultural and religious fracturing of communities, all pose new challenges for councillors.

The dynamic and rapidly changing environment within which councillors operate means that they are faced with finding new and innovative solutions to new and challenging problems of public policy. But they have to do so knowing that, certainly within the English context, their room for political manoeuvre is limited and the capacity to govern their areas is also limited in nature. Councillors have few hard governing powers, so when dealing with complex networks of public and private bodies they require skills of compromise, persuasion and negotiation so as to draw those beyond the council into some shared agenda for the locality's future prosperity. At the same time, councillors need to hold a whole host of public bodies to account for the policies they develop, the actions they take and the money they spend. The political skills of negotiation, compromise, coalition and alliance building, persuasion and simple doggedness are at a premium for our councillors and it is these soft powers that are their main resource when governing their areas.

The councillor is, above all, a political (though not necessarily party political) representative who holds office through a political process and whose position and actions are legitimised by the public vote. Councillors not only engage in governing networks to attempt to influence and shape what others do, they are also elected representatives of an area within a larger area – at least in the English context where councils are divided for electoral purposes into wards or divisions. The councillor needs to devote loyalty and operational activity to that ward or division, seeking to obtain resources for it, solve problems located within it, and deal with very specific problems and issues that arise from it. At the same time, councillors must balance the needs of that specific area with the overall needs of the council, reconciling local representation within a broader governing activity. Indeed, councillors live in close proximity with those they represent, govern and serve, and that proximity, that location of councillors within the communities from which they are elected, means that they are among the most accessible of politicians. Moreover, they also experience, first-hand, the outcomes of their own policy decisions or the policy decisions that government requires them to implement.

The life of the councillor is one big balancing act, or rather a constant process of reconciling competing pressures and demands, political and personal, and doing so while at the same time being under constant scrutiny from the local public and press and from higher levels of government.

Being a councillor has a profound effect on the private, public, family, work and social life of those elected to office. Yet, the support they receive for the various facets of their council work from the councils of which they are members is often inadequate and fails to recognise the demands made on elected members as politicians, case workers and local representatives. In addition, fear of being seen to be politically biased further limits the resources and support offered to councillors and places additional constraints on their room for manoeuvre. It is in closely observing how councillors operate under such constraints that a growing admiration develops of the work they undertake, of the commitment they display and of the achievements they secure.

This book has been a long time in the coming – as my very patient publisher will no doubt testify. It did not result from any one research project; rather it was something that emerged, at least in the thought processes, very early on in my political – rather than academic – activities. I first stood for election as councillor in a double by-election in 1984 at the age of 25. In my election material of the time I added a couple of years to that age because I didn't think anyone would vote for someone in their mid-twenties. It didn't matter, because the voters saw through the ruse and I lost that by-election, although my good friend and colleague, Steve Timms (now a long-serving MP), did win one of the seats. I was finally elected for the same seat at the full council elections in 1986, when my party won every seat on the council and I polled the highest votes in the borough. (I never checked that particular piece of information I was given, just in case someone was having me on.) Anyway, after working solidly for almost four years to win the seat and become a councillor – I hated every minute of it. But that didn't stop me being elected to a county council in 1993 and a district council in 1994. But on each council I was a one-term wonder – worked hard to get elected but couldn't quite make it as a councillor – although I did chair a major committee on the district council.

My inability to put up with the demands of the office with the same patience and tolerance as my councillor colleagues just served to increase my admiration for those who endure the workload, the interference with their life, the relentless round of meetings and the demands of the party whip. The book is intended not just as a contribution to the debate about the role of councillors and the office of councillor but it is also hoped that it will be a contribution to finalising what we want the office to do in this country and to developing a public respect for the office and its holders. It is to all of those individuals that have heard the returning officer say: 'I hereby declare that [insert name] is duly elected', that this book is dedicated and whose lives it explores.

Acknowledgements

It would not have been possible to write a book entitled 'In defence of councillors' without the co-operation, enthusiasm and interest displayed by all those councillors who so willingly gave their time to support my research and writing. To those and to all their colleagues who I spoke to and observed in a range of events that led to the book, a sincere thank you is due. Not just a thank you for support in the project but also a thank you for the time, energy, commitment you give and the personal sacrifices you all make to represent, support and work with your local communities. Without our councillors, our democracy and politics would be incomplete.

The book is dedicated to all councillors.

I'd like to thank Tony Mason from Manchester University Press. His advice, patience, flexibility and guidance made it possible for me to continue and complete this book. He is an excellent colleague.

Again, I have to say thank you to Julia, my long-suffering wife, and to my two daughters, Emma and Harriet – you three really don't know how much I owe you or how much you putting up with my mood swings when writing really means: thank you.

1

The constancy of change

Introduction

There have been many centrally inspired investigations, inquiries, reports, questions and examinations that have explored, expounded upon and deliberated, one way or another and from one perspective or another, the role of the councillor elected to serve as a political representative in local government (Committee on the Management of Local Government (hereafter HMSO/Maud), 1967a and 1967b; Committee of Inquiry into the Conduct of Local Authority Business (hereafter HMSO/Widdicombe), 1986a and 1986b; DCLG, 2007; Communities and Local Government Committee, 2013; House of Commons Political and Constitutional Reform Committee, 2013; TSO, 2013a, b). Many of those investigations were focused more broadly on local government itself, but no exploration of local government is complete without a serious consideration of what those we elect to our councils can and should do. Understandably, but frustratingly, each of those investigations has set out to understand the office of councillor by placing it in a contemporary setting, asking a series of contemporary questions, identifying existing inadequacies in the office (and often in the office-holders) and posing solutions from a contemporary perspective. That process, however, means that what we want from councillors will always face investigation, pressure for change and assessments based on the notion that the office is not fit for the current purpose, whatever that purpose may be.

These various investigations have asked some fundamental and recurring questions about the role of councillors, to which varying responses have been given. Those questions about councillors are typified thus: what do we want them to do? What is their purpose and role? What powers and responsibilities do we want them to have? Do we want them to be local leaders or take a lead from central government? Are they politicians and policy-makers or elected managers of public services? Who do we want them to be and what do we want them to look like? How many should there be and where? And, should they be professional paid politicians or lay, volunteer individuals? Each of these questions opens up a myriad of other questions, which will be explored in this book.

The answers given when the above questions have been asked about councillors have so far been incompletely formulated. They have often been merely a

product of their time, lacking in foresight or a clear appreciation of local representative democracy, local government and the contribution it makes to the
overall pattern and quality of English governance. While serious investigations
by commissions and committees of inquiry (see HMSO, 1967a, b, 1986a, b) have
been set to recast the structure, processes and internal and external workings of
local government and have also considered, in depth, the changing demands and
expectations of the office of councillor, they have addressed those issues from
pre-existing conceptions of the place and position of local government within
an overall governing system. Such system-imposed constraints on thinking have
shaped the ultimate outcomes of such inquiries and have reflected and reinforced
the subordinate position of local government and the inferior nature of local representative office, when compared to what are seen as higher levels of representation and political activity.

Not only have answers to questions about the purpose of councillors and their
roles and powers reflected the subordinate position of local government in the
political system of the country, they have also reflected an ideological view of
the role of local democracy and government. Both left and right of the political
spectrum have, for different reasons and with different intended policy outcomes,
arrived at the same conclusion about the position of local government and those
that serve at that level as elected office-holders. That ideological collusion and its
consequences will be explored in detail in this book.

The recurrent theme that underpins all questions about the role of the councillor is that this level of elected representative, unlike those at other levels of
government, is somehow under-developed, in need of constant reshaping and
reappraisal, disconnected from those represented, and is a product of a lower level
of governing capacity and ability when compared to central government. Such
views display a lack of clarity and understanding about the office of councillor that
often arises from a disregard for local representative democracy as a fundamental
underpinning to a wider democratic state.

Compounding the fluctuations that have affected thinking about the role of the
councillor is the reluctance in England, lamented by Sharpe (1970), to theorise
about 'political institutions and local government in particular'. That reluctance
and a similar disinclination to theorise about the role of councillors as well as local
government have, as we shall see, undermined attempts to answer important questions about the office of councillor. Yet the way we understand the office and what
councillors themselves do and think about their role are prone to continual pressure to change. Thus, we need to distinguish between those elements of the office
of councillor that may have an enduring characteristic and those that are shaped
by external pressure to which the role of the local representative must respond. It
is also necessary to distinguish between the office and the office-holder. Political
institutions cannot be judged solely by the actions or qualities of those that hold
them, they must also be judged by the powers, functions, tasks and responsibilities
that are located within the office and with the status and standing of that office.

The distinction between office and office-holder is a continual theme of this exploration and defence of councillors.

Pressure for change on local government exerted by other levels of government – whether that is central, regional or state governments – is a powerful force in determining the nature of the responsibilities that rest with the office of councillor and the balance between the soft and hard powers at their disposal. The constitutional position of local government partly determines how other levels of government can force change through legislation or may have to encourage or cajole change in the powers, roles and responsibilities of the councillor as a representative, a decision-maker and a governor of a locality and municipal institution. It is these other levels of government higher up in the chain of national governance that exert pressures for change on local government. This may be either through the broad brush of policy reform aimed at a range of policy areas but which in turn have an effect on the role of local government, or from policy aimed specifically at addressing weakness in local government and the officer of councillor, as perceived by those other levels of government.

Alongside how the centre may view local government is the pressure exerted by the shift from local government to local governance. This has been well documented by scholars such as Rhodes (1996), Kooiman (2003), Hajer and Wagenaar (2003), Stoker (2004) and Geddes (2006), to name a few. In contrast, less well documented is what the complexity of governance networks and a reshaping of the state has meant for councillors and for the activities they undertake, the pressures they experience, the interactions they engage in, the relationships they forge with communities and citizens and the way their roles and the expectations placed on them develop. Yet local democracy is representative democracy, and the councillor as a local representative occupies a central position in the dynamics of local politics. Representative, democratic local government and the councillors that are elected to it operate alongside, often in partnership with but certainly cognisant of, those local and supra-local bodies which now produce such a crowded landscape of provision and responsibility for the governing framework of the state. To these factors can be added an international dimension as the forces of urbanisation, globalisation and Europeanisation recast the contexts within which localities, local governments and councillors operate (see Le Gales, 1998, 2002; Kersting and Vetter 2003; Denters and Rose, 2005; Berg and Rao, 2005).

Another force for change on the office of councillor emanates from local communities and local citizens themselves. Today these display both assertiveness in presenting councillors with their views and unwillingness to simply accept decisions and policies to which they are opposed. Gyford (1986), writing for the Widdicombe Committee, stressed the uneasy relationship between what he called 'sectionalist politics' and representative democracy. Public assertiveness that challenges long-held notions of representative democracy, at least in the local context, now comes with official sanction as central government rhetoric has encouraged greater public participation in local government (DETR, 1998a, b; DCLG, 2006;

TSO, 2011). Greater public engagement with local government and enhanced public participation in local policy-making is a theme which echoes across Europe (Delwit et al., 2007; Michels and de Graaf, 2010). Yet such inducements to bring citizens and councils closer together place the councillor at the centre of tensions between representative and participatory democracy. They expose the councillor to competing sources of legitimacy: the public vote or the public at large. Part of the role of the councillor is now to manage those representative–participative tensions and to reconcile competing views and solutions to the same local problems.

Thus, the office of councillor does not exist or develop in isolation from external factors; it is not simply the product of what individual councillors do, or of what any one council expects of its elected members. Neither is it shaped by its location in a single place alone. Moreover, it is an office subject to differing political and ideological interpretations of its importance, role and place not just within the government of the localities but also in the governing fabric of the nation. Differing political interpretations of the purpose of local councillors operate within and beyond the locality within which they are situated and play themselves out within governance networks at all levels. There is, however, something deeper here than how party-political differences display themselves in the way councillors conduct their activities and develop the approach they take towards being an elected representative and elected member of a council. Rather, there is a collective view, taken by councillors themselves and by politicians at other levels of government – including those that have been councillors – about the very nature of the office of councillor, and those views shape that office and the role it plays in the governing of local communities.

But we have to go beyond the views of politicians, policy-makers and the public, beyond the findings of various commissions and inquiries and beyond the past and contemporary setting of local government if we are to start to answer the questions: what is the purpose of the office of councillor and what should councillors be able to do? Moreover, we have to move beyond any view of councillors that is inspired by the needs and opinions of central government alone if the governing capacity of the localities, and with it the office of councillor, is to be strengthened. Indeed, the temptation of political institutions and offices is to allow the contemporary setting to dictate the shape and purpose of political interactions and the architecture within which they are housed – particularly at the local level. That temptation is great for all politicians sitting within institutions other than local government. It is even more tempting when central government has little to restrain it when it comes to reshaping and redesigning other governing institutions – such as is the case for English local government.

In addressing the questions posed so far, the book examines the complex world inhabited by the councillor. It explores the experiences, expectations, pressures, problems, demands, motivations and rewards in relation to the individuals elected to serve as councillors. It also examines the office itself and considers not only what the roles, responsibilities, powers and functions of those we elect to our councils are but what they should be. This chapter goes on to set out the key themes of the book and those aspects that will be examined and explored throughout. The next section outlines the central issues which the book will examine in more detail. The third provides an outline of the broad constitutional context within which local government and councillors must conduct their activities. It does this to introduce a much wider discussion of the issue which is a constant theme of the book, a theme reflected in the title, the defence of councillors. The fourth section sets out some of the conceptions and misconceptions about councillors to set the background for the issues that the book will explore. The fifth section provides the structure of the book and details of the research on which it is based.

A complex and unbounded office

Much of what we know about councillors' working lives, the activities they undertake and the multifaceted nature of their roles comes from a number of single-council case studies (Birch, 1959; Bealey et al., 1965; Clements, 1969; Dearlove, 1973; Glassberg, 1981; Goss, 1988). Indeed, there is a rich, wide and deep source of such case-based material that seems, unfortunately, to have dried up recently. A common theme running through such material is an appreciation of how councillors are typical, commonplace citizens of their communities, but at the same time, they are also holders of a unique political position that separates them from the citizens whose trust, confidence and votes they have sought and been granted. We also learn, not surprisingly, that councillors are rooted in a place, a locality, a community that has been expressed and defined through a geographical setting – even though the council itself may be an artificial construct (Copus, 2010a).

Proximity to the locality distinguishes councillors from other types of elected representatives sitting on other governing institutions and is another virtue of the office. Many elected representatives sitting in regional and national chambers may be able to claim that they also live in the constituencies that they represent in the Parliament, but this is not considered a necessity or requirement of their office. The councillor, however, is of the locality in a way that is not expected of other politicians. Indeed, in some systems, moving from one part of the country to another would make it difficult to gain enough acceptance locally to make seeking election to a council an easy process (Verhelst et al., 2013).

Yet locality need only mean the council area and not the immediate community located within a ward or other electoral division; councillors do not have to live within the ward they represent, and in that respect, they parallel politicians elected to other institutions beyond the local. As Hampton (1970) pointed out, those that are politically motivated will find a convenient ward from which to represent their fellow citizens, even if that is on the other side of town from where they themselves live. Moreover, candidates from political parties have also distinguished themselves from other local citizens in that they are one of the less than 1 per cent of people across the country that chooses to join a political party (Kelly, 2010; Keen, 2014). Moreover, English local government is now fully party-politicised (Wilson and Game, 2011), with around 90 per cent of all councillors being members of one of the three main political parties. Thus, while attention is often given to increasing the numbers of women or ethnic minority councillors as a way of achieving a particular definition of 'representation' and 'representativeness' (see Pitkin, 1972), a bigger question of diversity and representativeness exists (certainly in the English context): what is to be done about the representation of citizens that are not members of political parties?

Newton (1976: 115–16) pointed out that while democratic theory makes it clear that the representative – in this case the councillor – should take into account the 'interest and well-being of those he or she represents', this says little about how they should act, how they define the interests of those represented, or what it is that the representative represents. It also says little about how councillors respond to and represent the perceived needs of sections of the community or the interests of gender, age, ethnicity or any other social categorisation. Thus, other tensions that must be reconciled include those between the community, the council, the party and the councillor as an individual with her or his own take on local political problems and priorities. Tensions between the roles of the councillor still remain to be satisfactorily explored, particularly as far as councillors' own perceptions and beliefs are concerned. To fully understand the developing roles of the councillor and to make sense of how and why councillors act the way they do, we must examine the attitudes, values and perceptions they have of the office they hold. Moreover, we must explore how these assumptions play into shaping the office of councillor.

An empirical investigation of the way councillors approach local representation, the sense they make of it and how they understand the experiences from which they develop their thinking, is a vital part of exploring the office of councillor. In addition, consideration must be given to theories of representation to further conceptualise the purpose and place of the councillor within government and governance and as a governor. Despite the continued centrality of the councillor to local government and democracy, the trends and patterns that have emerged in the development of their various roles are nevertheless under-theorised and under-conceptualised. We can reasonably assume that, over time, the conduct and behaviour of councillors, as well as their powers, functions and responsibilities, have altered from those that are traditionally associated with the councillor as an expression of the involvement of laymen in local representative democracy (Mouritzen and Svara, 2002).

In addition to the councillor's role as a political representative, two other dimensions have been referred to which also need clarifying. They are: the position councillors hold as decision-makers and as governors of a council area and the council as an organisation. The first of these – the decision-maker – could be taken as part of the role of a representative, especially given the existence of executive councillors of one sort or another across the world of local government. For the purposes of this book, decision-making is separated from the wider representative activities, role and purpose of the councillor, to enable an exploration of what decision-making means for a very specific political office – the councillor – in the very specific setting of local government.

Coupled with the above argument, the book will also stress the notion of the councillor as a governor of both a council area and the council as an organisational setting and bureaucratic machine. The concept of governor is used here again to distinguish a particular facet of the councillor's role from that of a representative and decision-maker. The term is not used to imply 'governorship' in the more traditional sense of the holder of the political office of 'Governor' (in the USA or Japan, for example), as a politician directly elected to executive sub-national office, normally at state level and overseeing other governmental agencies (Patterson and Caldeira, 1983; Reed, 1986; Adams and Kenny, 1989; Michio, 1997). Rather, the term governor is used in this book to denote the councillor as a politician engaged in controlling a large-scale enterprise (the council), either as an executive member or as a scrutineer, but one who also seeks to influence the world beyond the institution that is the council, to shape but not control the policies and decisions of others and to do this because they are the holder of an office by virtue of an electoral mandate. Thus, governor is used to indicate the outward-facing political role of the councillor when engaging in governance networks: a governor of governance.

Assessing how those holding the office of councillor act as representatives, decision-makers and governors, and what they achieve in each of these dimensions, provides a framework within which to consider the multifaceted nature of local political office. Moreover, it provides a way of conceptualising the varied roles of the councillor to examine the tensions experienced by the councillor in those roles; to analyse those local, regional and national factors that support or hinder the councillor in carrying out those roles; to explore councillors' role perceptions; and to examine how different and shifting political, institutional and democratic arrangements and trends have influenced the development of the office of councillor.

By taking the approach outlined above, we can systematically explore how the councillor as an elected local politician acts in relation to those that elect her or him as a caseworker, a gate-keeper to power, a negotiator or disseminator of and conduit for political opinion, and an overseer of the council of which they are a member. It also allows an exploration of how they interact with others within the complexity of governing networks.

Governing within governance

Councils and councillors do not inhabit centre stage in their locality but face a struggle for engagement themselves in a complex series of governance networks, as well as facing challenges from their own neighbourhoods (see Sorensen, 2006; Lowndes and Sullivan, 2008). The shift from local government to local governance places an additional burden on councillors, who must react to citizens' views as well as the policies of their parties, and transmit (should they so choose) those views into the complex, multi-layered networks within which councillors confront higher-level organisational players (Stoker, 2004). Councillors, by virtue of holding an elected office, have a legitimacy and moral leverage lacking in most of those with whom they must now work within the complexity of modern governance (Saward, 2003). Councillors' roles within governance networks require an outward-focused and combative style of interaction with those developing public policy and spending public money without a mandate from the citizen. This also requires councillors to forge new alliances and coalitions within diversified governing arrangements that mean they must operate politically beyond the comfortable and familiar confines of the council and its organisational structure for decision-making (Cole and John, 2001; Stoker, 2004). It is here that we need to explore the governing capacity that councillors and councils possess and how, if at all, they can enhance that governing capacity.

The governing capacity of the councillor and council can be defined as the ability to: focus resources (including legal, moral and political resources) and activity to transform their own political and governing potential and strengthen it so as to bring about political action; draw together coalition partners and allies around policy objectives; contain or exploit conflict; process and conceptualise policy problems so as to construct and implement solutions; innovate politically and take risks; and generate additional resources to take action that will influence or bring about change in the policies or behaviours of citizens, communities or private and public bodies. Governing capacity is either employed individually by the councillor or collectively through the council as a political and bureaucratic structure. Thus, the various roles that the councillor plays must be placed in the context of the council of which he or she is a member, as well as in the context of the wider governing network within which he or she must operate and interact with 'a more diverse and varied set of institutions and processes' (Stoker, 2004: 9). It is how councillors move beyond the confines of the council to influence or shape the actions and policies of others, often better resourced and geographically larger than the council, that opens up the prospect of democratising those networks and their participants.

In 2000, Burns asked 'can local democracy survive governance?' because, as he argued, local governance was inherently functionally fragmented and this was exemplified by how different organisations developed and formed formal or informal policy partnerships. Those policy partnerships could further fragment local democracy as an organisational arrangement, and it is worth quoting Burns at length here when he comments:

> it is essential that the local governance system has built into it the capacity to integrate and mediate the different fractures … and to ensure that it has the

organisational structures within which strategy can be developed. If these issues are not addressed, then the idea of local democracy as it has been advanced over the past two decades must be fundamentally altered.

(2000: 970)

Burns's central concern is still apparent: governance has fundamentally altered local democracy and it is now more accurate to refer to local democracies rather than local democracy, because the development of governance networks has allowed different forms of democracy to develop, within which councillors must continue to operate. What has emerged as a result of governance networks easing local government aside are four forms of local democracy: network, market, participatory and representative (see Haus and Sweeting, 2006). However, network, market and participatory democracies, of course, operate within a representative democratic framework at the local level and are not therefore forms of democracy which exclude councillors. Rather, councillors bring democratic legitimacy and processes to each of those forms and their related approaches to representation, decision-making and governing.

Given institutional arrangements and long-standing practices at the local level, participatory, network, and market forms of democracy can only develop to a limited extent. The different processes of democracy are therefore most appropriately thought of as variations within an overarching framework of representative democracy. But representative local democracy now sits within a much wider network form of democracy that extends beyond the territory of the council on which local representative democracy is focused. While the concept of governance has recently been questioned by Stoker (2011), and despite extensive studies of governance and the impact of networks on local government, councils have always, to one degree or another, had to work alongside or co-operate with a host of external agencies, partners and organisations. What the concept of governance crystallises is that councillors and councils now compete in a series of ongoing contests with organisational players over whom they have little 'governing' control but with whom they must interact, negotiate and compromise in order to shape the preferences of the network participants to share the preferences of the elected council. It also recognises that much governing through networks goes on without democratic input. It is the consequences of this contextual hog-tying of councillors and the council of which they are a member that shapes much of the activities and effectiveness of councillors as representatives, decision-makers and governors and to which we shall return throughout this book, particularly in Chapter 4.

Constitutional context and local government

There is another dimension to the world of the councillor that has to be considered for the contextual setting which it provides. That is the constitutional position of any system of local government. As a clear level of government subordinate to the centre, local government in England lacks even the most basic constitutional protection, including the right to continued existence. While this is not unusual in a unitary state (with or without a written constitution), it is not a necessary corollary of such constitutional arrangements. But, for England, it is the British central government that ultimately decides the shape, population size, responsibilities, powers and functions of councils and the number of elected members a council will have. It is central government which can, and does, merge, amalgamate or abolish individual councils, or even entire layers of local government. Moreover, it is the centre that decides the powers, functions, tasks, roles and responsibilities of the office of councillor.

While central government will consult with councils and local communities about the nature of local government, it is not bound by the outcomes of such consultation, nor are citizens given the final say over what happens to their councils or councillors. The British unitary system is based on top-down parliamentary sovereignty not a bottom-up citizen locality-based democracy which respects and provides political authority to its institutions of sub-national government and to those individuals elected to them as councillors. Further, English local government, like many of its overseas counterparts, is a dual-purpose institution. First, it provides an additional layer of democracy, political representation and engagement to that provided by parliamentary politics, and it allows for the diversity of political views and opinions expressed by communities to find outlet in an authoritative and elected body. Moreover, those elected to serve on councils have a mandate granted to them to represent their fellow citizens, make local political decisions and govern a council and its area. Councillors do this, of course, from their specific constitutional position and cognisant of the associated legal and financial constraints placed on them as a result of their constitutional status.

Thinkers such as De Tocqueville, Mill and Toulmin Smith have argued that local governing institutions are essential to freedom and liberty and can act as a barrier to an over-powerful central state, and moreover that local government is an integral part of any democratic system. But if it is to fulfil those worthy aims, local government must have power, responsibilities and freedoms for its councillors. Within a representative system of government, representative institutions, including those at the local level, have a premium over a wider interpretation of local democracy – that is the myriad of interactions that take place between citizens and communities within the confines of the boundaries of any one council. Local democracy is a linked but distinct concept from local government, and they both have a place in the overall democratic fabric of any society. But those councils legitimised by the public vote are in a governing position to make choices between competing demands and to reconcile competing views within the locality. Yet the question remains: do councils and councillors have the constitutionally defined position to make those choices, develop local policy to solve local problems and to act in a governing fashion within their localities?

Second, and alongside its politically representative and governing role, local government is also responsible for the provision or oversight of public services vital to nations where the state has taken the major responsibility for social welfare, social cohesion, the development of infrastructural integrity and economic development. Local government does not need to be the direct provider of the public services for which it is ultimately responsible. Governance theory, as we have seen, has explained the effects of a neo-liberal hegemony that pervades much thinking about local government and the role of councillor, which was given spur through the now fading fashion of new public management (NPM). Neither governance nor NPM gave much credence to the political or elected role of local government and councillors, whatever constitutional position it holds.

The stronger local government and councillors are and the greater the power that rests with local political leaders, the harder it is for neo-liberal advocates to depoliticise and constitutionally neuter local government by transforming the model of democracy within which it is located from a representative to a market form. In the latter, democracy is not achieved through the activities of candidates, parties, communities and voters, but rather through citizens acting as consumers or customers of public services, around whom the usual paraphernalia of customer-focused private enterprise can be constructed in the public realm.

The link between new and developing models of local government and the neo-liberal project for depoliticising local government must be made, not just because it reflects a current trend of thinking about the purpose of local politics and local politicians, but also because the constitutional status of local government influences the range of strategies that central authorities must devise to ensure they can influence the form, process and outcomes of local politics and the activities of councillors. A sub-national governing system with a strong constitutional position poses other tiers of government a different set of questions and challenges compared to a system where local government is constitutionally weak. In the English context, local government is collectively and individually a constitutionally weak entity, and consequently, councillors are constitutionally weak politicians, especially as their powers and their ability to take political action rests in the hands of the centre. The book addresses that constitutional frailty in Chapter 7 and provides a solution in Chapter 8.

Past, present and future

An objective of this book is to build from past approaches, understandings and expectations of what the office of councillor is about to then move through the current contemporary setting and to use both to theorise and conceptualise the office of councillor. The complex and often chaotic world that is local politics is given form and some shape in the representative institution of the council to which councillors are elected. But the council is only one part of the dynamic of local politics, although it is one that has experienced a shifting importance since the inception of democratically elected government. Gone are the days when local newspapers would report, verbatim, the speeches that councillors made in council (Jones, 1969; Hennock, 1973), because the status and standing of councillors has declined, and along with it the public resonance of their pronouncements and debates.

The idea of the sovereign council had diminished long before council executives arrived in English local government as a result of the Local Government Act 2000. Indeed, the party group meeting – or at least the group meeting of the ruling party group – had long replaced council as the place where important local decisions were made and policy developed and decided upon (Copus, 2004). Although local democracy is still representative, and the council meeting, of one sort or another, is the place where councillors do much but by no means all of their business, the councillor is no longer the only voice in town. Now councillors are confronted with a complex array of groups, communities and individuals organised or not organised, all of whom seek to influence what the councils do.

Yet the journey from where councillors were in what, for convenience if not accuracy, are often described as the 'golden days' of local government, somewhere in the late Victorian period, to where they are now is an informative and necessary part of understanding the office. It is also necessary to understand this journey in order to appreciate why the office of councillor and councillors as individuals face their current contemporary status and standing. Attention will be given in this book to examining the public image of the councillor, which is often the product of negative media reporting and government rhetoric and criticism rather than a reflection of the work councillors undertake and the sacrifices they make in carrying out their duties.

It is not unusual for councillors to get a 'bad press' given the commonplace anti-local government rhetoric which emerges from central government (irrespective of political control) and groups such as the Taxpayers' Alliance and from the national and local media. Stories of increases in councillor expenses, of trips abroad paid for by the council-tax payer, rumours of corruption and the constant whiff of scandal are the stuff on which a folklore about councillors has been steadily developing. Even the government's recent abolition of councillor pensions announced in the 2013 local financial settlement, which allocated funding to England's councils, was a practical outcome of a rhetorical shaping of public perceptions. The announcement by then local government minister Brandon Lewis MP (2012) was couched in terms of a £7 million saving for the taxpayer (thus posing councillors as receiving a pension from the pockets of the local taxpayer). But a key part of the rhetorical thrust was that councillors are and should be lay volunteers who *should* give willingly of their time for little or no reward and certainly not for a pension. The official mind and the idea of councillors and a 'bad press' are examined in Chapter 7.

Yet, by contrast to the rhetorically shaped set of public perceptions and image of the councillor, we know little of the reality of their experiences or of the intense nature of the pressures, demands and activities to which they are subject, or how those that seek to represent, serve and govern at the local level manage the work–life–council tensions (see Barron et al., 1991). We also need to explore more how councillors set about energising political action and change within their communities or deal with the growing expectations they face from those communities and what effect this has on other facets of their lives. The book will challenge the negative public perception, an almost cartoonesque caricature of councillors, by exploring the experiences of councillors and the political and public life that they lead. It will do this partly to deliberately rebalance public perceptions and also to understand the effect such an image has on the office of councillor and the individuals that hold that office, as well as on local democracy and politics more generally.

There is an element of local democracy and politics that takes place with little or no link to the council, representative democracy or formal, traditional representative politics. That parallel democracy that operates around the activities of neighbourhoods, communities, self-help groups and other bodies is not the subject of this book, but it is an aspect of local politics that the councillor will be aware of and may even be engaged in to some degree; it is a facet of local politics and democracy that will brush up against representative democracy as the occasion dictates. However, it is councillors that are the focus and subject of this book and this parallel local democracy will only be explored where it engages with councillors as elected representatives and the council as a governing institution.

While it is neither possible nor desirable to strip the office of councillor from its institutional setting, the book focuses more on councillors as elected representatives than on local government as the architectural structure that houses the office. It does this in order to crystallise an understanding that recognises competing visions of local representation and to allow us to think about the role unhindered by existing preconceptions and ideas, and to avoid viewing what councillors do as simply a product of the organisation in which they are located. But the book far from ignores local government as an organisational setting, as it would be wrong to isolate councillors completely from the representative body to which they are elected.

Thus, by considering the office of councillor as multidimensional and occupying multi-spaces, we can examine it not only for its current role and expectations but from a normative perspective. Equally, by somewhat dislodging the councillor from the council, we can understand the office from a new viewpoint, unconstrained by contemporary ideas or pressures, allowing new ideas about how it might develop to emerge. The book develops ideas about how the office of councillor could be constructed not only to meet contemporary pressures but also to contribute more broadly to a strengthening of local political representation and action and to the governing of a locality.

Structure of the book and research

The book does not draw on one research project alone. Rather it draws on a number of related research projects in which I have been involved and which span a number of years. Those projects were both national and international in nature, but the common thread running through each was that it explored the roles, responsibilities, attitudes, assumptions and political lives of councillors. So, the book uses as its basis the results of a collective body of research and draws on a range of research findings from linked but distinct projects. In addition, the book employs the results of qualitative research which was conducted to supplement the existing data. The following research was carried out just for the purpose of the book: eighty-seven interviews, twenty sets of participant observations, nineteen focus groups (of six councillors each), nine group discussions (of varying sizes) and documentary analysis of council material. In all, some 237 councillors took part in the research specifically for this book. Such research methods and drawing on different projects is designed to provide a deep, full and rich understanding of political action and interaction and of the reasons why and how councillors behave in certain ways.

In addition, the book deliberately draws from an eclectic range of sources, projects, events, meetings – some planned, some chance – interactions, informal discussions as interviews, social interactions, and informal observations and settings. It also unashamedly makes use of the wide range of interactions that I have had over the last twenty-five or so years as a researcher, working with councillors on research projects, training and development events and by attendance at conferences, seminars, workshops and other events with councillors.

In developing and researching the book, the approach adopted is that every event and interaction involving councillors is a research event. The book is therefore almost a work of political anthropology; I have lived, eaten, worked and played with councillors in their natural habitat; he can interpret and understand their strange language and their curious customs, their symbols and signs, the modes of interaction they adopt with other councillors and with citizens, and the meanings they attribute to phenomena and events. Above all, I have the utmost respect for the office of councillor and for the individuals that hold that office. The intention of the book is to let councillors themselves speak through its pages and in so doing to test our understanding of the local elected office that they hold.

The discussion and analysis in this book does not employ the usual technique of presenting and exploring data by variables such as age, gender, ethnicity, disability, employment status, educational attainment, type of councillors (executive or councillor), type of council or even party affiliation. Many will criticise such an approach, but the risk of such criticism was taken because the intention behind this book is to explore the common and shared experiences of all councillors and to understand what it is about the office and its duties that cuts across such variables and across the various facets of councillors' lives. It deliberately seeks an

undifferentiated view of the councillors' worlds and their understandings, interpretations and perceptions of the office they hold. It does this to present a picture
that all councillors should recognise and on which those policy-makers seeking to
understand the office and its holders can draw, especially if seeking to yet again
reshape and reformulate the office. I stand ready for criticism by fellow academics
for not employing the usual variable analysis.

The book takes the approach to the research and writing outlined above to
enable the formulation of a new model of the councillor as a politician and a new
model of local government for that politician to inhabit. The book is an empirical analysis of the lives and experiences of councillors in today's local politics,
but alongside that, it is a conceptualisation and discussion of representation in
its local manifestation and an exploration of the councillor as a representative, a
decision-maker and a governor of a locality. That discussion is set within the context of the pressures already outlined that impinge on what councillors do, can do
and are expected to do. Councillors can and do, however, shape the roles they play
and give preference to various aspects of the political tasks they undertake, and
they prioritise how they will focus their energies across the functions they have to
perform. The book will also account for the way in which the office of councillor
is shaped by external forces, not least of which are the views held by central government at any one time about the role and purpose of local government and the
councillors that are elected to serve on it.

The book tests the idea that although the role, purposes, functions and powers
that rest with councillors are granted and open to change by central government,
the immediacy of that office enables councillors to develop strategies to effect
political action, shape the activities of their councils and other organisations, and
bring about or resist change through political influence. At the core of the office
of councillor is a political purpose that can overcome restrictions and restraints
placed upon it by higher levels of government. By the interactions that councillors
engage in, they influence and shape the actions of organisations more powerful
and better resourced than the councils of which they are a member. Yet the very
immediacy of the councillor to the communities governed and represented also
shapes the activities councillors undertake and the effectiveness of those activities.

Unlike any other level of elected representative, councillors must balance a
broad governing perspective with the need to work closely with communities and
to stimulate community action. Councillors must develop networks both to mon-
itor what is happening locally and as a means of developing a critical mass of
influence (Rao, 1994), and their ability to do so will determine their wider ability
to influence the broader governing network within which the office has always
operated. To understand how councillors undertake these political activities, the
book will explore the link between action and innovation by councillors.

Most studies of innovation in local government focus on management or service
delivery (Osborne, 1998; Borins, 2001a, b; Newman et al., 2001; Andrews et al.,
2003). Where political practices are explored for innovation it is often around the

theme of democratic renewal – that is, how changes and developments in the practices of citizen engagement have been employed to refresh and enliven local democracy (Leach and Wingfield, 1999; Lowndes et al., 2001a, b; Stoker, 2006). What these studies explore are innovations in the processes and practices of democracy, especially those designed to engage the public more in either local elections or interactions with the council or with councillors. What this book will explore, however, is whether and how councillors take political action and whether, given the limitations on their office, they can innovate politically when faced with changing demands and new sets of problems (see particularly Chapter 2).

Political innovation differs from the concept of the political entrepreneur in two important ways (see Leighton and López, 2012). First, the councillor has not created any new form, organisation, party, structure or group as a way of seeking power, although they may be involved in encouraging the formation of tenants' or residents' groups by others. Second, political innovation is located in the immediacy of social, political and policy problems for which new, creative and imaginative approaches are required. In seeking to deal with the immediate rather than to generate new ideas to challenge a status quo or to produce a new set of institutional rules, the political innovator fills the space left by the political entrepreneur seeking large-scale political change. That is not to say that political innovators cannot also be political entrepreneurs, or vice versa, but that the concept of political innovation, and local political innovation particularly, reflects the reality that so much of what is expected of councillors and what they do is shaped by others or is a response to pressure from others for change in political practices and effect.

If a local political office can be restructured and its purpose, powers and responsibilities altered or downgraded by constitutionally more powerful levels of government, we are left with a straightforward and stark question: why do we elect councillors at all? In addressing this question, this book will often challenge, question and indeed criticise councillors across a range of issues that concern the way they conduct their various roles. But this book is, above all, a celebration of the 18,000 or so individuals across England and the rest of the UK and the countless number of their colleagues overseas, who willingly, assiduously and continually sacrifice great portions of their lives to take on the office of councillor and to serve their fellow local citizens. Moreover, the book intends to confront a rhetorical trend which is undermining local democracy, the office of councillor and councillors themselves in the public and political mind. It is for many good reasons, therefore, that this book is entitled 'In defence of councillors'. To act in defence of councillors, the book explores the challenges councillors face in operating in a turbulent political environment and it examines the composite elements of the office of councillor in order to address and understand the purpose of the office and why we have councillors.

To address the questions that have been set out above, we need firstly to explore what are currently understood to be the roles of the councillor, and the next chapter examines those in detail. It does this to assess how councillors set about effecting political action and on what and whom they focus their activities. The third chapter explores the tension councillors experience as party politicians with a set of political objectives they wish to put into action but who are faced with navigating a complex and rapidly changing environment. It compares the ideological councillor to the councillor acting as pragmatic governor. It does this by introducing the concept of *RealLokalPolitik*. The fourth chapter then moves on to explore how councillors make sense of, engage with and bring some democratic accountability to the array of inter-organisational relationships and interactions that is categorised as local governance. It undertakes this investigation also to assess the strategies councillors adopt to influence the activities of those over which they have no direct control, and whether and how they democratise and bring government to governance. The fifth chapter explores just why councillors do it; that is, why they stand for office, what motivates them to seek office and what they hope to achieve. It also examines the journey to the council chamber that councillors undertake. Chapter 6 examines the nature of the impact that holding the office has on other facets of the councillor's life. It accounts for the proximity councillors have to those they represent, govern and serve as a unique feature of this particular political office.

In Chapter 7, what is termed the 'official mind' (the view of councillors held by policy-makers at central level) is examined for what it tells us about whether or not there exists disdain or delight at higher levels of government about councillors and their office. The chapter also examines the way in which the local press report the political, public and private life of the councillor. It does this to understand the impact of some aspects of media reporting on wider public perceptions about councillors and their office. In Chapter 8, two potential models are presented of the way the office and powers of councillors could develop over time. The first is based on an extension of the existing system of executive and scrutiny roles and processes; the second is a 'fantasy local government' with councillors as real governors of their localities. These two models are presented as a way of suggesting alternatives to the limitations and frustrations attached to the current configuration of the office of councillor. Chapter 9 concludes by drawing the main themes of the book together in an unashamed celebration of the contribution councillors make to the governance and government of the country.

2

Reappraising and rethinking the office of councillor

Introduction

Much of our understanding about the office of councillor and the individuals that hold that office comes from assessments and analysis of the various roles that they are required to undertake. Those roles and the expectations associated with them vary according to their source: government and policy-makers, the council to which councillors are elected, individual citizens, communities of place and interest, political parties, business, third-sector groups, the media, academics, and councillors themselves. Understandably, considerable attention has focused on the relationship between the councillor and those that are represented (Eulau et al., 1959; Pitkin, 1972; Eulau and Whalke, 1978; Barron et al., 1991). While it is necessary to explore that relationship in order to conceptualise representation, it is only one aspect of the numerous and developing roles that the councillor undertakes, and it is only one of the sources of tension experienced by the councillor. Indeed, it has been recognised that the tensions inherent in the varied roles undertaken by councillors are not always mutually exclusive (see Lepine, 2009: 2–3) and are therefore difficult to reconcile. Such tensions include different sorts of relationships with citizens and parties, concerns with both local responsiveness and national priorities, and the political and managerial roles that councillors assume.

If we limit our consideration to the relationships councillors have with those they represent we are left with an incomplete picture of the multifaceted office of councillor. This picture does not allow us to account for how councillors act in a governing fashion, nor does it allow us to understand the full potential of that office as a political institution from which political action and change can be stimulated. Therefore in the studies that have explored what councillors do, it is common to assess their activity by reference to a number of roles (see Heclo, 1969; Jones, 1973; Corina, 1974; Newton, 1976; Rao, 1994). Indeed, there is a rich and deep literature that focuses on using role theory to develop our understanding of the office of councillor by considering the roles that attach to the office.

One of the many frustrations emerging from contemporary fascination with local governance over local government has been that it has stunted understanding of local government and local politics. Moreover, that focus on governance has also put a brake on explorations of developments and changes in councillor roles and conceptualisation of how councillors perceive their own role as an elected representative. As contemporary policy interest never shifts far from a focus on councillors and what they do or don't do, or can and can't do, as part of policy concerns about local government (see Communities and Local Government Committee, 2013; TSO, 2013a), it is time to reassess what we know of the roles of the councillor. Indeed, that reassessment is necessary to enable the identification and separation of the continuing and underlying features of the office from the contemporary demands and pressures that are experienced by councillors and that so often shape those roles.

In examining the roles of the councillor we need to consider if and how the trends that have influenced the shape and direction of local government as a whole have also altered what we expect from councillors. The pressures of urbanisation, globalisation, Europeanisation, increasing austerity and constraint, alongside increasing demands on services and growing participatory pressure within a representative system, have all shaped the demands made on local government and local political leaders and the expectations and roles of the councillor (see Denters and Rose, 2005; Loughlin et al., 2011, Mossberger et al., 2012).

Concerns about political accountability, democratic governance, citizen engagement and the quality of local democracy are at the heart of the debate about the transformation of expectations of what councillors can achieve and how they should conduct representation, governing and decision-making (Berg and Rao, 2005). Yet it is likely that the outcome of the debate about what we expect from councillors will reflect the politics of interactions between local government and other tiers of government, and particularly their policy objectives and attitudes to local government. Thus, while councillors are expected to respond quickly to changing expectations and demands on their office, how that office develops and the priorities it must address are not in their hands to decide

Each social, political, economic and contextual change that occurs around local government has implications for the role of the elected member, not only for the way they conduct their business as councillors, but also for the way they relate to external networks and contacts and how they develop innovative approaches to new problems and energise political action. Discussions about the changing role of the councillor, however, tend to stress the priorities and directions of the contemporary policy framework within which councillors are located. It is therefore refreshing to see discussions about what councillors can or should be doing to encourage innovation, experimentation and risk-taking in their political office (see Jones and Stewart, 1985; Stewart, 1992; Clarke and Stewart, 1998; Pluss and Kubler, 2013).

We shall see later that the reality of the office of councillor is one that balances a focus on the provision or oversight of public services with forging political action and change through the use of local political office.

It has been common to consider the roles of the councillor as part and parcel of their holding of a representative office, that is, their role as a representative somehow defines the myriad of other roles they undertake (Jennings, 1982; Rao, 1994; Drage, 2008). While this view is understandable, and political representation is clearly central to the office, representation itself, or rather the holding of a representative office, is the legitimising factor that enables councillors to carry out a range of other, albeit associated, activities and roles. Representation allows and legitimises but does not define what councillors do in their political office. It is also understandable to generalise so as to conceptualise the roles councillors undertake, but it is necessary to do so against the backdrop of a maturation process which moves, for the councillor, through a number of related stages, from the newly elected to the mature councillor (in years of service). That journey of accumulating experience of political office over time is paralleled by movement into and out of various leadership offices as the councillor's career path develops (Verhelst et al., 2013). Indeed, given an all-out, non-proportional election, it is possible that long-standing opposition councillors may be propelled into leadership office if they win control of a council. In that situation, councillors must mature politically and must do so quickly.

With that dual maturation of time and leadership office in mind, it is time to review the characteristics and categorisations that have defined councillors. That review will provide a framework within which further conceptualisation of the office of councillor can be set and within which new and fresh understandings of that office and its potential for promoting political action can be developed.

The next section examines how the role of local government generally is reflected in perceptions of the role of the councillor and how general agreement about the purpose of local government inevitably shapes the roles, functions, powers and tasks of the councillor. The third section provides a review and critique of what we currently understand about the role of the councillor. It suggests that stressing a distinction between what they do within the council and what they do outside it produces a false dichotomy which needs to be rectified. The fourth section explores, in detail, how councillors perceive their roles and shows that there can be a disjuncture between what councillors think are the most important aspects of their work and their ability to focus on these aspects. The chapter concludes by suggesting that the cause of such a disjuncture is the messiness and complexity of the political world in which the councillor operates. It further suggests that it is time to move on from an understanding based on neat and tidy role distinctions to a framework which enables us to fully grasp the intricacies of the office of councillor.

Councillor roles as a framework for analysis

Government inquiries and academic analysis have explored the various roles of the councillor in an effort to add clarity and definition to the tasks and responsibilities of the office, something which the Maud Committee in 1967 reported as being sadly lacking (HMSO, 1967a). In a majestic and comprehensive analysis of the Maud Committee's own failings, Jones (1975: 135) rightly criticises Maud's notion that the central role of the councillor is to be a manager. Yet, it is to be a manager of a very particular kind – a senior manager focused on broad policy and strategy (HMSO, 1967a, para 109: 30). Maud also struggled with the concepts of policy and administration and the oft-quoted notion that members decide policy and officers implement policy. Indeed, Maud went as far as to argue that:

> Policy cannot be defined and indeed, it should not be defined. Some issues are, to reasonable men, so important that they can be safely termed 'policy issues'. But, what may seem to be a routine matter may be charged with political significance to the extent that it becomes a matter of policy. Other routine matters may lead by practice and experience to the creation of a principle or a policy ... In advising on major issues officers are clearly contributing to the formulation of policy, but in shaping administrative decisions officers may also, even if less obviously, be formulating a policy.
>
> (HMSO, 1967a, para 143: 38)

Maud further argued:

> It is members who should take and be responsible for the key decisions on objectives, and on the means and plans to attain them. It is they who must periodically review the position as part of their function of directing and controlling. It is the officers who should provide the necessary staff work and advice which will enable members to identify the problems, set the objectives and select the means and plans to attain them.
>
> (HMSO, 1967a, para 145: 38)

What this major government-inspired inquiry was refreshingly open and honest about was that its analysis was made in relation to the 'major enterprises of the local authority' (p. 38). In other words, its understanding of the office of councillor was set firmly within the confines of what a council does as a service-based enterprise, not any potential it may have in governing an area. Maud did, however, stress the need to shift members' attention away from the day-to-day administration of services – which was the rightful preserve of the officer – towards the planning and control of major projects. But, in a powerful counter to Maud, Jones (1975: 137) contends that:

> The member is often more at home with the details of administration than with policy; indeed the cynic would hold that it is all some members are fit for. But, the administration of policy usually concerns the councillor more significantly than the policy itself. It is what most worries his constituents, whose queries and

complaints to him are mainly about how the carrying out of policy affects them, their families, their homes, and their areas; and the more specific the impact, the more intensely felt is the anxiety. Broad policy issues rarely elicit responses from constituents. Further, the councillors themselves find more satisfaction in involvement in services that have an effect, in a concrete and personal way, on people than in handling broad matters, setting priorities and allocating resources. Members like to deal with detailed administration because they recognize that this is what their constituents want them to do, and it is what they enjoy doing.

Here, Jones neatly summaries the key tension for members – while, even at a senior level, they are not managers but 'representatives', they believe that their continued tenure in office depends on the quality of the services provided by the council. Moreover, members will attempt to anticipate the reactions of the public to decisions they take and the nature of the public services delivered to the public (Gregory, 1969). Thus, public services are part of the councillor's world and, even in regard to broad policy objectives, their activities and functions often relate to public services.

Councillors have a role beyond public service provision, however. They are politicians who take political action in making decisions about the allocation of scarce resources, arbitrate between competing expectations, values and views, set a long-term agenda for change within their councils and communities, navigate through complex and controversial local issues on which widely differing opinions may exist and ultimately decide who wins and who loses in resource allocation. Yet, that highly political process takes place within an organisational setting – the council – that is shaped, structured and organised with a specific institutional arrangement devised with the sole purpose of facilitating the delivery of public services. Indeed, if every councillor disappeared tomorrow – after the deafening cheers from officers had died away – it would be difficult to spot which service had automatically ceased to be provided. So, is elected local government merely a quaint hangover from a bygone democratic age which can now safely be replaced by service managers? And if it is not, in what space do councillors carry out a more specifically political role? Are they politicians at all?

The Widdicombe Committee provided an answer – of sorts – to those questions when it emphasised the subservient constitutional position of English local government, thus:

> Although local government has origins pre-dating the sovereignty of Parliament, all current local authorities are the statutory creations of Parliament and have no independent status or right to exist. The whole system of local government could lawfully be abolished by Act of Parliament. Central government is not itself sovereign, and indeed its powers are – or may be – circumscribed by Parliament just as much as those of local government. In practice

however central government is drawn from the political party with a majority in Parliament and its de facto political strength is accordingly much greater than that of local government.

(HMSO, 1986a, para 3.3: 45)

The committee's investigation into local government was set at a time when a number of Labour councils across the country were challenging the political and governing supremacy of the centre. Those councils engaged in a series of political stand-offs with the centre over its economic policies and policies towards the financing of local government. Labour councils often saw themselves as a bulwark between the communities they governed and an over-powerful central state – at least an over-powerful state with which they disagreed (see Carvel, 1984; Livingstone, 1987; Blunkett and Jackson, 1987; Lansley et al., 1989). It is of little surprise that a committee of inquiry formed by a government facing constitutional and political challenge from councils claiming that their mandate was as strong as that of the centre should conclude that, far from being a governing institution, local government lacked even the basic right to continued existence.

The committee did, however, give a nod towards those systems of government – normally with written constitutions – that 'legally entrench the existence of those institutions that are most important to their political system, so they cannot be removed by a simple vote of the legislature' (HMSO, 1986a, para 3.4: 45), which, in the committee's analyses, included local government. It also noted that just because Parliament could abolish local government didn't make it acceptable for it to do so. The committee confirmed that, as well as deriving its very existence from Parliament, the position of local government in the political system was governed by the custom and conventions of parliamentary sovereignty, which itself was subject to the contribution local government made to the overall good government of the country (HMSO, 1986a: 45–6).

The position of local government was summarised thus:

> It follows that there is no validity in the assertion that local authorities have a 'local mandate' by which they derive authority from their electorate placing them above the law. The electoral basis of local authorities lends added authority to actions they take within the law, and to any proposals they make for changes to the law, but does not provide a mandate to act outside or above the law. Local authorities may properly lobby for changes in the law, but in their day-to-day conduct of affairs they must act within the law as it stands.
>
> (HMSO, 1986a, para 3.6: 46)

Little has changed since Widdicombe in the official view of the constitutional position of local government and of the councillors elected to it. So we are left wondering if the original notion in Chapter 1 that councillors are able to find space for political activity and to effect political action and change has already been nullified – at least in the central official mind (Chapter 7 explores the official mind in detail). But councillors are still elected political representatives with a relationship to and with their voters and communities and with a degree of discretion to develop local public policy. It is to these aspects and a more detailed analysis of councillor roles that we now turn.

At the heart of understanding the complexity of councillor activity and interaction is the idea, posited in Chapter 1, that although the office of councillor develops in terms of powers, functions, responsibilities and tasks as a result of external pressure from higher levels of government and public expectations and attitudes, councillors are not prisoners of those circumstances. Indeed, councillors are able to overcome restrictions on their office (and local government generally) to develop strategies that enable them, singularly or collectively, to effect political action, shape the activities of their councils and other organisations and bring about or resist change through political influence and action. Moreover, councillors are able to generate and develop a critical mass of interlinked networks across their wards or divisions and across their council areas (and within their councils) and beyond, and they are also able to accrue a critical mass of political resources to enable them to effect political action.

To understand the roles councillors undertake and how far they can effect political action we need to recognise the spatial scales within which councillors operate and to define dimensions of 'local' as they exist for councillors. First, councillors operate within the local context of their wards or divisions, that is, the electoral sub-division of the council; second, they operate within defined communities of place within those electoral areas – what might be termed the *sub-local*; third, there is the *council-wide* locality where the councillor operates on a stage that fills the entire geographical area that is the council; fourth is *a sub-regional* dimension that is the communities or identifiable geographical divisions that emerge because of economic, political or social purposes that extend beyond the boundaries of the council area but are contained within part of a region as it is understood in any national context; fifth are *regional* settings, either the artificial regions that England has been divided into, or more meaningful regions such as those of Belgium, Italy, Spain, or the German Länder; sixth is the *supra-regional* level, that is, those identifiable geographical divisions for economic, political or social purposes beyond the boundaries of a region but that are not national entities; and finally, the *national* stage. Councillors can and do operate and conduct political affairs at each of these levels, but for those that operate beyond the council, such activity is a result of a political choice to move in and operate at different supra-council levels of activity.

Locality has so far been described only as a geographical concept, but communities of interest and identity are most definitely features of the representative landscape – but they are not features that are catered for by the electoral system. Yet G. D. H. Cole and the Webbs came to believe that functional representation of people as workers in their trades or occupations was as important as territorial representation (see Webb and Webb, 1920). The argument rested on the idea that people cannot be fully represented just as voters and that their activities at work needed to be directly reflected and represented in local government and beyond. Indeed, it was trades or professions that would be, for the Webbs, the focus of representation and the mechanism through which representation would become a stronger and more effective process. Such debates took place, however, against the backdrop of a much more homogeneous society than today and were concerned with class rather than with ethnic, gender and sexual identity politics and the representation of presence in that regard (Phillips, 1995). Today, however, it is commonplace for representation to be defined and expressed in microcosmic terms rather than from a Burkean perspective, and this is an issue to which we will return in Chapter 7 (see also Pateman, 1970; Pitkin, 1972).

In advance of discussing competing versions of representation and representativeness in more detail, the following comments from councillors about their relationships to minorities and minority concerns are illuminating:

Minorities are under-represented in all walks of life, in jobs and in politics. How can you expect anyone to relate to the council if it's run by old, white, men: stale, pale and male? We need a diverse council to reflect the community and until we can get that I will make sure that minorities are not marginalised, overlooked or ignored. (Labour councillor)

Women, younger people, black and minority ethnic people and LGBT people and groups have specific needs and need a specific voice and that voice best comes from themselves. Until those voices are spoken by people themselves being elected then councillors must channel these very specific views and interests and stand up for them. (Liberal Democrat councillor)

The Somali community around here is always being shafted in favour of the white working-class; someone has to stand up for them [Somali community]. (Labour councillor)

We shall return to interpretations of representation later, but it is clear from these comments that a developing role for some councillors is to 'represent' minority interests, however they may be perceived and interpreted. Not unrelated to this developing sub-role of minority representation is how past analysis of councillor roles has tended to look at distinct aspects of the activities councillors carry out and to separate those activities into policy, people and processes (Jones, 1975; Newton, 1976; Rao, 1994). That sub-division of councillor activity is a good starting point but, as we shall see, it also masks some of the complexity of councillor roles, especially when taking the spatial scales described above into account.

Roles, relationships and responsibilities

The dynamic nature of local politics, the way it changes over time, the new and emerging problems of localities and the local manifestations of cultural, political, economic and socio-demographic developments and international trends or change inspired by other levels of government, all mean there is a continuing need to reassess the role of the councillor. Councillors themselves need to constantly rethink what they are able to do to secure political action or to work around the constraints on their office to find innovative ways of dealing with the challenges on any of the spatial scales on which they operate. Flowing through all the previously explored roles of the councillor is the need to accrue resources, allies, networks and skills that enable the development of original approaches to the issues faced by the councillor, the council and the community. As we shall see later, however, not all councillors see innovation as part of their role behaviour.

At this point, we need to distinguish between role perceptions and role behaviour (concepts explored in more detail in the next section). The former include those tasks that are seen as important by councillors, while the latter are those that they fulfil well and indeed prefer (Klok and Denters, 2013). There can, however, be a disjuncture between councillors' perceptions of their role and their behaviour (Heinelt, 2013a, b). Klok and Denters (2013, citing de Groot, 2009) maintain that, as representatives, councillors have an *external*-facing set of roles towards citizens and communities and an *internal* set of roles in regard to the activities of the council, each of which has associated perceptions and behaviours. That external–internal dimension to the role of the councillor provides a useful way of compartmentalising the focus of councillor attention and activity but, as we shall see, we must not conclude from this that there is a neat and tidy distinction between citizen-focused and council-focused work. The reality is far more complex and blurred, and we can see this when we start to examine in detail the representative style and focus of the councillor.

In making the distinction between representative style and focus, Eulau et al. (1959) separated the criterion of judgement used by the representative towards the act of representing from the body or group to which they gave preference (or perceived themselves as linked to, or prioritising) when conducting political activity. They drew attention to how representatives could act in a number of roles: (i) as free agents, or *trustees*, of the electorate's interests; (ii) as *delegates*, placing the wishes of the voter (or, as it turns out, some other delegating body) at the centre of their political attention, in some cases even acting as though bound by those views; or (iii) as a *politico*, in other words, as a *trustee* where possible or as a *delegate* when required. Rao (1994: 33–4) took the distinction further by showing that distinguishing between various aspects of representation enables us to tell whether councillors act more as *delegates* (bound by and to others) or as *trustees* (acting on their own independent and informed, even if politically slanted, judgement) when it comes to the voters' interests. Moreover, such distinctions enable us to judge where and when councillors act in the interest of the community (the external focus), as a *constitu-ency servant* or *mentor*, or where and when they act as servants of a political party.

Before Rao's conceptualisations, Jones (1975) had noted that distinctions in councillor representative focus are often difficult to disentangle when it comes to the act and processes of representing. The councillor may act as a representative of a broad section of the community, a particular organised group, another local authority or individual citizens. Since Jones wrote, and as we have seen above, the choice of representative focus has widened considerably and today councillors will focus not only on a section of today's often fractured local communities but even on sections within them, an example being Respect Party councillors, whose focus is not just mainly ethnic minorities but Muslims in particular (see Clarke et al., 2008). Indeed, councillors may speak not only on behalf of certain groups or organ-isations, as Jones (1975) noted, but also on behalf of linked groups, leading them to promote the interest of certain groups, such as environmentalist organisations. Finally, councillors may also represent the interests of a number of other author-ities – again identified by Jones (1975) – but now there are not just other elected councils to consider (including the emergence of combined authorities) but also a myriad of bodies to which councillors are appointed and which make up today's complex local governance networks (Stoker, 2004; Bevir and Rhodes, 2006), all of which could themselves be 'represented' by the councillor in other forums.

When examining the various focuses for councillor activity, account must be taken of the relationship councillors have with their political parties. Newton (1976: 122–4), recognising the importance of political parties in English local government, categorised the strength of the councillor's relationship with the party as that of either a party rebel, faithful or abstainer. As a result of his work in Birmingham, Newton placed councillors into five role types:

i. the *parochial*, who focuses on her or his ward and the individuals within it
ii. the *people's agent*, who also focuses on the problems of individual constitu-ents but does so within the context of a broader, city-wide governing per-spective, thus bringing together two spatial levels of representation and an external focus
iii. the *policy advocate*, who expresses a preference for broad policy issues and governing the council as a whole, an internal focus
iv. the *policy broker*, who is concerned with matters of broad representation of the council as a whole but also acts as a mediator in the policy process, an internal focus
v. the *policy spokesperson*, who sees herself or himself as speaking on behalf of the electorate on general policy issues, an external focus.

Coming to similar conclusions, Gyford (1976: 133–41) saw councillors as hav-ing the potential to choose to act as *tribunes* of the people, focused on individual casework and ward-based issues, or as *statespeople*, focused on broader policy problems and maintaining patterns of party-political control of local councils. Heclo (1969) saw the councillor as focusing their activity as a *committee member*, specialising in the business of the council and the running of the council as an organisation and so dedicated to shaping its aims and direction (see Karlsson, 2013a), a *constituency representative*, focusing on local concerns and with attention fixed on the lowest spatial level within which councillors operate, or as a *party activist*, approaching the work of the council and representation with the interests of the party at the forefront. Corina (1974) developed five typologies to explain the nature of the councillor's relationship with his or her party. The *party politician, ideologist, partyist, associate* and *politico-administrator*, each of whom varies in the connection and closeness they have with the party and in how they interpret its role and purpose within the conduct of council affairs. Simply put, some councillors are more inclined to place party and ideology above all else, while others see the party and party group as assisting them in some aspect of their own council work and, of course, in their re-election (see Verhelst et al., 2013).

That relationship the councillor has with his or her party is a powerful determinant of councillor activity (Copus, 2004). The party politicisation of local government, however, is far from an English phenomenon and is something that has occurred in many national settings (see Bäck, 2004; Maisel and Buckley, 2005; Fallend et al., 2006; Reiser and Holtmann, 2008; Phillips, 2010; Copus et al., 2012). A focus on party, of course, means that council work is conducted in such a way as to minimise criticism and maximise benefit to the party concerned, not just locally but regionally and nationally. Indeed, where national political parties are present, the council and local politics become yet another stage on which national party battles can be fought and where councillors can display the credibility of their party in government, a credibility which they hope will reflect on their party's ability to govern at the national level.

The concentration on the relationship councillors have with their parties is understandable, but it means that what has been absent from much of the exploration of councillor roles is any recognition that he or she may have some responsibility for securing the accountability of local political leaders or for securing political action or innovation in governing their localities. The Maud Committee (HMSO, 1967a, b) and the Widdicombe Committee (HMSO, 1986a, b) did give some consideration to the councillor's role in securing accountability by recognising that councillors must hold the local council bureaucracy up to public gaze and examination. But this is accountability of the administrative machine of paid officers and not of the political leadership of the council.

The fact that councillors may almost eschew a role in political accountability (or at least do so publicly if they are members of the ruling group or administration) is explained by the role councillors play as representatives of their party. If accountability is to be effective, any questioning, criticism and challenge of the political leadership has to be an open and public process. If this is the case, then a strain is placed on party councillors and their loyalty to their party. It is for this reason that accountability interactions between councillors and a council leadership are often confined to private party group meetings.

Prior to the Local Government Act 2000 there was no serious expectation that councillors would act as the vehicle through which accountability of the local political leadership would be secured. Although opposition councillors would seek to challenge, undermine and criticise the ruling group for its administration of the council, much of what took place in open public council meetings was political theatre with little or no effect on the actions of the ruling administration (Copus, 2004). Activity related to public accountability was confined to one type of councillor – the opposition member. Yet the 2000 Act placed a responsibility on all councillors – whether in the majority or minority – to hold the council leadership to account and to use overview and scrutiny committees as a resource in securing that accountability (see Stoker et al., 2003). Party loyalty, however, makes the expectation that councillors will develop an accountability role a difficult one to meet.

As a Conservative councillor commented in interview:

> The council has a Conservative majority, which I fought for, a Conservative leader, whom I voted for, a Conservative cabinet whom I voted for and is implementing Conservative policies which I support. I don't want to challenge that; all I want to challenge is our socialist opponents who want to waste council taxpayers' money on grandstanding political schemes.

Thus, given the existence of powerful council executives, we are left wondering how political accountability is secured through the office of councillor. When it comes to councillors developing their role as scrutineers, it is clear that deeply ingrained and long-standing patterns of political behaviour and relationships – inter- and intra-party – display some considerable resilience to the redesign of the architecture of political decision-making (Copus, 2008). Past political practices in English local government, where group loyalty and discipline required councillors of the same party to act as coherent unified party *blocs*, are incompatible with the new role expectation of executive scrutineer. To be effective scrutineers, councillors must question, criticise and challenge the political leadership and do so in public, even if that leadership is from their party. Whether councillors conduct such a role or not does not detract from the fact that they are now expected to be vehicles through which powerful executive local leaders are held to public account.

The role of scrutineer is not just an internal expectation but also an external one. This is the case because powerful local political executives will act in a governing fashion so as to at the very least influence the activities of a range of organisations within governance networks. We are left, then, with the question: who is it that holds not only political executives but also those myriad of players in complex governance networks to account for the decisions they make, the policies they develop and the public resources they employ?

Councillors are among the few individuals in any governance network that come with an electorally legitimised mandate secured by virtue of the public vote. Thus, they have a right to explore the effects that the actions taken by others – without such a mandate – have on the public realm and how they use public resources to secure their own objectives. Taking the scrutiny role to its fullest external extent means it is a strategic device for councillors in promoting political action and a way through which they can influence and bring about change in organisations beyond their council, a process which is explored in more detail in Chapter 4.

What we have seen from the exploration of what is known about councillors' roles is that councillors do have some freedom over where to place their main focus of attention or interest. It is that freedom of movement we now turn to in more detail.

Perception, behaviour and political action

It is the choice available to the councillor to turn their attention to specific aspects of their work or onto specific groupings or focuses for their representative activities that allows them to shape their behaviour to match where they place their political priorities. However, in the work of Klok and Denters (2013: 66–73), we see that, across Europe, the relationship between the role perceptions and role behaviour of councillors is a complex one. In an international survey of seventeen European countries, Klok and Denters asked councillors how important the following tasks were to them:

- defining the main goals of the municipality
- controlling municipal activity
- representing local society
- publicising debate on local issues
- explaining council decisions
- implementing a party programme
- supporting the executive
- mediating conflicts in local society
- promoting the views and interests of minorities and women.

                                        (Klok and Denters, 2013: 66)

They went on to measure behaviour by asking councillors how they would define their 'contribution' to the tasks above (Klok and Denters, 2013: 67). The findings showed that particular internal and external roles – defining council goals and local representation – were of equal and utmost importance to councillors' perceptions of what their office means. They found that surprisingly less important for councillors was controlling municipal activities and explaining decisions to citizens – again a mix of internally and externally focused roles. The tasks of implementing the party programme, supporting the executive, mediating conflicts and promoting the views and interests of women and minorities were less but not unimportant to councillors. But Klok and Denters conclude that although councillors see certain tasks as more or less important, this does not mean they have the ability or position to have an input to those tasks, and they go on to comment that it is not 'that difficult to see these task as important (role perceptions), but it is much harder for councillors to have a high contribution to these tasks' (2013: 73).

In their important work, Klok and Denters uncover not only a disjuncture between role perceptions and behaviour but also a major source of frustration for many councillors – across Europe – that they are not adequately able to contribute to areas they perceive to be important. It would also be the case that those councillors who can make a contribution are senior, executive members, thus adding to the frustrations of other councillors, who see their role perceptions choked off by structural arrangements. Klok and Denters (2013: 73) give the example of defining the council goals (an internal process), where only 16 per cent of councillors indicated that their contribution here was very great, with 38 per cent seeing it as moderate or less; although defining the council goals was seen as the most important role for councillors, it was placed fifth in terms of relative contribution.

Klok and Denters (2013: 74) did find that, with this example to one side, there was a 'very small' difference between the perceptions of importance of the other roles and councillors' contribution to them, a difference that still indicated that importance did not match contribution. While, by their own admission, their figures show a slight variation between attributed importance and contribution, the intensity of the frustration experienced by councillors cannot be displayed in figures alone. The source of the disjuncture between the importance of a role (perception) and contribution (behaviour) to that role is found in factors such as: the relative powers, roles, responsibilities and functions of councillors; the executive and non-executive distinction between councillors, leading to power and influence imbalances; ruling and opposition status; personal qualities, skills and abilities; organisational structures; links to external bodies; the range of services provided by or overseen by councils; and the influence, role and power of senior council officers. Not only can these factors limit the input councillors have to what they see as important aspects of their office, they can also intensify any frustrations they experienced.

Councillors faced with, for example, an expectation that they will 'represent requests and issues emerging from local society' may find their ability to do just that blocked by council procedures, backbench status, party discipline, or a determined chief executive who wishes to avoid the particular issue or who has an alternative vision. A councillor seeking to solve a casework problem, secure resources for a particular project, deal with competing and conflicting views within the locality – and sometimes dealing with all these issues at once – will experience frustration and perceive obstructions and blockage to action that are intensified by the political and personal interactions and expectations involved. As a Labour backbench councillor in an interview explained:

> We [him and his two ward colleagues] had been fighting for ages to keep these shops open [council-owned property rented out to shopkeepers on a council estate] but whatever we did just didn't work. I had sleepless nights for weeks about the consequences for the estate and local people of the shops closing. Now they have and are boarded up with crappy corrugated iron sheets: it looks like a war zone; we knew it would be bad. The place just looks abandoned. My wife got shouted at in the playground when she was dropping off the kids once by someone who thought we weren't doing anything – that sort of thing happens, but it's not her who's the councillor. I've been trying to find new tenants and even trying to get the council to open the shops up and staff them as a sort of drop-in centre, so at least they're open and working until we can find a tenant; co-ops, volunteers, tried the lot. We won't give up but as councillors we just can't make anything happen. I go to a lot of meetings and vote on this and that – millions of pounds worth of stuff really – but I can't keep a couple of poxy bloody little shops open in my ward – I wonder what's the point sometimes.

This is a lengthy comment but one which displays the intensity of frustration and bitterness experienced by councillors when unable to achieve in an important role expectation – for both councillor and the community – that they will be able to make stuff happen, to effect political action. Added to this case is a feeling of failure for the councillor, that he has let the community down. The comment also shows that not every attempt at political innovation will be successful, but what is central here is that this particular member, like his colleagues internationally, is driven by a desire to achieve, to fulfil a role perception/expectation and by a determination not to give in. It is that doggedness often displayed by councillors that is a factor in political success – no matter what failures, frustrations or obstructions may be experienced along the way.

Klok and Denters (2013: 81) conclude that: 'the overall level of councillors' contribution [to their tasks] is perceived by them as lower than the importance of these tasks'. They label this disjuncture 'role behaviour deficit'. But for councillors, the deficit between their contribution to a task and its perceived importance to them is a situation they can change by seeking innovative ways of securing political action and by developing the capacity and resources of their office. Moreover, the role behaviour deficit as it is experienced on a daily basis by councillors forces them to focus on developing ways around the barriers and obstacles to the action they wish to take or the action they wish to inspire in others. Later in the book we shall see just how councillors have overcome the role behaviour deficit identified by Klok and Denters (2013).

Conclusion

Examining the multifaceted roles of the councillor provides a way in which the office's powers, functions, tasks and responsibilities can be understood for how they influence the councillor's ability to take political action. The nature of their office inevitably means that there is an internal focus on the working of the council: the organisation, provision and quality of public services, the budgetary process, overseeing and holding to account a bureaucratic machine, the co-ordination of organisational efforts to achieve either management goals or political objectives and planning, leading and directing the council. On the other hand, there are those broader representational activities which focus the councillor's attention on the local community and beyond, and which are external to the council as an organisation but are an integral part of the councillor acting as a representative: promoting or pursuing the interests of all, or sections of, a community, providing leadership to communities and local groups, acting as a conduit for political opinion and views on local issues from the community, championing particular geographical areas, interacting with organisations in governance networks, pastoral work and being a lightning rod for local political activity that originates outside of the council and outside of party politics. Of, course input to these processes depends on the councillor's status either inside or outside the ruling party and on the council leadership, which will shape but not determine the effectiveness of the councillor's input to these internal and external tasks.

The internal–external dimension to the role of the councillor is a useful way of conceptualising the activities and focus that councillors develop. But the dynamics of local politics means that there is no clear cut-off point between what is internal and what is external activity, as the reality is far more blurred at the edges. As we will see later in the book, viewing councillors' activities in committee, party or administrative processes (internal) as somehow separate from their community- or citizen-focused activities (external) creates a false dichotomy, or at least an artificial division of the work councillors undertake and therefore doesn't help to fully illuminate the office as a whole. Yet the desire to bring clarity to the role of the councillor is understandable and it is something that those exploring role definitions, perceptions and behaviours have sought to provide. Indeed, in England, such role clarity is something that government inquiries of one sort or another have sought as a valuable commodity when considering local government reform.

We will see in the next chapter that to fully appreciate the nature of the office of councillor it is necessary to explore the messiness of councillors' experiences, the places within which they act and the roles they undertake. In so doing we must account for the councillor as a political office-holder firmly rooted within the communities represented and governed, but an office-holder who experiences first-hand the problems of governing with limited resources and capacity.

Indeed, when councillors are faced with an array of external organisations whose decisions impact on their communities and council, the messiness the councillor must clear up becomes all the more evident. Boundaries between internal and external duties and political work all but disappear when councillors attempt to bring order to external chaos by engaging with and trying to shape the direction of those powerful bodies beyond the council which themselves shape and influence, as well as determine, public policies. It is to that aspect we now turn.

3

Councillors and *RealLokalPolitik*

Introduction

The previous chapter's discussion of the roles of the councillor explored how councillors orientate themselves towards their various tasks and explained and separated those tasks to simplify the messy and dynamic exchanges of local politics. The conclusion was, however, that while such compartmentalising is useful, it can also mask the messy reality of the experiences councillors have as elected representatives firmly positioned within their localities. The blurring of the roles of the councillor and the difficulties of neatly distinguishing activities conducted within the council from those conducted in the outside world raises an important question about how councillors deal with the complexities, competing voices and opinions and tensions that emerge in their communities or councils.

The strategies councillors adopt in dealing with political conflict may reflect either a distinctive ideologically and party-based approach or a more pragmatic view of what can be achieved in the council and the community. If the latter is the case then a *RealLokalPolitik* emerges for councillors that recognises the constraints on their office that are constitutional, political, legal, resource-based, organisational, conceptual, expectational and personal. If that is the case we would expect to see a pragmatic, practical, flexible, responsive and innovative approach from councillors to developing action. Given these two possible views of the local political world – the ideological and the *RealLokalPolitik* – we need then to understand how and why councillors act either ideologically or pragmatically and what the possible consequences are of adopting either approach when it comes to working in the council and the community.

In recognising that the tasks councillors face are not neatly categorised as internal and external to the council, but that they also blur and overlap, two potential strategies can emerge for the councillor: the first attempts to maintain as much of a distinction as possible between the council and the outside world in terms of tasks, and the second tries to recognise and embrace the interlinkages between the council and the community. Councillors operate in either the council or the community and also cross the boundary between them because of the electoral mandate granted to them by the public, which legitimises their ability to make decisions and to act (see Wilson, 1999). But councillors do not inhabit centre stage in their own locality; rather, they face a struggle for engagement themselves in a complex series of governance networks where they confront players with greater resources and influence, who often have greater spatial coverage and impact than councillors and their councils. This theme is explored in detail in the next chapter.

Councillors also face challenges to their electoral legitimacy from their own neighbourhoods (see Sorensen and Torfing 2007; Lowndes and Sullivan 2008). This places a burden on them as they must react to or confront citizens' views or indeed transmit them through complex multi-layered networks to other policy players (Stoker 2004). By virtue of holding an elected office, councillors have a political legitimacy and moral leverage lacking to most of those with whom they must work within the complexity of modern local governance (Saward, 2003). And of course the same applies to the various communities with whom they must work and whom they represent. In acting as a representative and in developing a governing capacity in relation to a locality that enables the achievement of political objectives, councillors are required to operate at the interface between their council and its external environment. The extent to which councillors are successful in operating at that interface will depend on their ability to balance their ideological and party allegiances with the demands for compromise and negotiation that emerge when dealing with conflicting views and perspectives on the same issues from their councils and communities.

The next section of the chapter explores how councillors manage the tensions between the certainty of their ideological and party position and the uncertain compromise-demanding and messy world outside the council. It does this by contrasting the ideological and the pragmatic in the form of *RealLokalPolitik*. This discussion of *RealLokalPolitik* is also relevant to the next chapter where councillors' activities in governance networks are explored and it therefore provides a link to the analysis in that chapter. The third section explores how councillors display a preference for a zone of activity – inside or outside the council – and how that preference is displayed in political behaviour and action. The fourth section develops the discussion of the relationship the councillor has with the council and the outside world by presenting idealised models – the *lay* and *professional* councillor. It then illuminates these models with vignettes of councillor behaviour drawn from the research. The concluding section draws out the key points of the chapter.

Party, people and power

In the analysis of the roles councillors play, competing versions of the same office always emerge. Councillors are seen as focusing on their party, community or some policy field, with the third often reflecting the needs of either the party or the community. We have seen in studies (Copus, 2004; Bäck, 2004; Leach, 2006; Fallend et al., 2006; Heinelt, 2013a) that councillors' strength of party attachment results in, if not an ideological focus to their decision-making, then certainly one that displays party loyalty as at a premium. What Karlsson (2013a: 98) has called the *party soldier* and I (Copus 2004: *passim*) described in detail as the *party person* are those councillors that will place the loyalty demands of the party, the requirements of party discipline and the policy decisions of the party above the views of the local citizens. Indeed, the *party soldier* would cast their vote according to the opinion of their party group and not the voters. As Karlsson (2013a: 98) sums it up: 'A party soldier does not have a free mandate, but it is the party and not the voters that have the last word.' Indeed, as I (Copus 2004: 42) have described it, the *party person* places the party at the centre of his or her assumptive world. For them, the party is:

> Not just a vehicle to secure election (although it has that potential role), it is the only vehicle through which politics can effectively and legitimately be conducted. Moreover, it is also the place where politics and representation is conducted and the only body which can genuinely claim to be 'representative'; the party is local democracy in action. The organisation and activity of political parties and the approach to politics taken by party people, inextricably intertwine local democracy, representation, government and politics. Party has made local democracy, representation, government and politics its own realm, partly as a result of the strength of councillors' and party members' partisan attachment and partly as a result of the electorate's acquiescence in the dominance of political parties in territorial politics.
>
> (Copus, 2004: 42)

The party is not merely a political vehicle through which political objectives can be achieved, it is also a constant reference point in the activities of the loyal councillor, wherever he or she may be acting. Indeed, the party fulfils the social and personal needs of the councillor (and party member), thus disloyalty to the party comes with considerable consequences beyond the political. Karlsson (2013a: 100) concludes that *party soldiers* were 'more likely to be found among senior councillors and members of executive boards'. Seniority is defined in terms of council office and not age because, in Karlsson's analysis, 'older councillors seem not to favour the party soldier as a representation style'. He also found that *party soldiers* are more likely to exist in larger (more urban) municipalities. He uses the construct of *party soldier* alongside Eulau et al. (1959) *trustee* and *delegate* and, as I (Copus, 1999, 2003) have shown, the *trustee*'s freedom often translates to an adherence to the party line. It does so because, as a party member who contributes to internal debate and decision-making and who generally agrees with the outcome of internal party processes, the councillor's freedom to act (*trustee*) can be one and the same thing as being a party loyalist. Indeed, Karlsson (2013a: 98) agrees that: 'A trustee or delegate could be very loyal to their party, but they do not view the party as the final source of legitimacy for their mandate.'

The concept of the *party soldier* provides an ideal type dyed-in-the-wool party loyalist on which to base our understanding of how councillors support their party in the representative process. The *party person* extends that ideal type beyond a representative focus on the party to a relationship which reflects a depth and intensity of attachment and which sees the party as not just a separate political entity which exists for the purposes of political action and achievement but as something which sits at the centre of the councillor's life experiences far beyond the party political.

The extent of party involvement in local government varies, of course, from country to country, as does the organisational structure and settings for local government, the constitutional arrangements and sharing of power between institutions of government at different levels, and variations in local political opportunity structures. One similarity that exists, however, is that councillors, wherever they are located, cannot survive as representatives on an internally (to the council) set of focused tasks and functions. Indeed, in times of austerity, and with the neo-liberal critique of local government and the managerialism inherent in public value thinking together serving to depoliticise and undermine the importance of local democracy and representation, there are considerable pressures on a party-centric internally focused approach to being a councillor (see Bozeman, 2002; Jessop, 2002; Geddes, 2006; Cole and Parston, 2006). Indeed, even though many councillors – though by no means all, given differing national contexts – will be members of national political parties and among the senior party members in the locality, the sustainability of a party-centric ideological basis to their actions inside and outside the council is questionable. That is not to say that the tribal tendencies of party politics will not find ways to display themselves, even in the most inappropriate settings: they will. But what is called into question by the nature and extent of the activity councillors must conduct outside their council is whether they are able to secure political action and influence action taken by others while maintaining a strict ideological and party-centric view of the world.

A more pragmatic view of the world is needed by councillors operating in a complex and often conflictual external political environment, where demands for negotiation and compromise are made and where successful political action will rest on the construction of coalitions or alliances. Successful political action will rest on a realistic assessment of what is achievable (as opposed to desirable) and what, in any current set of circumstances, is not achievable – or at least not yet achievable. It is not that councillors must lose sight of any set of goals or betray a deep-seated view of the world. Indeed, they will not; rather it is that political action must rest on a realistic assessment of success or failure (see Stone, 1995).

Understanding political action has often rested on studies exploring the tasks, role and processes of political leadership (Kotter and Lawrence, 1974; Svara, 1987; Stone, 1995; Leach and Wilson, 2000; Rhodes and 't Hart, 2014). But the concept of political action also assists us in linking what we know of the role of the councillor (not just the mayor or leader) to their ability to bring about change and to address complex problems at different spatial levels, including changes in the views and actions of the political leader. So, to understand the success or other-wise of councillors in pursuing a course of action, an assessment is needed of any differences that occur as a result of action taken by the councillor (Stone, 1995). The reasons for the achievement (or failure) of a particular goal or the securing of a preferred policy preference may lie with the ability of the councillor to fully utilise the facilities and resources (formal or informal) available. Alternatively, a councillor skilled in building coalitions and engaging with citizens and a range of organisations can become effective in dealing with intransigent issues (Stone, 1995) and overcome barriers and resistance based on making a long-term and strategic difference (see Greasley and Stoker, 2009).

It is not just political leaders that have to attempt to shape, control and lead events and to use them to pursue policy and political goals; councillors, too, will be seeking to do just the same and, much as with political leaders, councillors will either be reactive or proactive in their approach to taking action. The pro-active councillor will be able to display a clear 'personal agenda as opposed to a reactive councillor, who is much more likely to lack any clear agenda' – personal or otherwise (see Leach and Wilson, 2000: 32). Again, as with the local political leadership, councillors require the skill to communicate, cajole, and convince a range of audiences: national and regional politicians, civil servants, quangos and public policy agencies, national, regional and local business, church and commu-nity leaders, and local citizens. But they must be able to do so in small, discursive settings where a clear recognition of the realities of any given situation (and an idea of how others see that reality) is a necessity for political action (Bjørnå and Aarsæther, 2009; Schaap et al., 2009). Moreover, the challenge of convincing an expert professional officer of a councillor's desired course, or spanning the polit-ical and managerial divide and the boundary between the council and the exter-nal world is facilitated not only by structure and power but by personal skill (see Skelcher, 2005; Lapuente, 2010).

Determination and imagination in pursuit of simple decisions or solutions to straightforward but problematic issues at the lowest level of spatial activity must be matched, for the councillor, with even greater determination and skill when it comes to long-term goals or visions, operationalised at higher spatial levels. The process of generating and garnering political support for a preferred goal, action or policy means the development and deployment of community networks as resources so as to add to the means available to take political action (see Boogers and Van Ostaaijen, 2009; Bochel and Bochel, 2010). If councillors operate solely from a party-centric view of the world in all interactions, their ability to accrue resources, seek innovative solutions and develop networks and support will be limited. Indeed, the interactions they have will be limited to those with whom they agree and who agree with the councillor's objectives and means of achieving them rather than from a more pragmatic or realistic course.

The theories and practices of *Realpolitik* emerge from policy-making in the world of international relations and diplomacy and explain the use of power, the exercise of practical politics and the realistic notions of what can be achieved, without the constraints of a fixed set of views (see Williams, 1989; Wayman and Diehl, 1994; MacNeil, 2000). *Realpolitik* is also often associated with securing objectives through the use of power – though not necessarily force – with little ethical or moral direction or concerns about 'right' or 'wrong', and so contrasts with an ideological view (see Kratochwil, 1993; Frederickson, 1993; Alkopher, 2005). However, an understanding of the international policy process that seeks to secure political objectives while at the same time accommodating the practical limitations on achieving those goals does provide concepts that allow us to understand local politics.

The idea of *RealLokalPolitik* enables us to examine how councillors reconcile the tension between adopting a party-centric view and the practicalities of interacting with communities and other agencies, which entails a pragmatic approach in order to develop compromise and wide support for political objectives. It also enables us to understand how councillors construct and maintain links with a range of individuals and organisations within and beyond their localities, some of which will have existed before election to the council (Lee, 1963). Even though election to the council elevates councillors above local citizens and provides a legitimised office from which to make governing decisions and to act as mediators of conflicting and competing interests, local politics is a very fertile ground for protest and challenge aimed at the actions of councillors by citizens (Lawson and Merkl, 1988; Brown, 2003; McClymont and O'Hare, 2008). Although the distinction between executive and non-executive councillor is an international one (John, 2001; Borraz and John, 2004; Reynaert et al., 2009; Wollmann and Thurmaier, 2012), meaning that different types of councillors are called upon to make different kinds of decisions, the mediation of interest and arbitrating between competing views remains central to what all councillors do and how they can take political action and secure wide-ranging influence.

In mediating and arbitrating between different interests, councillors must assess the possibilities of achieving the desired results and the costs and consequences of those results set within each and every practical and legal context of any local government system. Councillors' actions will be focused on securing the local public interest which they, as the elected representatives, will assess and develop strategies for achieving. In so doing, councillors will experience pressures to compromise their ideological or party-interest principles and to operate outside of such certainties to achieve what is practical or realistic given existing local and national constraints. *RealLokalPolitik*, however, is not a predictive tool designed to display the possible outcome of any issue arising in the local political arena. Rather, by acknowledging that councillors are faced with circumstances in which their ideological frame of reference will be challenged, it enables us to understand how they respond when faced with such challenges and how they do so at different spatial levels. *RealLokalPolitik* recognises the multi-level governing local body politic within which councillors operate.

Crossing the divide: the local body politic

Over their time in office, councillors will develop and express preferences for certain aspects of their work and for where, given a free hand, they would focus their time and attention. Councillors, of course, do not have a free hand in choosing what they do as they are subject to demands for attention from the council as an administrative and decision-making body, their constituents, local civil society, their party, the media, and, a wide and diverse range of bodies and organisations located within and beyond the council's boundaries. Yet they do have preferences for focus and for activities, tasks and responsibilities, as well as with whom they wish to interact and on behalf of whose interests they see themselves acting. A Liberal Democrat councillor in interview summed up this preference selection thus:

> When I first stood for council I didn't know what to expect, but I work for a mental health charity and I thought it would be a good opportunity to do something about mental health issues. I wasn't so naive to think I could cherry-pick what I would and wouldn't do and council work is so time-consuming and demanding that there are always several balls in the air at the same time. Constituents' matters to sort out, community groups, work on the hospital trust, then back to council papers, then the phone rings and it's Mr X with a problem about whatever. It is like being constantly battered with issues that you have to deal with that are sometimes related and sometimes not. So, I do try to keep mental health as a priority, I go to meetings, events, campaigns, even fetes and socials but no councillor can really control what is done and if you tried to do that you wouldn't get re-elected.

A Conservative county councillor commented in a similar fashion:

> I do a lot of charity work for the elderly and have always tried to put charity and elderly as my priority. But, I can't make it my only priority. To me, MPs seem to be able to act much more like politicians – I'm sure their priorities are not all of their own choosing though – but as a councillor if I don't go to meetings after six months I lose my seat and some of the meetings I go to are not ones which I'd give priority over attending something outside the council. Much of what we do seems so unrelated, but on the other hand, as an individual I have to join the dots, so to speak. I work full time, which means that I have even less time to focus council work on my own priorities. I'll give you an example and this is only an impression. I know our MPs very well and they don't seem to have half the official papers to read as we do; we're swamped in reports which are all of the same type – when I look at the documentation the MPs have, it seems to be from a much wider range of sources. Of course they are full time and have support. I'm not envious of their position, to be honest I wouldn't want to spend all my time in Westminster; I like the local connection, the closeness to people and to the issues we have to make decisions about

or think about and it's not all about the council. I'd just like to be a bit more in control of what I do here.

These two quotes express the frustrations often experienced by councillors in dealing with the variegated responsibilities and tasks that fall to them and the often-expressed feeling of a lack of control over the tasks that they are expected to tackle. Yet it is clear that councillors are also politicians, politically astute and aware and not only focused on local politics but national politics as well. As one Liberal Democrat councillor commented when the issue of involvement in the Syrian crisis was being debated in Parliament in 2014:

> A Labour Councillor asked if I was trying to create local division over Syria (by consulting local people on their views about intervention). It was quite the opposite. I was trying to ensure that we were all consulted.

The decision about intervention in Syria did not fall to this councillor's council. But, as a politician, a member of a national political party – one which was in government at the time – his attention was drawn towards a major international issue. Indeed, it was an issue that he used his elected office as councillor to solicit local opinion on and to channel that opinion to MPs and ministers. On the same day as the discussion he was holding on the Syrian crisis, the councillor was involved in dealing with a local music festival, a local community fair, constituents' problems and a meeting of the health and well-being board. In this case, however, there was no expression that the day, or issues, or the role of a councillor had somehow escaped his control. Far from it. The councillor in question has a high national (local government) profile which was developed from a firm base in local politics and from the base of being a politician in and of the locality.

Similarly, a Labour councillor in an English city was actively involved in the 'No' campaign for the Scottish separation referendum. He commented:

> The call went out from London that councillors had to 'do something to save the union', so I've been working the phones, calling voters in Scotland to get them to vote 'No'; that was interesting. We also are flying the Saltire from the town hall – another idea from London. We've had some complaints from people about that, though.

Again, at the same time as his engagement in a union-wide campaign, this councillor was also carrying out his duties as a cabinet member and a ward representative – after hoisting the Scottish flag over an English city he then went directly to his regular weekly surgery.

So far we have seen two views emerge. The first is of councillors experiencing a form of loss of control over their workload and priorities and, as a consequence, their political activities being dictated by the factors that make the most pressing demands on their attention. The second is of a more politicised approach which provides a focal point for organising the various levels on which councillors operate. Here the various activities are not separate but simply need to be carefully co-ordinated to give the councillor control over priorities. For many councillors, the Syrian crisis and the government's decision about intervention was not something they felt they should avoid just because their office is a local one. Nor was the 'No' campaign in the Scottish referendum – although in interviews some Labour councillors were uncomfortable in following the national leadership line. But what they were aware of was the ability to use a local, electorally legitimised platform to express a political opinion and take political action.

The examples above do not indicate a clear-cut internal–external division in the councillors' responsibilities. Admittedly, there are activities that lean towards an internal or external focus, but the point is the rapidity with which councillors swing between dealing with issues that may be council-focused and those that are focused on the wider world. The crucial point is whether the councillor is able to ensure coherence between these two worlds and how this is achieved in securing any form of political action and in mediating interests. It is necessary then to look at some examples of how councillors have done just that and the consequences of them failing to do so. In order to simplify the analysis, the discussion in the previous chapter about councillor roles is condensed into two ideal types of councillor and two ideal *genres* of councillor. But neither of these types has full control over their preferences and priorities and must also undertake activity outside of their preferred realm:

The *corporate* councillor – whose main preference is to devote interest and attention to the running of the council or to those tasks associated with what the council does as an organisation and to improve that organisation. It is a role focused on the administrative machinery and activities of the council itself. Attention is given to external factors and demands but they are not at the core of the councillor's activities.

The *associated* councillor – whose main interest is in interaction with the complexity of politics outside the council and in mediating interests and arbitrating between conflicting causes. The *associated* councillor's idea of political action is something which uses the resources and office of councillor to achieve a wider objective. The associate councillor immerses her or himself in the working of the council but in order to pursue a broader set of political objectives. They do not see running the council as the primary task, although it is an important one.

The *lay* genre (also see Verhelst et al., 2013) – views council membership as a voluntary process and believes that the focus of the councillor should be on clear-cut but limited activities around holding the bureaucratic and political administration to account and pursuing constituents' problems. The *lay* member does not see her or himself as a 'politician' and approaches council work by bringing an external, albeit elected, set of eyes to the activities of experts and professionals.

The *professional* genre – links together all aspects of the work as a councillor, whether it is internal decision-making or external networking, or interest mediation and arbitration or engagement in governance networks taking place in any and all settings and at all spatial levels. The *professional* councillor seeks to develop their individual capacity and resources to govern and to approach the work of a councillor politically and as a politician.

With these condensed typologies of councillor we can make the following assumptions: the *corporate* councillor will operate in a strongly *lay* genre because of a largely internal focus to the work of the councillor, and the *associate* councillor will act in a strongly *professional* genre because of a more politicised view of what can and should be achieved as a councillor. Each type of councillor and the linked approach can then be gauged against their willingness to innovate and to take political action. What we cannot yet assume is that any one type or genre will be more or less of a political innovator in their preferred sphere of activity. Figure 1 displays the ideal type and genre of councillor with the strength or weakness of attachment to internal and external council activities.

These ideal types provide a way of assessing how and to what degree councillors undertake action and seek to innovate when it comes to their roles in acting as decision-makers, representatives and governors of their localities. It also provides a way of understanding how councillors can enhance the powers of their office to strengthen their governing capacity and with that their influence, especially in relationship to those that present a challenge to their authority: civil society and the wider governance network, which we now explore.

The councillor in action

Councillors inhabit an office that is the product of traditional representative democracy and they display a strong attachment to the mechanisms and methods of operating associated with this form of democracy (see Sweeting and Copus, 2012). Such attachment to this model, however, does not mean councillors are restricted to operating within the institution to which they were elected or that they can isolate themselves from external pressures. If the tasks councillors undertook were

Strong internal	Lay councillor	Professional councillor	Strong external
Weak external	Corporate	Associate	Weak internal

Figure 1 Ideal type and genre: the office of councillor

so limited then the links between councillors as representatives and the local civil society from which they themselves arise would be loosened and community organisations would seek an even greater role in local affairs (Barnett, 2011). While councillors come with an electoral mandate and thus electoral accountability, there is no such mandate or system of accountability for community activists seeking to influence a council. The presumed authenticity of community voice cannot be challenged or a leadership changed, except by some small restricted membership.

In the accountability stakes, as Phillips (1994) noted, votes are absolute trumps. Although it is not so much votes that are trumps, as any organisation can 'elect' its leadership; rather, it is free and fair local elections open to all citizens that not only are trumps but also provide councillors with a greater authenticity than that claimed by community activists. It also provides them with greater democratic legitimacy for their actions than those actions taken by the players in governance networks (see Skelcher, 2005; Sorensen and Torfing, 2005; Klijn and Skelcher, 2007). Indeed, when councillors interact with citizens or business and public agencies to strengthen their own governing capacity (defined for our purposes in Chapter 1) and to enhance their ability to influence others, they are not just co-operating and working with others, they are transferring electoral legitimacy to those that lack it.

Governing capacity for councillors is strengthened by sharing electoral legitimacy with others and leaning on their resources by working pragmatically with community-based organisations or other public bodies as required, rather than through the construction of a continual coalition of support comprising the same members over time (see Stone, 1989, 1993; Mossberger and Stoker, 2001). Councillors can do this because the authority granted by the election provides them with the legitimacy to interact with others in a governing fashion, and as councillors lack the power to legislate to force local action, they must fall back on their elected position to imply authority. The authority granted to a council and councillors by election underpins the ability to take action, but councillors often struggle to employ that authority or its legitimacy. Or, more pointedly, they struggle to have it fully recognised and responded to by others when seeking to achieve political objectives or to generate change. The reality of being a councillor is that the office held does not necessarily guarantee that communities, community activists and private and public agencies or the council itself will respond to the councillor as a governor.

To understand in more detail how councillors take action, two specific vignettes are presented which set out and explore cases where councillors have been confronted with either a need or a desire to take action. It does this set against the ideal types and genres of councillor described in the previous section in order to assess the nature of the interactions that occurred in each case. The vignettes do not give all the details of the cases but focus only on the actions of the councillors concerned. The meeting referred to in the first vignette was observed as part of the research.

We expect your support

A ward represented by three Labour councillors (A, B and C) was designated as a possible site for a permanent gypsy and traveller site. The announcement caused considerable concern among residents, and a local group emerged to campaign against the location of the site. The campaign by the group was focused on the council – as the decision-maker – and played out heavily in the local press, which was a forum for letters and reports on the development of the issue. The campaign was well organised and supported locally, and as well as use of the local press to pursue their case, the campaigners demonstrated outside the proposed site with placards and banners, leafleted the locality and circulated a petition opposing the site. They made contact with the three local councillors soon after the proposal had become public.

Councillor A was away on holiday when the initial contact was made, via email, to each of the councillors for the ward and she was not due to return for over a week from the sending of that email. In that period, Councillors B and C suggested that they meet with the group to discuss the matter and it was at that initial meeting that the fault-lines began to emerge. Councillor B had no hesitation in supporting the campaigners. He commented that:

> The proposed site is not appropriate at all, its location makes no sense and it appears as if officers have just plucked the idea out of the air because they have to. There will inevitably be some problems and local people had a right to have their councillor stand up for them and I agreed that the site was wrong anyway.

The councillor explained that in the heat of the moment at a private meeting, he had made comments that a fellow councillor felt 'inappropriate' and an official complaint had been made about the comments. As a result, Councillor B was ordered to undertake equalities training by the council: an embarrassing position for a Labour councillor. But Councillor B threw his weight wholeheartedly behind the campaign against the site. His activity was, understandably, focused on convincing the council that the proposal should not be pursued, and his attention was given to internal meetings with officers and other senior councillors and attending planning committee meetings and a series of site visits in which he took council officers not only around the proposed site but the surrounding area. Councillor B, of course, echoed the concerns of local residents and, in his own admission, he:

> may have reflected to council colleagues some of the language and comments made about travellers by residents, who, to be frank, were angry, frightened and felt they were the bad guys; probably shouldn't say 'guys': bad 'people'.

Residents did make comments that, in today's culture wars, some of the terms used would be deemed offensive by some, but for others they would be just common sense, based on experience and reflecting their deep-seated anxieties. Councillor B had operated mainly quietly, behind the scenes and with a strong administrative focus as a way of dealing with the issue. He had also, however, made himself fully available to the campaigners, not only by attending events and meetings, but also over the phone, by email and visits to his home – which was inside the ward. In fact, one of the attacks from some of his fellow councillors that hurt the most was not the accusations of racist or offensive comments, but that he was only doing what he was doing because he lived in the area affected. There was clearly, however, a distance between Councillor B and the campaigners; he had not 'joined' the campaign and only attended meetings by request and to deal with issues pertinent to the council. He dealt with such aspects diligently and carefully. One of the campaigners went as far as to comment.

> Do you know, I've never voted for [Councillor B], I'm not a Labour voter but he impressed me with how hard he works. I know he has to be careful, being Labour and all and they seem to prefer the gypsies to residents who vote for them, but this chap's good. You can always get hold of him – he even gave us his work phone and email address (the only time Councillor B's full-time employment was mentioned). I wish there were more councillors like him.

Councillor C – who did not live in the ward – took a very different approach and it is rumoured, though denied, that it was Councillor C that complained to the chief whip of the group about Councillor B's supposed 'inappropriate comments'. Councillor C commented:

> At the start I was happy to go along to their [campaign group] meetings and to meet with them because when this sort of thing happens there is a lot of tension, stress and anger which has to be carefully managed before it gets out of hand. Travellers have rights and those rights are often overlooked. We also have a responsibility to protect and support people who may not be fixed residents or voters – it is morally wrong to ignore such groups, marginalise their way of life and expect them to conform to other people's norms. But fixed communities have rights too, what I have to do is to balance each of those sets and come up with a solution that is the correct one. But, traveller communities should not be subject to fear and hate and baseless generalisations.

Councillor C saw his role far less as one of working with the council and much more as trying to mediate and reconcile two very different sets of views on the issue. He attended meetings when requested, always with Councillor B, but with the intention, if not to convince residents of the need for the site to be located where proposed, then certainly to persuade them of the rights of the travellers and the correctness of making provisions and facilities available for them. On the one hand, his approach was to negotiate and to seek compromise, but at the same time, he stressed that his aim was to: 'protect an excluded group and ensure they weren't the target of racism and further exclusion'. His view of the local community was one of their privilege, albeit a relative privilege, against the traveller community's disadvantage and exclusion.

For Councillor C the issue was one of power and advantage, and for a while he walked a tightrope between his political world view and the increasingly anxious outcries of local residents. But tensions emerged and increased. In an interview, he made the comment: 'I'm sick of hearing the words "these people", and I challenge it every time'. The breaking point came at a public meeting organised by the campaign group (by this time, Councillor A had long returned from holiday but had kept away from the fray). At that meeting, after lengthy and increasingly angry exchanges between attendees and council officers and Councillor C, one resident made a straightforward comment to Councillor C: 'we have elected you and we expect your support. All I've heard from you is "their [travellers'] rights", what about us?'

Councillor C left while the meeting was still taking place after having made a comment in which he expressed 'shame' at the behaviour and comments made by some in the meeting, disgust at the 'racism' of some present, and 'embarrassment' at having to 'represent' such an area.

In an interview he commented:

> They have no idea of power, no conception of how power is used, no concern about how society is structured and certainly don't care about altering inequalities and unfairness. The whole business is about power and its use and I'm arguing with those that have power that they should include others in their view of what constitutes society. Do you know what my main worry is now, that the site won't meet demand and because of government cuts we will be stretched to provide services such as education for the children and will end up letting down a marginalised community. The government has to provide more resources and some of these council taxpayers will have to offer up a bit more to ensure fairness. I was sickened by some of the comments I heard and it just goes to show how much racism and prejudice there is to overcome. I hope the site goes ahead.

Councillor A, who came back from holiday to find things already in motion, candidly admitted that she was glad to have been able to take a bit of a back seat.

> It's a no-win situation and no one has won; Councillor C is universally hated and thought to be a traitor to the area (he'll probably try and get selected somewhere else for the next elections). He stood his ground and is right that we have to support marginalised groups – but he was in the firing line not me. Councillor B may have got carried away but he should never have been disciplined – especially as he was trying to hold the line between Councillor C and the ward and he did it very well for a while. Because they [campaigners] had already got two councillors involved I was under a lot less pressure to be involved. Look, the difficulty is this: we have to provide for travellers – and it's right we do – but people

get upset about traveller camps. I can step back a bit because of the way things worked out, but it's about making a decision based on everyone having their go and based on trying to find a solution that suits everyone. Battle-lines had already been drawn up, although they hadn't firmed up, when I got back – thank heaven for family holidays, ah!

We see here, between the two councillors involved, a very different perspective on how the issue should be approached. Councillor B was supportive of the campaigners (the electorate), prepared to work within the council but also alongside residents to pursue a particular course of action. Councillor C had a more politicised world view, initially trying to mediate between two irreconcilable forces and finally needing to choose a side. Part of his decision may have been based on Councillor B's support and work for the residents, and Councillor C balanced that by defending travellers and the need for a site; part of his position was based on a view of power, social structure and order and a desire to change the power balance, if only around one issue in one location, but with a longer-term world view and objective.

What is also shown here is how the relationship between councillors and their constituents does not just rest on the positions councillors take on a particular issue – an obvious conclusion. It also rests on whether councillors are perceived to be working for, part of, and integrated with a community. That issue is picked up in more detail in the next case from another council.

Here we go again

Councillor A, who declared himself a dedicated and committed socialist, had become concerned about what he considered to be 'irregularities' in the way the Conservative cabinet had been conducting its business. The cabinet had made a number of decisions which involved the expenditure of large sums of money – over £500,000 – on renovating a playing field, a bandstand and a club-house attached to the playing field. He also developed a strong suspicion about the way in which the cabinet was making decisions more generally. Councillor B was a Conservative councillor for the ward in which the field was located. While as ward councillor he expressed himself 'delighted' at what had been done, in interview he expressed 'disquiet' about how the decision had been made, and he shared Councillor A's concerns about cabinet decision-making. At no time did Councillors A and B discuss the issue together and they worked separately on dealing with the concerns they felt about cabinet decision-making.

Councillor A contacted senior council officers to seek copies of all information the cabinet were given on the field development scheme. He was sent – via email – a copy of the final report that had gone to the cabinet. He requested again all background and briefing papers that had gone to the cabinet. He received no reply to his email after two weeks, so emailed again. He received an acknowledgement but not a substantive response. He commented:

> I thought to myself 'here we go again' as I realised something was going on; they were taking a long time to reply, so I made a quick couple of phone calls, all very pleasant, I thought, asking for a reply and the papers. Nothing happened, so I rang again. Then I had a phone call, at work, from the Chief Executive saying that he had a very serious issue to discuss with me, that he'd already discussed it with the leader of the council and could I come in the next day to discuss things. Well, as it happens, I had a work presentation to make, so I said I couldn't make it then but to give me some dates or that we speak after a scrutiny meeting I was due in for the following week.

He added the following:

> The decision was good for the residents of [named ward]. I have one problem, though, there are far worse-off places than that area and places where £500,000 would have had a far greater impact. Not just my own ward, but across the district, and part of the problem is they [cabinet] are not assessing where there is real need. My view is that we spend that money where it is most needed and that would be to provide some, any facilities in some parts of the district, not just repair and upgrade what is there. If there is a smaller and smaller cake to go round, the hungriest should get at least a bite.

Councillor B had met with the council leader and the environment portfolio-holder to discuss the work on the playing field, but it became clear to him that even though he was the ward councillor, a good deal of discussion had already taken place and decisions had already been made before he was involved. As he commented:

> I'm delighted the work has been done, but I just got the feeling that things were not handled as they should have been, I can't put my finger on it – but the cabinet seem to operate like this and it was presented to me as though they were doing me a favour. I felt somewhat patronised, to be honest. But that's not the point; the point is something about the way decisions are made just isn't what one would expect.

Councillor A attended his meeting with the Chief Executive to find that the council leader, the chair of the standards committee and the council solicitor were also present. In his own words, he was greeted by the Chief Executive:

> He said to me 'I'm sorry you refused to meet us last week but am glad you have seen the error of your ways'.

In interview, the Chief Executive denied that these were his opening words but did feel that Councillor A had refused to meet with him and only changed his mind later.

Councillor A was then confronted with the accusation that he had been bullying and intimidating council staff by constantly harassing them and requesting information that, as had been explained to him, was not available to him as a councillor.

Despite what he saw as an 'attempt' to intimidate him and 'throw him off the scent', his strategy was to constantly and at every opportunity question carefully and forensically the process by which the cabinet had made its decision to spend the money on the issue at hand. He specifically focused on the nature and process of the advice that was being given to the cabinet by senior officers.

Councillor A commented:

I have to work full time and so I can't give everything to council work, but it seems to me I'd be a poor councillor if I let the suspicions I have about the way the cabinet is working slip by. I'm doing my job of a councillor if I ask about why and how things were done and also what advice and information formed the basis of those decisions. So, as a councillor I use council, scrutiny and full council to, well embarrass them [officers and cabinet members] and it's surprising how embarrassing a well-placed question can be. I stood up at one full council meeting and said: 'I'd just like to ask the leader and chief executive...' and before I could finish the leader shouted: 'here we go again' – I think I got to them. I can only get to them by being determined to find out what's happening and to keep plugging away – do the research and ask the questions. It's not just about the playing field work, it's about the whole way the cabinet and senior officers work together to exclude everyone else. I will hold them to account.

I joined the council to help people and to make sure things were done the right way, properly and openly, but doing the right thing is often lost in party battles. I'm responsible for some of that, because I always contrast the affluent areas with the less well-off to force home the point that some people in the district are being ignored and that's about resource allocation and that's party political.

Councillor B, on the other hand, who was retired but in his own words – 'I like to keep an eye on what's going on up there' – had seen his ward benefit from the playing field redevelopment, but he felt excluded from the debate and that the cabinet operated in too closed a fashion with too 'cosy' a relationship with the senior officers. His strategy was different from Councillor A's but was still fixed on a notion of accountability and openness, although not expressed in those terms. Councillor B sought alternative sources of advice; his wife had worked in a solicitor's firm for twenty-five years and he knew the partners well. He would not disclose confidential material but would discuss issues with them and also explore how decisions had been made and whether they had been made legally. He commented:

> I discussed all this with the leader and he knew what I was doing – he didn't like it and demanded that I prove I'd maintain confidentially – which was difficult but I got [named solicitors] to send some sort of letter and that appeared to do the trick.

Councillor B described himself as 'a dog with a bone. There are no votes in this and I make myself unpopular with some of my colleagues but if I didn't investigate that things were done properly I wouldn't be doing my job as a councillor.'

Action explained

What we have seen in these two examples is how councillors have taken very different approaches to dealing with the demands made on their office. In the first example, we saw councillors motivated by a desire to mediate between competing views but being forced by circumstances into taking sides. Given more straightforward and dispassionate circumstances, they might have arrived at different conclusions – but local politics is rarely straightforward and never dispassionate. In the first vignette we saw examples of a *lay corporate* councillor in Councillor B and an *associate professional* in Councillor C. We see how localities are an arena for not only a locally focused politics but also the exposition of a broad world view within a local context, which comes with consequences. Councillor C from the first case complained of late-night abusive phone calls, anonymous letters and a Facebook campaign against him personally.

In the second vignette we saw examples of a *lay associate* councillor in Councillor A and *lay corporate* councillor in Councillor B and we also saw how interests were being promoted, challenged and ways forward being sought that would benefit one group or another. In this case, unlike the first case, the councillors were able to take a more calculated, careful and less emotionally and politically charged approach to what they were doing. Yes, pressure was brought to bear, especially on Councillor A, but the intensity of the issue – focused mainly as it was on the workings of the council – lacked some of the political heat of the first example.

What is not shown in the vignettes is that these were not hermetically sealed actions and interactions that took place without any other interference or demands for attention. Far from it. Each of the councillors involved stressed that although these issues were the most immediate and, in the words of one councillor, the 'noisiest', and although they did demand attention and drain the councillors' energy, other matters could not be ignored. Not least work and family life, but also other council business, meetings, other smaller-scale, less noisy campaigns, party duties, ward casework and regional and national politics. None of these were squeezed out by the critical issue at the centre of attention for a given period. Indeed, two of the councillors were also dealing with other critical issues: one a long-running dispute between neighbours on a particular estate which had involved multi-agency approaches – mainly the police; the other where one of the councillors had a seriously ill relative about whom no details were given but who sadly passed away during the research.

What is clear is that it takes considerable effort on the part of the councillor to control the environment within which they operate, and that control can very easily slip away. The world view of the councillor may provide some certainty with which to approach issues, but it may not guarantee a certain outcome for councillors seeking to take action. We saw in the first vignette particularly how a pragmatic approach could also be taken, but this did get both Councillors B and C into trouble. But in the vignettes we saw all the councillors seeking to deal with situations not of their own making and to balance beliefs against the uncertainty of their surroundings and the complexity of the demands made upon them.

Conclusions

In understanding the day-to-day experiences of councillors it is necessary to remember that, above all, they are politicians that inhabit a political world. While councillors will deal with the minutiae of case work one moment, in the next they will be engulfed in a major local issue, then be immersed in the details of council budgeting problems and then find themselves part of a national political debate using the council chamber and their elected office to add weight to their comment and opinion. The political interactions in which councillors are involved are shaped partly by their own preferences for a focus on one aspect of their work or another – whether internal or external to the council – or are shaped by circumstances which demand that councillors engage with, or become involved in, activities on which they place a low priority or would rather avoid altogether.

The varying level of control councillors have over their engagement with facets of their work is evident, and it is not a surprising conclusion that events dictate much of what councillors are able to achieve. Yet the options open to councillors in taking political action to resolve the problems they face may be either bounded by ideological concerns or limited by what is practically possible or pragmatically desirable. Effective political action relies on the ability of the individual councillor to travel between the preferred zones of action – the council or the external political world – and in so doing bring together a critical mass of resources to achieve a given political objective.

We have seen that councillors do have preferred arenas for action, with our *corporate* councillors favouring the council as an institution and our *associated* councillors viewing the outside world as their setting for action. In addition, a councillor can act as a *lay-volunteer*-oriented councillor who seeks to hold the machinery of the council to account or to pursue constituents' grievances but does not see membership of the council as transforming them into a politician; rather they remain at one and the same time part of but also distanced from the council of which they are a member. The *professional* councillor, on the other hand, sees the office of councillor as a resource to promote or pursue a broad governing agenda for the locality – ideologically based or through the prism of *RealLokalPolitik*. Neither the *lay* nor the *professional* councillor, however, is immune from pressures to operate outside their preferred arena or to take on tasks that they would rather leave to their colleagues. Again, as with much of the day-to-day experiences of the councillor, proximity to the voter and local circumstances can shake the councillor's preferred approach to the office and confront their world view with the realities of practical politics or the consequences of divergence from an ideological position – as our first vignette indicated. In Chapter 7, the idea of *lay-volunteer* and *professional* councillors is explored in the context of the contemporary policy debate.

In setting out to use the resources of the office of councillor and the limited power that is associated with it to instigate action or prevent change (in itself an action), councillors can operate from a pragmatic or ideological standpoint. But the complexity of the political world inhabited by councillors and the limits on their resources and powers and what they can realistically achieve suggest that councillors may be most effective operating within a framework of a *RealLokalPolitik*. Within that framework, councillors will construct a set of pragmatic goals and actions based on negotiation and compromise, so as to respond incrementally to the needs of citizens or communities. Such a view may lack the superior feeling of being directed by a moral compass, but at least the actions of the councillor are not bounded by ideological certainty.

As we shall see in the next chapter, the ideological–*RealLokalPolitik* distinction is not limited to helping us understand how councillors act in relation to the council and their community. It also provides a way of understanding how councillors can seek to overcome the limitations of their office when they interact with a complex array of organisations beyond the council. Again, in this context, councillors face a stark choice – operate in every interaction within governance networks as a political ideologue with an overall goal of political transformation, or develop a pragmatic approach to extend the scope of influence so as to act as a governor outside the council by seeking to influence the outputs and outcomes of players within external networks. It is to that set of interactions we now turn.

4

Councillors: bringing order to chaos

Introduction

We have seen in Chapters 2 and 3 that councillors develop a preferred focus of attention for their activities but that they are not totally free to indulge their preference for working with constituents, or on policy development, or pursuing the strategic government of the council, or on their externally focused work. Indeed, councillors must span a range of activities that can be broadly summarised as: one-to-one advocacy (pursuing constituents' interests); giving voice to a community; acting to promote strategic external government; and espousing, promoting and pursuing a set of political views. With the focus of action for councillors condensed in such a way we can see clearly that each of the four areas of action requires the councillor to look beyond the council if they are to be effective. In this chapter, we explore how councillors engage with the complex world of public and private bodies and interests that comprise the external environment in order to see what strategies are developed to enhance councillors' influence in arenas where they have little or no control.

The office of councillor, while being an elected one, does not hold centre stage in the locality. Rather, councillors face a struggle for engagement and influence in a complex series of networks that ripple outwards from the council and the immediate locality into a far wider geographical and political framework of decision-making and policy development (see Sorensen and Torfing, 2007; Lowndes and Sullivan, 2008). Rather than making decisions as authoritative politicians with powers to enact change, councillors must interact in networks of different size and scope to exert pressure, pursue influence and attempt to shape decisions and policy with a vast range of individuals and organisations in complex multi-layered networks within which they confront higher-level players (Stoker, 2004; Denters and Rose, 2005; Sorensen and Torfing, 2014). The task for councillors is to develop the capacity and critical mass of resources to shape the behaviour and decisions of others and to shape and influence the external world through acts of diplomacy rather than control. Seeing the councillor as engaged in diplomacy with competing organisations with different scales and spatial organisation and unequal resource bases fits well with the idea of *RealLokalPolitik* explored in the last chapter. The art of diplomacy, the negotiation and compromise required to gain some form of strategic advantage, will see councillors increasingly exposed to pressure to adopt a pragmatic, rather than ideological, approach to secure strategic advantage or influence.

Councillors, by virtue of holding an elected office, have a legitimacy and moral leverage lacking to most of those with whom they must now work within the complexity of modern governance (Saward, 2003; Bekkers et al., 2007; Klijn and Skelcher, 2007). The electoral legitimacy and authenticity of the councillor to act and the link they have to those they represent (see Pitkin, 1972) was considered in Chapter 3 and its impact on the councillor is further explored in Chapter 6. In this chapter, the focus of attention is on how councillors interact with those they wish or need to influence beyond the confines of the council. It examines how, if at all, councillors are able to employ their electoral mandate and the office they hold as resources through which to express and use their authenticity as political representatives to effect action in arenas where they lack the power to control.

As the organisational landscape of local government changes and as government shifts the powers and responsibilities for service provision and strategic governance across that landscape, councillors are increasingly required to act within multi-layered networks. Councillors are presented with the task of channelling into a range of public policy players either their own views (as a trustee), the articulated and general citizen view (as a delegate) or the decisions and polices of their party (as a party loyalist). The idea of *RealLokalPolitik* as requiring a pragmatic and incremental approach to what is achievable will, more realistically, see councillors employ a combination of their own, citizen and party views as leverage when they seek to influence and encourage others to make certain decisions, take certain actions, or move in a policy direction to bring them into alignment with a set of political or policy objectives. Councillors' actions require of them an outward-focused and diplomatic style of interaction when attempting to shape the behaviour of those developing public policy and spending public money without a mandate from the citizen. It also requires a willingness, on the part of councillors, to forge new alliances and coalitions within diversified governing arrangements – outside of the council (Cole and John, 2001; Stoker, 2004).

How do councillors go about forging coalitions and alliances and then employing those, alongside their electoral mandate, as leverage when interacting with a range of organisations and individuals and when seeking to shape the decisions and actions of bodies over which they have no direct governing control? The electoral mandate provides a tool to strengthen the councillor's position in such interactions, but how councillors conduct their representative activities determines whether the engagement they have with any private or public body will have an impact on what the latter ultimately does. Moreover, in understanding the office of councillor and the ability to take political action attached to it, we need to explore whether the councillor's electoral status, any support networks they have and the support they get from their councils is sufficient when they are trying to convince others of how their resources and actions should be employed (Perri 6 et al., 2002).

To have an impact beyond the confines of the council, councillors must develop individual and collective strategies to transform locally based political resources into a means of making a significant contribution to any governing network. It is how that process operates and its effectiveness for securing political action by the councillor that the chapter examines. The next section considers the electoral legitimacy of the council and councillor and how that provides a justification for action which is lacking to all others within governance networks. The third section examines how and how well councillors act as a link between the wide range of organisations that comprise governance networks and contrasts that diplomatic activity with the idea of the council as an authoritative political body. The fourth section examines the strategies councillors develop to extend the reach of their political influence beyond the council. It also considers the implications for local government of the changing organisational landscape that councillors must now navigate. The conclusion section draws out the implications of the governance narrative for the narrative of local government.

The source of local sovereignty

If the office of councillor comes with legitimacy to act and a legitimacy to try to shape how others will act, then a link must be made between councillors, the council and citizens in an electoral chain of command. While the electoral chain of command theory has been rightly criticised by Dearlove (1973: 25–31) as inadequately reflecting the attenuating role of political parties in local democracy, the linkages that the theory explores provide a starting point for understanding how councillors can operate in a diplomatic fashion in complex networks of influence. As Dearlove (1973: 26) explains, with the electoral chain of command theory: 'causal connections are posited between electors, councillors and officers and the vote is regarded as the starting point of a chain of command'. If we place parties at two points in this chain between electors and officers thus: *electors, parties, councillors, parties, officers,* we can see that parties at one and the same time weaken the link with electors but also provide electors with a clear reference point for understanding their councillors' actions and so also strengthen the link.

When parties are placed between councillors and officers they act as a source of strength for councillors in facing a powerful, well-resourced and professional administrative machine. That is not to say that Independent councillors cannot adequately hold officers to account (they can, see Copus et al., 2009; Copus and Wingfield, 2014), merely that parties provide councillors with an additional link in the chain of command – one which flows two ways, from the councillor as something to which the councillor contributes and to the councillor as something which expects his or her loyalty (Copus, 2004; Copus and Erlingsson, 2013). As a result of the 2014 English local elections, just over 90 per cent of all councillors in England come from one of the three main political parties, thus the voters have placed national political parties in a position to act as a strong link in that local chain of electoral command, a chain where votes are absolute trumps and are the only legitimate and justifiable way of ascertaining the wishes of the people (Green, 1990; Phillips, 1994). Thus, there is a link between councillors and parties which is sustained by the act of voting and the transference of a legitimacy to act politically from the voter to the councillor.

Dearlove (1973) rightly points out that the chain of command is also predicated on local government having high levels of discretion at its command. The decline in the standing of English local government in particular has been well documented (see, for example, Jones and Stewart, 1985; Young and Rao, 1997). But when that decline began, English local government was already at a very low point compared to much local government overseas (see Reynaert et al., 2005; Denters and Rose, 2005). Categorisations of local government systems (see Page and Goldsmith, 1987; Hesse and Sharpe, 1991; Goldsmith and Page, 2010) also stress the discretion available to local government within different systems and under different constitutional arrangements as a key factor in local government independence or relative standing in the face of regional or central government. Where that discretion is low, the electoral chain of command theory is weakened, and that is certainly the case for English local government.

If, however, we place parties at the two points in that chain of command suggested above, and if we then focus not on the discretion that councils have in regard to the services they have been made responsible for by other layers of government but on their political legitimacy in seeking to influence others, then we start to see that the electoral chain of command has some utility (Dearlove, 1973: 29) as a characterisation of local politics. Electoral turnout – low as it is in England compared to other nations – does not damage the theory as it is not intended to explain the working of elections but how legitimacy (and accountability) is accrued and transferred from one link in the chain to another. The chain of command does not disregard the low salience of local elections for voters in this country, but the ideas on which it is based are not damaged by single country exceptions, such as England's position at the bottom of European local election turnout (Rallings and Thrasher, 2013). Rather, where voting does take place, there is always a transfer of power and responsibility from the voter to the councillor and his or her party, whatever the turnout. The chain of command underpins, therefore, the legitimacy of councillors to act outside the council and to employ political discretion in negotiating, persuading and affecting how others behave and the decisions they make.

Thus, given the electoral legitimacy of the councillor, we can assume their influence extends beyond their ability to hold a council bureaucracy to account and into wider governing networks and to those whose size and scope extend beyond the council's area, whether they are public, private or third-sector bodies. Thus the electoral chain of command becomes: *voter, party, councillor, party, council official, external agency* and *environment*, and while the chain may not be perfectly linear, more like a chain mail of interconnected linkages, each one takes the councillor

back to their link with the voter. Thus, despite the complexity of governing networks, and despite the low level of political and governing power held by councils
and councillors, we can still trace a legitimacy for councillors to act from the chain
of command, indicating that elected local representative democracy does indeed
have a role in shaping what unelected and often unaccountable networks do.

Stoker (2004: 15) points out that the 'governance account' (that literature and
narrative that accounts for the competition experienced by the elected council in
the governing of an area) argues that the complexity of the interactions that now
make up the local policy landscape does not mean local government has ceased
to matter. Rather, it no longer has the dominance locally that it once experienced.
Local government no longer 'acts on its own' (*ibid.*: 16) across a range of policy fields. Stoker (2004: 16) goes on to identify a shift from 'overhead representative democracy', where citizens controlled councillors and politicians controlled
bureaucrats (the electoral chain of command), to forms of accountability that
stretch beyond this into governance. Governance recognises the complexity of
'intergovernmental networks' (Stoker 2004: 19) and the rise of 'multi-level governance'. Other challengers have imposed themselves in competition with local
government acting as 'new lines of accountability' (*ibid.*: 17). But the councillor
still has a legitimacy that others lack from open and inclusive electoral processes
that deliver a mandate to govern.

Because they are assessing a shift from one model to another, or assume community participation as a more authentic pluralistic democracy than representative
democracy (see Foley and Martin, 2000; Lowndes et al., 2001a, b, 2006; Newman
et al., 2004a, b), accounts of governance and public or community participation
in local government do not adequately recognise the importance of the council
as an electorally legitimised body. Consequently, inadvertently or otherwise, such
accounts can undermine local representative democracy. Indeed, it is because
local government has lost dominance locally as provider and controller of access
to public services that its electoral linkage to the public can be transformed into a
source of legitimacy for councillors to exert influence in governance interactions
and take part in the only game in town. Councillors have two moral levers available
to them: their democratic mandate and the legitimacy it provides, and the linkage between councillors as elected representatives and the citizens they represent.
In contrast, claims to legitimacy and authenticity made by unelected community
activists are themselves challengeable for lack of accountability and inclusion.

Rather than fundamentally undermining the position of local government, the
existence of challengers, either service providers and decision-makers or players
claiming some relationship with a section of the community, provides an opportunity for councillors to employ their mandate to hold these disparate and potentially chaotic elements to account. Indeed, if other service agencies and public and
private sector bodies lack real lines of accountability, then any perceived weakness
in the electoral chain of command pales into insignificance. While other actors
and agencies within governance networks may conduct public consultation, they

do so without the same political link and the overhead chain of command that exists between citizens and councils. Even initiatives such as service user groups or panels, discussion forums and surveys or social media campaigns do not provide a chain of command or any form of direct accountability. Thus, as such bodies have moved into the territory that was once the domain of local government – large-scale provision of public services, decisions about the expenditure of public money, the development of public policy and developing an organisational and institutional structure to suit the geographical demands of its service administration (Copus, 2010b) – new territory is opened up for exploration by democratically elected councillors.

The opening-up of that new territory means that to the legitimate tasks of the office of councillor can be added that of scrutineer – not in the narrow inwardly focused sense of overview and scrutiny within the council but as an externally focused set of processes – largely in the control of the councillor. These will be based on negotiation, discussion, compromise and the seeking of explanations and justifications of the decisions and actions of others. Indeed, as one councillor in an interview expressed it: 'Scrutiny needs teeth, it needs to be able to force outsiders (public bodies) to attend and it needs the powers of enforcement of its reports and recommendations.' What is being proposed here, very simply, is that councillors can lead and govern, not through the direct provision of services by their councils but through holding those that do provide them to account and being able to shape how they operate to bring them into alignment with an overall vision for the locality. The governance narrative to which Stoker refers, while part of the justification for the demise of authoritative local government, can also assist in refocusing the role and activities of councillors.

The thin (representative) democracy that Barber (1984) critiques can be thickened and strengthened considerably, not necessarily by large-scale public participation, consultation and deliberation, as such a framework provides a forum for the self-selected and self-interested and a local war of all against all, but by local representative democracy, which avoids these pitfalls. Democracy and accountability of any thickness is, however, absent from great swathes of the public landscape and so councils must increasingly become a setting in which the accountability of others can be secured by councillors acting as political representatives interacting with bodies beyond the council and meshing previously unaccountable bodies into the electoral chain mail of command. It is to how councillors interact to achieve accountability and influence in networks collectively, and with their network partners individually, that the chapter now turns.

Councillors: authority and influence

As elected politicians granted a mandate by the voters, councillors are now faced with the task of influencing the decisions and actions of independent players within a web of relationships (Klijn and Skelcher, 2007). Given the complexity of the inter-relationships between these independent players, the sovereignty and authority of the elected council, if it is to continue to mean anything at all, has to be employed in new ways by councillors (Sorensen, 2006). Governance scholars have given attention to how local government can secure the democratic anchorage of governance networks so that their performance can be assessed and overseen by local government and how the democratic deficit inherent in governance networks can be mitigated (see Skelcher, 2005; Torfing et al., 2009). The question remains, however: can vicarious democratic legitimacy accrue to these networks collectively and the independent players individually, simply through the presence and actions of a formal or informal relationship with an elected official – the councillor?

If we require our governors at national and local government level to be elected to secure legitimacy and the authority to act, then it is questionable that legitimacy and democratic viability, inclusivity and accountability can be transferred to others by elected bodies, by interaction with a councillor or a council. Moreover, the role of the councillor, when operating within any form of network, is not merely to provide the veneer of democracy and accountability to those that have no electoral mandate. If the governance narrative describes how elected local government has lost its position within localities and has been replaced by the activities of unelected and unaccountable bodies that have no direct political linkage to citizens, then the role of councillors is not to provide what these networks lack. The role of the councillor becomes twofold: first, to hold such bodies answerable for their decisions and actions, and second, given councils' lack of governing powers, to attempt to mould the activities of the independent players to match the policy preferences and overall political vision of the council as an elected and democratic body. Or, as one councillor in an interview very clearly posed it: 'how can we as councillors who have been elected, be relegated behind those who haven't and how, without the power to get them to do what the people who have voted for us want, can we control them?'

A strong local representative democracy would indeed enable elected councils and councillors to control the activities and policies of those that casually operate within governance networks developing public policy, making decisions and spending public money, with no real democratic mandate – anchored or otherwise. Currently, however, elected councillors must settle for diplomatic activity with their unelected counterparts as a way of securing influence. The difficulties involved in securing that influence are a major source of frustration for many councillors, as illustrated below:

The LEP (Local Enterprise Partnership) is not elected so how do we hold it to account? I worry that the presence of councillors on the board only gives the LEP a legitimacy it doesn't have or deserve. It is doing the work of the councils and its money ultimately comes from what should be with the council. What I do is to give a voice to the community at the LEP, not just to the council … the LEP area is so big that it tends to overlook local areas or, worse, does things that will, in the long run affect some areas very badly. Councillors have to be part of the LEP as a strategic body, but we have to make sure that what it does reflects the needs of our own areas and the views of our voters. It is very difficult in a formal setting to do either of these things – especially given the focus of the LEP. (Labour councillor)

The LEP is just an example of where councils are being engineered out of any responsibility or control over what goes on and we are the ones that have been elected! The LEPs are not answerable to us or to anyone really and we can take part in the discussion, that's true, but we [councillors] are thinking about a range of things and services and issues, whereas the LEP is focused on one thing only and that narrow focus, while important, can ignore how decisions, policies, services have to link up. I've been told a few times at LEP meetings 'yes, interesting, but that's really to do with the council'. I mean, how can you operate like that – sometimes it's said in a sort of dismissive, that's not important enough attitude; other times it's done because others there – that aren't councillors – are thinking from a narrow perspective. It's quite dangerous, really. (Conservative councillor)

I go to these LEP meetings and they are extremely important and it is right that the people that are there, as business leaders, have an important input to the issues that are being considered. I know there are council leaders, like myself there too. But, you can't give our election to those that have been appointed. The issues discussed should be discussed with those on the board and people like them, but it should be elected councils that make the final decisions. (Conservative councillor)

Yes, I attend the meetings, but I find I get more say over what happens by meeting and discussing things privately with board members, separately. I meet the chair of the LEP regularly, outside the meetings, and we discuss problems and solutions and the needs of the area – not just my council either. It is much more conducive to being able to help his [the LEP chair] thinking develop. I've sat in formal meetings and listened to him say almost what I've said to him in private and I know he'll bring others from the private sector on board too. Now I'm sure they are sitting there thinking exactly the same about me, though. (Conservative council leader)

It is also evident that while councillors do place weight on the elected office they hold in their attempts to wield some form of influence over other bodies, that is not always responded to positively by the non-elected elements they face, as a councillor sitting on a probation trust commented:

I'm the only one on the Trust that has been elected to anything, but that appears to count for nothing at formal trust meetings. It is very difficult to get others to recognise, not only that I represent a council, a party and my voters but that I come to the table with a mandate and yes, I do, indirectly refer to that, as subtly as possible, just to remind folk that it matters. Also, I do it to see how they respond and to use it as a way of trying to get the rest of the board to come along.

I'm there because I'm a councillor and I am always trying to get the trust to think about what they do from a political point of view and to get them to share what I know my colleagues [councillors] think about the issue before us. Look, we [his council] have a range of policies about community safety and other related service areas that address what we are trying to achieve for the people that use the probation service. Our policies also address the political agenda we are trying to achieve. The Trust is one way we can achieve those objectives but only if it comes along with us. (Labour borough councillor)

The same councillor also admitted to the importance of private meetings with the chair of the trust and with individual trust members and officers. It is clear from the examples given by councillors that they tend to operate on trusts and boards in very similar ways to how they operate within their councils. That is, councillors use the formal meetings and settings of any partnership bodies of which they are members as a forum in which to follow a formal meeting agenda, debate the business before them, pronounce on policy matters and attempt to encourage and convince others that they should support a particular decision, and then to make decisions. There is a key difference, however, and that is the absence of the certainty that is provided by a party group agreeing prior to a public and formal council meeting what decisions to take in public, although some LEP members who were councillors did admit to discussing the issues with the other councillor members of the board before the formal board meeting. Given that the councillors were from different councils and parties, the purpose of this was not to agree a 'whip' but rather to share thoughts about the matters before the meeting and to consider the local government implications and input.

Councillors also operate on partnership bodies in a way that is similar to how they act at their own councils. In this alternative mode of operation we see councillors employing informal negotiating and influencing techniques and, indeed, operating very happily in informal settings. Councillors thus interact with other non-councillor board members and employees of the partnership bodies outside of official meetings, to build support and convince others that a particular decision should be made or policy developed. Indeed, one councillor was remarkably candid about this process when she said:

I do here what I do at the council: meet privately with officers, come in and out (although that's not quite as easy, yet, as it is at the council), talk to staff and the experts here and try and convince them of what I'm thinking – or let them convince me otherwise. (Liberal Democrat borough councillor)

Another councillor showed a different approach and saw those working at the LEP as a potential resource for her in her wider council work. She commented:

I will be in the office speaking to the director [of the LEP] and especially the person who deals with the European grants but also with some of the other really

good people they have there to help me as a councillor. They are always happy to
give advice and as long as what I ask is within their remit, I've never had a problem getting help – as long as it's somehow connected to economic development.
(Conservative county councillor)

It is no surprise that councillors operate within the various partner bodies in
the same way as they operate at their council base. If both a formal and informal
approach to gaining influence works in the council, then it is reasonable to assume
that it can be effectively employed in other non-council settings. Moreover, if
councillors hold offices outside the council because of their council membership,
which they hold in turn because of their election to the council, then any sense
of frustration at not being able to successfully influence partnership bodies of
which they are a member will magnify any sense of democratic distance and lack
of accountability. It is at this point of frustration that councillors will fall back on
their role as scrutineer, responsible for ensuring the accountability of an unelected
body, particularly if councillors are present on that body in numbers.

I question, challenge and ask for explanations, especially as there are so many
that are not elected, as councillors, I mean. I use it [a water customer liaison
panel) to stand up for local people and try to get the best possible service for
them. But they have to answer questions – actually that is what this thing is here
for, really. (Liberal Democrat city councillor)

What must be kept in mind is the sheer variety of purposes, shapes, size, scale
and interests of the bodies on which councillors find themselves sitting, or which,
even if not members, they must attempt to influence. Moreover, shifts and changes
in the governance landscape arising from the government's creation of new organisational configurations, or the abolition of existing ones, provide councillors with
an additional problem – bringing stability of purpose and direction to a potentially turbulent landscape. Councillors, of course, are well aware of this shifting
landscape and recognise the importance of navigating it to ensure they develop
a continual stream of influence, whatever the setting. As one Labour councillor
commented: 'I was on the RDA [Regional Development Agency] now I'm on the
LEP – all that's changed is the initials they use.'

As central governments come and go, and as the public agencies which they
create often come and go with them, councillors must revise their strategies
for interaction and influence and employ them in new settings. But, as public
agencies are reformulated and their activities and responsibilities reconfigured,
the council remains the only body with a democratic mandate to act. Yet central
government fails to recognise the importance of that mandate and of the democratic underpinning that it grants to councillors – other than by the offer of a
given number of seats on trusts or boards. The diminution of the role of local
government and councillors continues while the powers and responsibilities

of councils and other public agencies are reconfigured around them. Thus, the interactions of councillors within and between these public bodies take on a strategic importance.

Any time and energy councillors invest in studying the landscape and understanding the purpose and objectives of the public agencies with which they must interact comes at a premium, but one worth paying. Indeed, councillors' membership of any form of public agency provides them with the opportunity to align such bodies with the broader policies and objectives of their council and to strategically join together the disparate decisions taken by others. The irony here is that an elected official is attempting to influence unelected officials, rather than the other way around. If councillors are able to influence and shape the overall framework within which these bodies operate and effectively co-ordinate policy and action into a cohesive direction, then they are acting as meta-governors (Jessop, 1998; Sorensen and Torfing, 2009). To do that, however, councillors scattered across various bodies must act cohesively and co-ordinate their actions and the actions of other councillors. Such co-ordination of action becomes increasingly difficult when council membership of some boards or public agencies is spread across several different councils. Indeed, it may be unachievable because of political differences.

The success of democratic anchorage rests on councillors actually having influence and not on their mere presence within networks or on boards, trusts or whatever other configurations are used in place of the democratically elected council. It also rests on councillors having cohesive strategies for influence that join up across a range of bodies and for their activities in all levels of interactions outside the council to be seen as a strategic priority for the council. Without that, there is not so much democratic anchorage, but councils and councillors acting as a democratic buoy which merely indicates the presence of the council as it bobs up and down in a sea of undemocratic, unaccountable and unelected organisations that control great swathes of public policy and public spending. So, is it anchor or buoy?

Strategies for influence

The range of what are often termed in local government 'outside bodies' to which councillors are appointed indicates the complexity and varying importance of the organisations councillors must interact with and seek to influence. 'We have 150 outside bodies to appoint our 48 members to and only half of those members are on outside bodies. The problem is in a lot of cases the member doesn't even get notification of meetings, let alone actual agendas.' That comment, made by a Conservative county councillor, summarises the reality of the situation for many councillors and councils when it comes to the ability and opportunities they have to structure and focus their actions to have some influence over the bodies that have replaced the elected council in great swathes of the public sector. Another councillor added: 'it is difficult to get co-ordination across councillors from different councils let alone have any observable influence or be able to use our democratic position to achieve solid results.'

Do councillors therefore attempt to have influence within one body, or do they try to produce a cohesive and strategically targeted influence across the public and private sector that provides the potential for, but not the actuality of, democratically anchoring the bodies with which they interact? Moreover, do councillors use their mandate and their knowledge of public opinion from their own political networks or the council's consultation and engagement with the public to pursue particular policy options within governance networks? As I found, (Copus 2010b: 584–6) councillors do not see themselves as bound by the views of their voters when operating outside the council, much as they do not see themselves as mandated by the voters to act in a particular way in the council itself. The world of governance, much like the council, is not a place in which the specific views of the voter are pursued. Rather, networks are a place in which 'the established patterns of representative and political leadership behaviour are extended to new settings for the purpose of securing elite policy preferences' (Copus, 2010b: 585).

Councillors are, however, more likely to employ the results of public consultation exercises undertaken by their councils as a way of securing influence with external bodies, rather than using their more general political mandate as leverage (Copus, 2010b: 586). We also see councillors acting as 'trustees' (Eulau et al., 1959) of both the public and their councils rather than being mandated and expected to act as a 'delegate' of their council when interacting in governance networks. As many councillors appointed to the higher-level public bodies are themselves leading councillors who set the agenda for their councils and their groups, they are free to pursue a broad set of objectives as they think fit. But we return to the question of the effectiveness of their input in terms of having an influence and to anchoring the practices of others into some form of democratically inspired direction. We have already seen that there are three ways in which councillors can operate within networks, but that does not mean that they are acting in a coherent fashion or with a strategic set of objectives. The research for this book suggests that there are three ideal types of councillor when it comes to developing strategies for effective action and influence within governance networks:

The *casual councillor* operates as an individual, detached from the council and only representing it and the voters in the broadest of senses. The councillor may sit on a board of an outside body – of some considerable importance – but acts solely as a member of that body. That is, the councillor receives agenda, minutes and reports and in formal settings processes the work presented to her or him by the officers of the organisation concerned. The councillor acts as though the only requirement is to make the decisions that the organisation itself is charged with making and to operate with a focus only on those responsibilities. There is no attempt to pursue either the overall objectives of the council or to promote the articulated views of the voters on particular questions. No informal process or discussions are used to set or shape an agenda and only formal meetings count from this councillor's perspective. Here there is little chance of any real success for the councillor in having a strategic influence through the body of which he or she is a member.

The *single-focus councillor* sees the activities of any outside public and private organisation on which he or she is appointed as an opportunity to shape what those bodies do, the policies they develop and the decisions they take. The councillor will use formal and informal settings to draw the actions of the particular bodies into alignment with the council's policies in those specific areas so that the outcomes match policy objectives of the council. Much stress is placed on the informal processes of influence and in building support across the membership of the board concerned to ensure decisions favoured by the council are made. The councillor here recognises the importance of controlling and shaping an agenda before decisions are placed in a formal setting for ratification. Indeed, this councillor has transferred the processes of party decision-making into an external body. However, there is no attempt to draw the threads together into a broader strategic and coherent whole, no matter how many outside bodies the councillor may be a member of. But the leverage provided by elected office is employed and so too is the pursuit of community opinion. The councillor here sees each body as an entity to be influenced separately.

The councillor acting as *governor* recognises the interrelated nature of the actions of bodies on which they sit and actively attempts to draw them into alignment with the overall policy direction of the council. The councillor operates so as to question, challenge and seek justification for actions of public agencies of which he or she is a representative of the council but also uses the informal processes to shape the policy agenda across a number of bodies. The councillor particularly skilled in this approach will also endeavour to influence indirectly those bodies on which he is not an official council representative, through negotiations and discussions with councillors who are members of other bodies or by approaching public and private organisations to which he or she is not associated, and organising discussions and debates with those bodies by simply employing the mandate that attaches to the office of councillor as leverage.

It is no surprise when looking at these modules that we see parallels with the *corporate* and *associated* councillor and the *lay* and *professional* genre of councillors identified in Chapter 3 when the relationship of the councillor with the council was explored. What we see of councillors when operating outside the council is that they transfer an operating mode that matches their operational relationship with the council of which they are member. What is clear from the three ideal types is that the mere presence of councillors operating as formal members of external agencies is no guarantee that those bodies will be anchored in any democratic

fashion. Nor is it a guarantee that, merely by interacting with such bodies, councillors will take on the role of governors: that is to see their political duties as bringing shape, form and direction to the interactions of organisations within networks
and to networks themselves and to do so with a set of political objectives in mind.
Councillors must see this role as a distinct feature of their office and be politically inspired to act in a governing fashion by specifically focusing on the external
world and influencing, shaping and holding it to account. Without that process,
there is no democratic linkage within the system and the democratic chain mail
begins to degrade.

Councillors as individual politicians will interpret the roles, responsibilities and
functions they play both inside and outside the council in ways which suit their
own conceptualisation of those roles. Unless governing through other bodies or
holding them to account is part of the councillor's governing assumptions, there is
little chance of that councillor being engaged in a process of bringing democratic
oversight to governing networks. A Labour councillor summed up the governing
frame of mind when he commented:

> Partnerships are the name of the game and the level of cuts in our budget means
> we're able to do less and less, so we have to work with anyone and everyone, but
> it's how you do it that matters. As a council we know what we want to achieve,
> health, housing, crime – drugs particularly, improving the economy, getting
> business working here, the environment, trying to hold on financially while the
> health service takes more and more public money and isn't accountable, work-
> ing with the police, the private companies that run the public utilities, and for
> every quango the government says it's abolished, another seems to spring up; all
> of that just can't happen, it has to be joined up, co-ordinated somehow and not
> just that but challenged. That's what's left to local government – being govern-
> ment in a very broad sense.

That view contrasts starkly with another Labour councillor from a different
authority, who said: 'it's a mess; we [local government] have nothing left, or very
little that isn't shared with someone else at some point – we have all these meetings and some councillors go to more meetings outside the council than for the
council, but they can't do anything. I look after my ward and try and make sure the
council works properly; that's all you can do.'

These are two very different views of what it is to be a councillor, but it takes
more than a councillor having an understanding that the diminution of the sovereign council as the governing body of the locality can somehow be compensated
for by engagement with the bodies that have replaced its role and powers. The next
step is for the council as an institution to embrace a wider governing perspective and to be organised to support the actions and innovations of those councillors who perceive governing to be their role so as to maximise the influence they
can have within wider networks beyond the council. Thus, councils must stress

the 'government' in local government and see democratising, shaping and holding to account the networks with which they are faced as an essential role for all councillors.

Conclusion

Local government is confronted with a continual struggle for influence over the decisions, policies and resource expenditure undertaken by unelected operators within their locality that make up the networks through which much public policy is developed and implemented. The council and its councillors have a mandate granted by the voters in an electoral chain of command, which links voters to parties, councillors and the council and then into the disparate and diffuse networks of those engaged in public policy development and decision-making. The idea that the council is a sovereign political body within any one locality has broken down, if it was ever a reality in the first place. But the fact remains that of all the numerous agencies that operate alongside local government today, the council is the only body with any direct political legitimised link to the community through the mechanism of the public vote.

It is commonplace today to criticise that link and claim that community activists are somehow more authentic than elected councillors, or that public agencies that are not elected are somehow better placed to make decisions about key areas of public policy than an elected council. But none of those claims can replace that direct line of accountability that rests with the council and its members. The transference of the democratic legitimacy of the council to all players within networks, however, is not an automatic result of interactions between elected councillors and their unelected counterparts with whom they must do business. Rather, it is something which must be planned, co-ordinated and strategically focused by the council and not left to the skills and inclinations of individual councillors. If councils are to govern in governance networks, nothing can be left to chance.

Councillors are well aware that their office is sanctioned by the public vote and that this provides them with a moral and political lever to be used within external networks and to shape the actions of particular public agencies. Moreover, when councillors see themselves as governors of the networks within which they operate they also adopt the same relationship with their council as they do with the electorate: that of trustee rather than a delegate of the council – freedom for manoeuvre for the councillor in governance networks means a degree of independence from the council. But councillors do not necessarily always see their role in broad strategic terms; rather they may see it simply as being a member of a board on which they are expected to do no more than proceed through a formal agenda placed before them. Yet there are councillors that see their role much more as a politician who must join together the component parts of external networks into some broad cohesive direction and through diplomatic manoeuvres bring them into alignment with their own and their council's political objectives.

Governance may describe the process of interaction between independent but interconnected agencies (Atkinson and Coleman, 1992; Rhodes, 1997; Pierre, 2000), but the implication of a term that sounds like 'government' is that there is something democratic and accountable within those interactions. But it is just that: an implication. The existence of councillors within networks can at best add an element of direction and bring the activities of those bodies into some form of alignment with the direction preferred by the elected council – even if the boundaries of public agencies extend beyond the boundaries of any council. At worst, it provides no more than a democratic veneer to the actions of agencies that develop public policy, spend public resources and impact on the well-being of communities, but which are not directly chosen by the public or have the virtue of a direct mandate.

When acting externally, councillors face much the same problems as when acting internally to their council. Time, resources, advice and support are required to enable councillors to use networks of partners as a way of developing their own governing capacity in much the same way as they are needed to enable councillors to operate effectively within their own councils. Indeed, councillors tend to take with them to public agencies the practices and approaches that they employ within their councils. This means that much of the potential for developing governing capacity can be lost to procedural demands. There are most certainly councillors who operate as strategically focused politicians operating beyond the scope of their councils to attempt to influence and shape the activities and polices of those bodies with which they and their councils interact. But unless the council as a whole is structured and organised to ensure councillors undertake such activity as a role expectation and then supports councillors in meeting that activity, success in democratising and directing networks is far from guaranteed.

So we are left with a scattered pattern of councillor action when it comes to engagement in governance networks and to attempts to influence or bring some form of democratic accountability to those networks and the individual agencies within them. Councillors have yet to fully embrace the idea of governor as a distinct role and function, and until they do so, their ability to aggregate preferences, influence unelected bodies and provide a distinct policy framework within which others should operate will remain unfulfilled. But, as we have seen, councillors must strike a balance between those aspects of the current role and its expectations and other aspects of the role to which they give less preference but are expected to undertake. Some councillors see governing the area through networks as a way of taking action to achieve their political objectives; others see it as an undesirable process that is eating away the control of the council over the provision of public services; and still others see it as a distraction from running the council and holding it to account.

The success of councillors operating as governors within networks, or indeed recognising it as a legitimate undertaking for them in the first place, depends on a number of factors: councillors' own motivations for standing and staying in office; what it was they sought to achieve through council membership; their willingness and ability to be politically innovative in approaching the office of councillor and using it to effect change; the effects of council membership on their public and private lives; the time they are able to devote to council work; and their own views about what action they need to take to achieve their political objectives. It is to these factors we now turn.

5

Why seek to serve?

Introduction

In Chapter 1 we saw that the roles and functions of the office of councillor are shaped by a range of external forces, and councillors' preferences for concentrating on certain roles are not for them alone to settle. Those forces include international trends and developments in the world economy or the process of urbanisation, the demands and changes that central and regional governments make to local government, and the demands and expectations of individual citizens and communities. The previous chapter also showed that the strategies and approaches councillors themselves develop as politicians attempting to influence, or govern, beyond the confines of the council depend on the priority they give to this aspect of their work. There is therefore a constant pressure on the councillor to perform a series of disparate roles within the limited time available and to respond to changing demands and expectations. This results in the office of councillor having few, if any, boundaries.

The 18,000 councillors across England and their countless counterparts elected to municipalities across the globe, as well as all those who present themselves as candidates to the voters in the hope of being elected as a councillor, do so with varying expectations of what they can achieve and of the demands that will be made upon them. Some that have never presented themselves before the electorate will, when standing for the first time, have a clear indication of what the role may entail. These candidates may have been long-time members of political parties, they have worked alongside councillors and interacted with them at party meetings or other events. In addition, once the decision to stand was made, they would have had their enthusiasm stoked by the pressures of the competition of the selection process. Even so, the mature party member will still lack the insider knowledge of the sitting councillor about the procedures and process of the council and what can and cannot be achieved with the office, inside and outside the council.

The candidate who is either very new to his or her party or was selected with the promise that the seat was 'unwinnable' and that all that was required was a paper candidate to keep the enemy pinned down, may have a very unclear view of what is expected of them or what they can expect to achieve. The Independent candidate, with no local party structure through which to absorb the basics of the role, may be even less well prepared for office – assuming that there are no other

Independent councillors on the council with whom he or she can discuss candidature and role tasks and expectations before standing for election. In addition to a pre-existing level of role uncertainty for the potentially new councillor, there is the mix of factors that may have motivated the councillor to stand in the first place and which may therefore act as a focus for their attention immediately after election. The councillor seeking re-election will not only have a clearer idea of what can and cannot be achieved, they will also have had experience of the frustrations, problems, demands, challenges, barriers and personal and employment costs of being a councillor. Yet, whether new or old to the council: they stand.

The casual disregard and in some cases downright hostility which is often meted out to councillors by the media (which is the subject of Chapter 7) sets a background against which councillors must operate and shapes the environment within which they must attempt to achieve their political objectives. However, councillors are politicians rooted in their localities, living in close proximity to those they represent and for whom they must make governing decisions. They are close (in some cases, as we shall see later, dangerously close) to communities and individuals with whom they interact as governors, caseworkers, representatives, advisors, policy-makers, advocates, decision-makers, community champions and the overseers of public services (Heclo, 1969; Newton, 1976; Gyford, 1976; Rao, 1994). That proximity and its effects on the life of the councillor are explored in the next chapter. What is examined in this chapter is the question for all councillors: why do it? The chapter also considers what encourages individuals to present themselves to the local electorate and to do so time after time.

The next section examines the reasons why, for some of our fellow citizens, the time becomes right for them to stand for election to the council. It does this by setting out the characteristics of the particular journeys to the council that come together and result in the decision to stand: the slow burn, the big bang and the resister (the latter is a term also used by Barron et al., 1989, 1991). The third section then examines, in detail, what it is that stimulates councillors to seek office and what they hope to achieve on election. It also looks at what party, ideological, political, personal or community-related factors must come together to provide the stimulus to seek election. The chapter concludes by setting out what can be learnt from what stimulates some to stand for the office of councillor.

The time was right

There are difficulties in identifying and understanding what it is that spurs individuals to seek political office. These difficulties arise from what Norris and Lovenduski (1995: 167), using data from the 1992 British Candidates Survey, referred to as the intangible, 'hidden', 'complex' and fluid nature of a set of deeply personal factors stimulating a person to place themselves before the voters. Some early social psychology claimed that certain personality types were prone to seeking elected office (Lasswell, 1960; Barber, 1965); other studies take a rational choice approach (see Schlesinger, 1991) and suggest that motivations to seek office can be categorised thus: personal, ideological, public service, single issues and representation (see Norris and Lovenduski, 1995: 165).

More recently, the 2010 Local Government Association (LGA) census of councillors throughout England showed that the most common reason for standing for election was a desire to 'serve the community' (NFER, 2011: 11), with some 88 per cent of respondents stating this as their reason for standing. Other factors which led councillors to put themselves forward were: the desire to promote change (52 per cent), the councillor's 'political beliefs' (50 per cent), because they had been asked to stand (28 per cent), and being motivated by a single issue (12 per cent) (NFER, 2011: 11). The LGA survey also found that there was a party-political dimension to the responses, as the report stated that Labour councillors were: 'notably more likely to have become a councillor because of their political beliefs (74.2 per cent) and to change things (63.7 per cent) and were less likely to have become one because they had been asked (15.9 per cent)' (NFER, 2011: 11). Conservative and Liberal Democrat councillors, on the other hand, were: 'more likely to have become councillors because they had been asked' (31.4 per cent and 32.6 per cent respectively) (NFER, 2011: 11).

Understanding the route into the office of councillor has focused on the notion of 'political recruitment', that is, the process through which individuals are deliberately 'selected' to join the political elite and by which a series of selection (formal and informal) processes are employed to filter the potential members of that elite who then begin to navigate the various political offices available. Verhelst et al. (2013: 28) (citing the work of Prewitt, 1969 and 1970, Marvick, 1972 and Brady et al., 1999: 153) suggest we can understand the nature of the local political recruitment process best by focusing on the background of those recruited and the characteristics that the recruiters seek. Verhelst et al. (2013: 29–30) go on to point out that particular weight is given to the idea that certain types of individuals, from certain social strata, who might have experienced a process of political socialisation and mobilisation, are more likely to be looked upon favourably by local political recruiters (Budge and Farlie, 1975; Van Liefferinge and Steyvers, 2008). A process of political apprenticeship further enhances the opportunities for certain groups to be selected as candidates for council and is thus seen as narrowing the social base of those that stand for election (see Reynaert, 2012 and Verhelst and Kerrouche, 2012).

Verhelst et al. (2013: 30) point out that the classic model of elite recruitment is, however, rather deterministic and fails to account properly for the complex array of personal concerns and circumstances, individual expectations and political aims, and the detailed, complex, shifting, sometimes deliberate and other times accidental factors that set an individual on the path to presenting her or himself before the voters to become a councillor. There is a deep well of personal motivations and circumstances which stimulate, or which are simply opportune, that must come together before the ones chosen to join the elite are ready to be considered for selection. Political parties, for example, will offer to their members various inducements to stand for council, such as support in electioneering and with the costs of campaigning, organisational resources and structures and a long-term political vision and the possibility of a long-term career (see Ostrogorski, 1902; Michels, 1915; Birch, 1959; Clark and Wilson, 1961: 134–5; Lee, 1963; Jones, 1969; Glassberg, 1981; Panebianco, 1988: ch. 2).

The inducements offered to members to stand for local office are no free ride, however, as parties expect the loyalty of their councillors to the party programme once elected. The local party group on the council will place a high premium on councillor loyalty and thus a dilemma is ever present for the party councillor about whom or what they represent and to whom they owe their ultimate allegiance. A reasonable assumption is that the stronger a councillor's ties to his or her party, the more the councillor is able and willing to represent it – but in doing so perceives that the voters are also being represented because the party operates in the voters' best interests. But are councillors stimulated by party interests and motivations alone when it comes to the decision to seek office? The LGA figures above would suggest otherwise, so it is also necessary to search for those common factors that are part of the decision-making journey that leads all councillors, of any party or none, to office. It is the individual councillor's journey that provides a detailed picture of why and how there is the constant flow of political interest from individuals prepared to campaign for and fill the office of councillor. The research resulting in this book identified that the journey to becoming a councillor had distinct sets of characteristics, which might be categorised as the *slow burn*, the *big bang* and the *resister*.

The slow burn

The *slow burn* refers to a person who started out with no ambitions to stand for council and either became active in a party or in a community organisation out of interest or general commitment to a cause. During the slow burn, there is a long period of continual political engagement and activity and a growing commitment to local politics – whether in a party or not – and an increasing involvement with political colleagues and a gradual taking on of more positions of authority and responsibility within a party or other organisation. Over time, the cumulative effect of this greater involvement on the longer-term life choices of the potential candidate and political activist (the term is used here solely to mean someone active in politics and not with its more pejorative connotations) steers that person towards council candidacy.

The key feature of the slow burn is that, on entering politics, there is no prior desire to be a councillor but rather a growing realisation that there is a logical journey that takes an individual to the council. The journey is not the same for all councillors, and what prevents all activists from becoming councillors is a stage-of-life decision, a lack of interest in taking activism to elected office, or the absence of a tipping point. For the slow burner, the arrival of a tipping point is what causes the final decision to stand for election to council. That tipping point will manifest itself in a number of ways: a dramatic party-related incident which spurs an individual to candidacy; an opportunity arising to stand for a seat; a change in life circumstances; shifting political allegiances; a case of revenge; final agreement from a spouse; or, more prosaically, as one councillor described it: 'the time was just right'. Indeed, that comment was repeated by many of those that had finally made the decision to seek office and was a way of summarising the end of a deeply personal journey – which may, even for the councillor concerned, have had no clear defining eureka moment, rather a gradual realisation that standing for council could either no longer be avoided or that inexplicably the time had just arrived.

The same councillor added:

> I'd been in the party for 20 years and done just about everything you could think of, held all sorts of offices and worked in every election over those 20 years, not missed one; I'd done it all except stand for the council. One of our councillors stood down and I decided to have a go. A couple of people suggested I should but there were two others interested, but they were both from outside the ward and they selected me. I'll certainly be standing again; I don't see the point of doing just one term, unless for some reason you can't carry on.

The big bang

In contrast to the slow burn is the *big bang*, which is a route to the council that is planned and is always the objective of the individual who joins a party or who decides to present themselves as an Independent. Even if the right time does not present itself for some while, or political circumstances are not right, the intention to stand is always present, and indeed it was the motivating force in becoming active in local politics in the first place. The big bang may be mitigated, of course, because a party's rules may set out a minimum period of membership before being eligible for selection (thus giving selectors more time to assess the worthiness of the candidate). The Labour Party rules, for example, stipulate that a candidate must have been a member of the party continually for twelve months to qualify for candidacy (Labour Party, 2013: 22). Local Conservative associations and Liberal Democrats have been known to recruit candidates on the doorstep – who were not existing members – or have advertised in the local press for candidates.

A Conservative councillor explained thus:

> I'd always wanted to be a councillor – long before I joined the Conservatives; it was just a feeling I have had for as long as I could remember – I was one of those obnoxious 13-year-olds that was going to be Prime Minister (no insult intended

to our Foreign Secretary) and if I couldn't do that I'd be a councillor. I don't know why or when the ambition gripped me – it's just always been there. I'm in my third term now and will just keep going as long as the party and voters will have me.

These views were echoed by a Labour councillor:

I love politics, I always have. I joined the party as soon as I could and stood for election while at university. Politics and being a councillor was more important than getting my degree – which I did, by the way, just, and that was mainly due to being a councillor. But I had to do it; I always knew I was going to stand. I don't have any ambitions to be an MP or MEP; there's something about being a councillor that always attracted me – it can be bloody frustrating but I can represent my party as an elected representative and that's a great feeling.

The resister

The *resister*, on the other hand, claims never to have had an interest in standing for the council and, more than that, has continually over the years spurned opportunities and advances to stand. It was not part of the reason they had become involved in politics or what they intended to contribute to it or get from it; it was not a motivating factor in their political world view. The resisters present an interesting case and they can be found among party members and Independent councillors alike. With no ambition to stand, and with their rebuffing of constant requests by colleagues, they eventually crumble, after what one councillor called 'an intense period of moral blackmail', and do what they are told is their duty and finally agree to stand. Often, they stand when promised that the seat in which they have been selected is not winnable – many resisters are councillors for unwinnable seats – yet they did win.

Surprisingly many resisters interviewed expressed the desire to stand again, as one Liberal Democrat put it:

It's like that old song 'I didn't wanna do it, I didn't wanna do it, and all the time you knew it, I guess you always knew it; you made me want to', and what made me want to be a councillor was being a councillor – I was determined not to do it and was quite rude to folk when they tried to get me to do it, but I did and I want to carry on.

A Conservative councillor commented:

I told them I did not want to be a councillor; they promised I wouldn't win and I did and I told them at the count: I'll do this for four years only then find some other mug, I have a career, a family and a life outside politics that is more important to me than being on the council. But, after a while, I realised this is an important job; it needs to be done and done properly. I'm coming round to standing again – if they'll have me.

Some resisters also reach a tipping point as a result of the 'intense period of moral blackmail' referred to above. But besides their general reluctance, as one councillor who displayed the characteristics of a resister explained:

> It is and continues to be a privilege to be a councillor. I did not go into this par-
> ticularly willingly or expected to win, but it is a privilege and while I'm here I'm
> going to make a bloody good job of it: that's the right thing to do.

'Making a good job of it', however, is not just a case of working hard and being assiduous in council work, it is also linked to a recognition of what can and cannot be achieved in local politics. Indeed, 'making a good job' is linked to the concept of *RealLokalPolitik* described in Chapter 3 and to the idea that councillors are stimulated by the desire to take political action. But if the ability to take action is tempered by the constraints on the office of councillor and by the nature of the powers and responsibilities that attach to it, then we need to understand whether potential councillors are aware of this. In other words, what expectations do they have of the office and do those expectations have a role to play in deciding to stand for council? Moreover, we need to explore if the growing realisation of the realities of the office have any effect on decisions about whether or not to remain a coun-cillor and seek office again.

It is time now to examine in more detail why so many people are prepared to contest local elections and then to explore the demands of the office that spill over from the official world into the more private and personal world of the council-lor. To conduct that examination, it is necessary to turn to the councillors them-selves and to their explanations of motivations, stimuli, experiences, frustrations and success. We do this by exploring how the political and personal worlds of the councillor collide and, as we shall see, the political is most certainly the personal and the personal the political.

Resistance is useless

Three models have been set out in the previous section to help understand the combination of factors that need to come together for individuals to recognise that the time is right for them to present themselves to the voters for election as coun-cillor. Those models were the slow burn, the big bang and the resister, and they provide a way of assessing the explanations councillors themselves have provided of what it is that stimulates them into political office. This analysis also helps us to understand how they deal with the 24-hour-a-day job they have as a councillor. The process of assessing and making sense of the reasons councillors give for standing for council is assisted by also examining whether councillors display the traits of the *lay* or the *professional* councillor (see Chapter 3). Indeed, we could assume that *lay* and *professional* councillors are stimulated into seeking office by different concerns, motivations and expectations of what they can achieve once elected. In addition, in order to fully understand the nature of the office they hold, we need to assess how closely council candidates' expectations of what can be achieved match their experiences of what they have been able to achieve.

A reasonable expectation is that being a councillor provides power, resources, status and organisational support to enable the taking of political action, collectively and individually, and at very least provides a platform from which to espouse and pursue an electorally legitimised set of beliefs and values. Indeed, a constant view expressed by councillors is that they expected, on first election, to be provided with a source of material support for the actions they wished to undertake and which for some had stimulated their entry into elected local politics. It is here that we find that the desire to take action – sometimes based on anger at a particular local set of circumstances – was tempered by a realistic view of what could be achieved. When standing for the first time, councillors are not as naive as to think that they will inherit the mantle of a powerful politician able to push buttons to make things happen. What they do assume, however, is that the organisation to which they are elected will provide them with a base of operations and a reservoir of support and resources upon which they can draw. Many, however, are disappointed with what they find available, and that will be explored later.

Whichever route they took to the council – slow burn, the big bang or resister – on initial election, all councillors had an expectation that they would be able to achieve something – even if that was articulated in very general terms, such as in the following examples: 'I wanted to give something back to the community' (Labour councillor); 'I have lived in this town all my life and this is a way of giving something back' (Conservative councillor); 'I wanted to do something practical, long-lasting and worthwhile' (Liberal Democrat councillor); and 'I love the place where I live and the people and just wanted to get involved and do some work' (Independent councillor). It is among the big-bang grouping that we see the articulation of a clearer stimulus to seeking office from the outset, and it is among this group that we more often than not see a set of specific objectives which are related to a political party programme. Among this group we also see the characteristics of the *professional* councillor rather than the *lay* member. But those stimuli are related to a party-related and ideological view – tempered with some realism: 'I want a more equal, fair society which cares for those in need' (Labour councillor); 'I want to get my country back from the EU and every victory helps do that' (UKIP councillor); and 'I believe in small state, low tax and freedom and I wanted to do something to achieve those beliefs' (Conservative councillor).

Thus, for the big bang to occur, a particular set of political objectives, values or beliefs must simply exist alongside the opportunities to stand for office. The big bang will require little pushing towards the council as political activity is a passion, a driving desire and interest, which sees the individual motivated to seek local office as a logical way of pursuing those beliefs. There is no resistance to standing for council; indeed there is an active seeking out of the chance to stand and to pursue a set of political goals. A Conservative councillor explained: 'I stood for the council three times before getting elected and if I hadn't won on the fourth occasion, then I'd still be standing now.'

It is, however, not just the party member who experiences the big bang, as Independents too can harbour a desire for council membership that is actively sought. As one Independent councillor and former council leader commented:

> Not only did I want to be a councillor, I wanted to lead the council – a difficult ambition seeing as I detest party politics and everything it means, but Independents have always been strong here. I run my own business and so could get the time to do it. I was elected first time, because I know so many people here and was leader within 4 years. I just always thought that being a councillor was a good thing to do; it's hard to explain; I'm not political so it's not that. It's about, service I suppose and, if I'm honest, a sense of fulfilment – it's just a worthy, if underrated, task.

The above is not to say that the resister and slow burn are not party politicians. They are, and they are committed to their parties as intensely as any member. What distinguishes them is that they come to a slow and growing realisation that elected office is a requirement in order to secure what they believe in politically. And even having realised this fact, some will still resist taking that final step to office. Among these two groups, we see both *professional* and *lay* councillors: the Independent former council leader quoted above displayed all the traits of a *professional* councillor – although in interview rejected that description. What is evident is that, for many of those who long resisted the blandishments of their party colleagues, friends or neighbours to stand for council, resistance was ultimately futile; many of those who proclaimed that they would neither seek nor accept the nomination of their party did so in the end.

In delving deeper, it becomes clear that neat distinctions between motivations for becoming a councillor cannot be readily drawn. Rather what exists is a basket of reasons relating to the individual's decision to present themselves for selection and election. It is necessary, then, to identify and sort those reasons into broad categories so that we can understand what it is that stimulates individuals to become councillors. The research indicated that the following grouping of stimuli exist:

- **Public service**: councillors can be motivated by a deep sense of public service, of pursuing the public well-being, of giving up their time, energy and own resources to provide a service to their fellow citizens, and in so doing, make a series of personal, family and employment sacrifices out of a sense of duty. But it is a public service of a very specific sort that comes with elected office, as councillors want to achieve certain political goals to secure their vision of the general well-being, and political power is required to pursue and promote that vision. Political public service is therefore distinguishable from voluntary, community or charity work – although councillors are often engaged in some form of this type of activity – which may often have been part of the stimulus to them seeking elected office. A moral sense of public service as motivation to become a councillor is not some relic of a dim and distant philanthropically orientated view of local politics – it is a contemporary stimulant to local office.

- **The democratic spirit**: linked to public service, councillors often have a deep-centred belief in the democratic system and in deliberation and the democratic way of resolving political differences. They also have a firm belief that engagement in the democratic process is a duty, or a privilege, and either way, is not something that should be taken lightly. Local elections as a source of legitimacy are highly prized by councillors stimulated by the democratic spirit and are seen as fundamentally the right way of allocating political office in any democracy. That is not to say that such a spirit is not strained when their opponents win seats, but acceptance of the results of the voters' choice is a vital part of any functioning democracy. In addition, the democratic spirit acts as a motivation to office because it imbues a desire to participate in the democratic system of government at the local level. The spirit was articulated by the use of words such as: 'privilege' or 'honour': 'It is an honour to serve'; 'I'm privileged to represent the people'; 'it was an honour to be elected'.

- **Ambition**: the desire to achieve for personal growth and success and to stand out in some way as having secured victory in open competition is a motivator for some. Moreover, the victory is not necessarily the end result, and further personal advancement and growth may be secured through a council career. Ambition, and political ambition in particular, does stimulate the seeking of the office of councillor and, for some, achievement of office alone is sufficient motivation.

- **Status and reward**: linked to ambition to a degree, but status is more about being distinguished from others – even though the office of councillor today is much maligned, it still offers a status and public recognition within the community. The office separates the holder from other local citizens and, as a county councillor summed it up: 'there are over 800,000 people in this county and only 60 councillors on this council and I'm one of them'. Reward comes in many forms but some, it must be said, are indeed motivated to stand for office by the idea of financial reward flowing from the councillor allowance system or for other income that might accrue from other offices that might be available. One former council leader, who had been deposed in a group coup, complained bitterly that: 'not only did they take the leadership away from me [they being his opponents within the group] they took everything. I was taken off the Police

Authority [since abolished by the Police Reform and Social Responsibility Act 2011], the Fire and Rescue Authority, the bloody lot, everything. It has cost me my living; we relied on that income as a family and it's all gone.'

While these four categories are ideal types and in reality stimuli to seek office will be the result of an individually more complex interplay of factors, the categories do reflect two sets of stimuli: the first, positive, public and other-regarding, the second, narrower, private and self-regarding. However, it was the set of stimuli that reflected the public service and the democratic spirit that were overwhelmingly found in councillors' explanations of why they sought and continued to seek office. Where the self-regarding stimuli were present, they were most often an ancillary response to the more positive motivations, and matters such as status and uniqueness or reward, for example, were seen as an added bonus. Councillors also show that their motivation may be stable or developmental when faced with continuing in office. In other words, their original motivation may continue to be the spur to seek re-election, or a shift occurs as a council career develops and as the experiences of council work expand, so new stimuli to continue in office take the place of the original reasons.

Of note is that councillors are motivated to stay in office even if they lack any leadership position or the likelihood that they will achieve it. Not only does the role of a backbench councillor not deter those holding it from seeking re-election, it is often a positive reason for continuing as a councillor, as exemplified by the following comments:

I have never been interested in taking on a cabinet post; the leadership role doesn't attract me, too much detail and far too many meetings. I prefer to work in and for my ward and deal with my scrutiny stuff and that way I can see the effects of what I do on my ward. (Liberal Democrat councillor)

I've seen what the leader and cabinet members have to do and the workload they have and good luck to them. There's too much of a borough-wide focus there and I am happy to carry on in the community and to be able to work for people locally. (Conservative councillor)

I will continue to stand for as long as the party and ward want me – I've told the local branch not to expect a leadership contender or an important, powerful councillor, just someone who gets on with what's needed round here – they seem happy with that – they'll let me know when they're not. (Labour councillor)

I believe in being a councillor, it's hard work but there's a sort of privilege that goes with it, that goes with looking after a very specific area – I know the council has to be run and the district as a whole has to have a direction and that's what the leader and cabinet are there to provide. I say my bit, absolutely, but I enjoy my work and I know and my family knows that I wouldn't enjoy what goes with being in charge. (Conservative county councillor)

Such councillors may be what Glassberg (1981) called 'classic parochials', and the term 'parochial' is often used in a pejorative sense by some councillors to belittle their colleagues who place the needs of their communities and wards above the council-wide focus. However, not only do such parochials play a vital role in binding a council tightly to the communities it is supposed to represent and serve, they also find the pastoral (Copus, 2004) role of the councillor as vital as any governing, political or leadership undertaking. Such councillors still desire to take political action, it is merely the location of that action that differs from their colleagues who may operate with a broader governing orientation. One of the central factors which inspire councillors initially to seek and then to retain office is the idea of taking political action – or, as it was more colloquially referred to in interviews with councillors: 'getting something done'. It was the notion of action towards a certain goal – either a broad, overarching political goal, or a single-issue objective, or a community- or ward-focused objective, or a desire to improve a particular service or the lot of a particular group that underpinned the desire to stand. Whatever the scope of the political action envisaged, doing stuff, making things happen was a central factor for councillors in seeking and staying in office.

So, what we begin to see is that whatever collection of factors and personal circumstances come together at a given point in time to provide the impetus for individuals to seek the office of councillor, those reasons can be either political, community or altruistic and other-regarding or more self-centred and self-regarding. It may also be more helpful in the long run to consider the 'reasons' why councillors stand and continue to stand in addition to 'motivation', as the latter refers to more psychological factors and a set of tests to explain behaviour, whereas 'reasons' allows us to focus on the complex set of issues that come together to result in someone standing for office. In this way, it is possible to distinguish between but also account for what it is about individuals that stimulates them to stand for council, the recruitment process as conducted by political recruiters, and the personal circumstances that must support the other two factors.

A Conservative councillor illuminated the distinction between these three processes, but also how they come together, and it is worth quoting his comment at length:

I had a personal crusade to get the local kebab shop to clear up after itself and to take responsibility for the litter – now I know it wasn't their fault that people throw boxes and wrappers all over the place, but they do and they buy the stuff at this particular shop. It took a while, but I think I made them realise that as part of the community they had a responsibility to do it – the owner's children go to the same school as my children and when they were younger they'd been to birthday parties, that sort of thing. Eventually they did take responsibility and things are much better – I always go there now with my friends.

But, that was just part of things. I was always interested in politics, nationally and locally and the EU and at work and socially I'd argue from a particular – as

I found out – conservative point of view. What surprised me and my family and friends when I decided to stand was that all the things we get angry or passionate about are political, but we don't always look at them as though they are. So I'd argue about standards in schools, especially my own children's, the quality of the library, what's happening at the local hospital, the state of the streets and why certain roads never seem to be cleaned or repaired – all these sorts of things. These are all political issues about which political decisions are made but people, including me at one time, just don't see them like that.

Then a councillor asked me to go to something about being a candidate that the council were putting on one Saturday morning – a sort of put up or shut up challenge, I suppose. I'd often gone to his surgery and moaned about one thing or another, so it was his way of saying 'have a go'. I did some research, looked into what it would mean and went and chatted to a couple of councillors – I had joined the Conservative Party by then – and after a while I ended up thinking: I can and want to do this. The final thing was talking it over with my wife – she just said: 'look, you're always moaning about something, so this is a chance to actually do something'. Another put up or shut up – so I put up. It all seemed to fall into place: the kids were getting older – teenagers – and didn't want to be seen with daddy too much; work is busy, I'm in insurance, but I don't travel much and my immediate manager is really good about being flexible – I do a lot of home working. It took me a while to realise, however, that I'd been recruited – a bit like when MI5 or 6 or the Russians used to recruit people at university. The councillor I moaned to a lot was quite clever – if he'd said straight out – well stand then, I don't think I would have done.

I'm glad I stood, I enjoy it and it works; it's a shame it took me so long, but I suppose I had to realise it was what I wanted to do.

In this lengthy quote, we see how for some, but by no means all, councillors, there is no one clear reason to seek office. Rather, significant events and experiences come into alignment and lead to the council chamber. In this case, we see that an overriding general political interest, coupled with contact with councillors – initially outside of a political party – and the recognition by party members of the arrival of a potential candidate on the scene, resulted in candidacy and election. The potential interest to stand for council was always there, it simply had to be brought to the fore and the direction to the council chamber pointed out by a recruiting sergeant. One thing is clear, however, political action and bringing about change and improvement is what stimulates many to seek the office of councillor.

Other councillors have a far more straightforward journey to the chamber; for them, a more classic recruitment process takes place, especially for the big-bang councillor who has long intended to become a councillor. Here, the potential councillor deliberately steps into a position to be recruited and, as a result, becomes a vital player in the process, openly making their availability and willingness to stand known to recruiters. In addition, an apprenticeship is served in various local party offices, attending social gatherings, working in elections and other campaigns, again placing the big-bang candidate in front of the recruiters. Indeed, the tactic here is to enter a position where the potential candidate cannot be ignored and it is almost impossible not to recruit them. So, in addition to the classic councillor recruitment models and those that rely on a more porous, less deterministic process recognising the 'dynamic interaction of candidates' supply and selectors' demands (Verhelst et al., 2013: 30), there is an additional element of self-recruitment or self-selection. The party member wishing to be a councillor can assist the recruitment process by promoting their willingness and ability to stand for council and creating a dynamic that contributes to their requirement; the contribution to the selection process made by the willing recruit should not be overlooked.

Whether a willing or reluctant recruit, once a mandate is secured from the voters, the councillor is then faced with the necessity of managing the workload with which they are confronted and doing so in a way that balances their role as a representative and the tasks it brings with the political objectives they have set for themselves. It is clear that what councillors gain is the ability to take political action with a legitimacy provided by the public vote. It is the desire to secure public legitimacy and political office that distinguishes councillors from others involved in wider political activity. It is the democratic spirit with which councillors are imbued and the public service ethos which they display that is at the heart of understanding who stands and why.

Conclusions

When exploring with councillors the question of why they do it, we open ourselves to a myriad of answers, but, as we have seen in this chapter, councillors fall into three main categories of candidate: the big bang, the slow burn and the resister, and each of these types has a different relationship with the notion of becoming a councillor. The first is stimulated by politics and a deeply held set of core political beliefs on which they want to take political action, and one way of doing that is to become a councillor; the second has a much longer journey and reaches a personal tipping point, beyond which they become ready to stand for council; and the third actively resists all blandishments to stand but eventually finds that resistance is useless. These categories are not confined to party members but also explain why some wish to become Independent councillors. Moreover, the process of political recruitment is not confined to political parties alone but is also conducted by those seeking to support Independent candidates for council election (Grant, 1971, 1973; Bottom and Copus, 2011). But for any recruiter, the potential recruit must be ready to be selected.

While we can distinguish general patterns of behaviour and characteristics that lead an individual to become a councillor, those patterns often mask a complex dynamic and interplay of reasons that stimulate individuals into recognising that the time is right for them. It is necessary to understand these patterns and the characteristics they display, otherwise we rest too much on the notion that councillors are simply recruited by those selectors seeking individuals who reflect their own values and background. While it is no doubt the case, as we have seen, that the councillor population is not a microcosm of wider society – and the argument will continue about whether any democratic system should be based on microcosmic representation or traditional representation – we must go beyond perceived biases within the recruitment process and recognise the complexity of the factors that lead to an individual deciding to stand.

When we think about the categories of candidate identified above, we cannot assume that council office will be secured for all candidates – that is down to the electorate. Thus, the big-bang candidate may be perpetually frustrated, or the slow burns' and resisters' periods of burn and resistance may be of different lengths and may ultimately be frustrated by the electorate. What is being argued here is that any individual who finally seeks office will display certain characteristics by which we can understand how and why they came to candidacy and even to office. Councillors, understandably, have a desire to effect political action, but they also display a desire for personal growth and a willingness to invest time and energy in that process, and they have ambition that requires a public display of achievement – election. No matter how much councillors may be belittled or their office publicly undermined, the status that goes with elected office has meaning, and with status comes the recognised position to take action – this is not status for its own sake but status as a resource. There is also no doubt that councillors are imbued with a strong sense of public service or duty, linked to a democratic spirit. Taken together, these latter two factors direct the individual to seek elected office as a means of taking action – that office is the mandate through which service can be given and is legitimised. Councillors are, above all, democrats, even though they may intensely dislike 'the other lot winning'.

The reason we are continually able to fill the 18,000 council seats across England and the council seats across the globe is that citizens who are committed to their values and beliefs, with a clear vision of the good life and what it takes to produce good governance, and who are wedded to and in close proximity with their communities, put themselves before the voters. They do so because the time is right and they themselves have made a personal decision about what constitutes the right time. Once that decision is made and office is secured, those elected as councillors must come to terms with the demands of the office, the expectations and pressures from fellow citizens or their political parties, and the constraints, restrictions and limitations on their office and how that affects their ability to take the action they wish to take. Above all, they must then deal with the need to balance their roles, tasks and responsibilities as a councillor with all other facets of their life, and it is to this aspect that the next chapter turns.

6

A 24-hour-a-day job: when worlds collide

Introduction

A unique feature of the office of councillor is the proximity and immediacy councillors have to their constituencies, their voters and the communities they represent, govern and serve. That proximity distinguishes them from elected representatives at other levels of government. Unlike them, councillors cannot escape to another part of the country for weeks at a time to make decisions affecting others while being protected by distance that makes accessibility difficult. Councillors must live, work, shop, relax (possibly), socialise and be a connected part of the communities for which they have an elected responsibility. Being a councillor has been regularly described in interviews for this book as a '24-hour-a-day job', a job that has few, if any, boundaries between the political, personal and private and which rests on the everyday accessibility of the councillor as a politician but also as a citizen. Now, while politicians at other levels may choose to be close to those they represent, it is just that: a choice and not an expectation. Indeed, the councillor's proximity to the public is not an expectation, or even a requirement, rather, it is a fundamental feature of the office. While that proximity may be masked in larger, anonymous urban areas, particularly large cities, the councillor is still part of that community and area and is part of it on a daily basis.

So, we can take proximity and fuzzy boundaries between the various spheres of an individual's life as unique features of serving as a councillor, and both these features have a consequence for those elected as councillors. Those consequences are all the more stark given the view expressed by the current government that councillors are volunteers and not full-time politicians (TSO, 2013a), a view which is at the centre of the debate about the future of the office (explored in more detail in Chapters 7 and 8), and a view which conflicts with the reality of the steadily increasing number of hours councillors put into their office (Maud, 1967b; Robinson, 1977; Widdicombe, 1986b; Young and Davies, 1990; Bloch and John, 1991; Young and Rao, 1994; NFER, 2007, 2009, 2011). The idea that councillors are somehow part-time volunteers not engaged closely with their work, as a proper politician as an MP would be, is partly a corollary of the location of councillors close to those they represent. Unlike the councillor – even those in the largest of cities, a full-time politician, a proper governor, a skilled professional leader and representative would have distance – physical distance – between them and their constituents; that separation is needed so the politician can rise above those that are governed.

A consequence of the councillor's location within the community is their easy accessibility for individuals and communities. The physical closeness introduces casualness to the interactions between councillors and citizens and an element of familiarity born, if not of contempt, then of a realisation that councillors are of the community itself. The absence of physical barriers or distance between the councillor and the community introduces a particular dynamic between councillor–citizen–community that has few, if any, boundaries. The absence of boundaries or the blurring of the political/official personal/private spheres of a councillor's life makes demands on their time and places a strain on their balancing of the political and personal features of their life that is an acute part of their experience.

Barron et al. (1991), in a ground-breaking study of the public and private life of the councillor, held up the private world as a proper area of study. The qualitative research they conducted with councillors and their spouses aimed to collect a diverse range of experiences from the councillors and was designed to go beyond and beneath anything that could be uncovered by qualitative surveys. The research for this book has been explained in the introductory chapter and differs from that of Barron and colleagues in three important features. It does not focus, as they did, on gender; rather it seeks to identify and explore the shared experiences of councillors from all backgrounds. Second, the research has an anthropological dimension in that it was conducted not only in specific research interview settings but also in gatherings of councillors in their natural habitat – council meetings, party groups and other party events, conferences and from observations of councillors in public and social settings. Finally, it does not compartmentalise the life of the councillor; rather it explores the point at which boundaries blur. This chapter intends to add depth and richness to our understanding of the blurring of the boundaries between the spheres of councillors' lives and add to an understanding of how those experiences affect what councillors do.

The chapter unashamedly presents the realities of the life of the councillor – in this chapter, more than any other, the councillors speak for themselves and present and defend their actions, the work they do, their experiences and the frustrations of the office they hold and the effect that office has on other aspects of their life. The chapter does this partly because, without such a detailed understanding, we cannot go on to understand fully the purpose of the office of councillor, and partly because those from other levels of government wishing to reframe and reshape the office can only have a chance of producing a positive outcome if they fully understand what being a councillor means to those that take on the role. With that knowledge, sensible decisions can be made about strengthening the councillor's role and the office more generally (some of these are discussed in more detail in Chapter 8). In this chapter, the councillors' experiences of their office, and what sense they make of those experiences, is explored. The chapter allows councillors to tell their stories as a deliberate celebration of the 18,000 of our fellow citizens across England (and their counterparts elsewhere) and recognition of what they contribute to their communities, the overall governance of the country and to the fabric of democracy both locally and nationally.

The next section briefly examines the nature of the various settings within which councillors act. The third section goes on to examine, in more detail, how a crossover point emerges between the formal political/policy role of the councillor and other aspects of the councillor's life and how these boundaries blur and even merge. The fourth section then explores the strategies councillors develop to manage that crossover. The chapter concludes by drawing together the main findings.

Proximity to people and place

Councillors act in separate settings and venues, what have been called elsewhere 'theatres of representation' (Copus, 1999, 2004), and these theatres are both formal and informal in nature. My theatres of representation (Copus, 2004: 192–4) were either open (e.g. the full council, a council committee, public meeting, or the media) or closed (e.g. the party group, the local party or private meetings with officers, other councillors or external bodies where the public was not, or could not be, present to observe). Thus, the different theatres have different levels of secrecy and transparency, allowing councillors to act differently in different settings. The issue here is the degree to which a councillor's actions are visible and therefore observable by the public; the councillor can act either in front of the public or away from the public gaze. Therefore any theatre within which a councillor acts can be judged for the privacy or otherwise that attaches to it, and this in turn will give an indication of the nature of the interactions within those settings.

There is one constant feature of all the theatres of representation identified above – they are political arenas where councillors act as the elected representative or governor of a locality. It is possible to extend these theatres into areas that are less obviously political and less obviously places where the councillor is engaged in political debate or action which has a political objective. In that way, we can start to identify more clearly the point at which boundaries between the political and personal begin to blur and at what point they might merge or vanish altogether. What the analysis is trying to identify is how far council work penetrates into the more private spheres of councillors' lives and what effect that penetration has on those other spheres.

To enable a consideration of the way in which council work seeps into other aspects of the councillor's life, three areas are explored: work, family and social life. These areas do, of course, blur themselves and cannot always be compartmentalised, and each will flow into and affect the others to some degree. In turn, however, they will affect and be affected by the duties that the councillor has to carry out. We need to see if councillors cross the boundaries between aspects of life or whether they operate within a boundaryless world altogether.

The office of councillor has attached to it a series of formal expectations of action in traditional political theatres of the council, but in speaking to councillors, it becomes clear that the power of that formality can spread to interaction with the public, such as in advice surgeries. As a Labour councillor summarised:

> If I'm at a meeting, scrutiny or council, then I'll be standing up for what I believe in, which is what those who voted for me also support – that's what a representative democracy is about. Even when I'm dealing with casework, I can get access to officers and also to, say, the hospital trust, in a way that others can't – that's why they come to me, that's the job. So, in my surgery it is sort of formal, not the way I do things, because people have to be at their ease, but come to think of it, it's also pretty formal. I'm in a special room at the school, table, chairs behind where I sit; three chairs the other side where folk will sit; it is quite formal, isn't it? But, people still can talk to me normally, I'm not an official in that sense and I see that part of things as then going to the right officer to sort out the problem – it's not always that straightforward, but I do it because I have an access people don't – officers have to talk to me on my terms.

What we see here is the formalisation of two specific roles, the political in the council and the pastoral role that is casework. In the quote above, they are shown as part of a function requiring a traditionally inspired view of processes. The description of the surgery and its setting out in a ritualistic fashion was something raised by and familiar to the majority of councillors. Although councillors recognised the formality of the surgery setting, not one councillor suggested sitting on the floor on beanbags and lighting joss sticks to ease the mood. Although most claimed that they wanted to make sure those who approached them in this formal advice setting were at ease and able to communicate properly, joss sticks and beanbags would probably make people more, not less, tense. One Liberal Democrat stated:

> When people come to see me they are either at the end of their tether, angry, or browbeaten or a combination of all three. Some do come to me as the first port of call; when I ask who they've spoken to, I'll often get told: you. So, councillors are not the last stop any more, sometimes we are the first and actually, I think that's ok. The problem is anger, if people are shouting or abusive or waving their fists (I've had that) I have to remember: it's not me; it's what's happened to them that they're angry at. I have three surgeries a week – sometimes they're packed and sometimes no one comes – but you have to do it; not everyone has the internet and some people just want to see you, even if they could phone.

Sometimes I feel like I'm counselling rather than being a councillor – I sit, I listen, I make sympathetic noises and they go away and then come back next week to have another go. Thing is, this all takes time. Ok, 3 hours a week doesn't sound much – that's just the surgery – I do much more than 3 hours a week on casework. When no one comes, though, that's 3 hours I could have used for something else – even if just being with the family – I've always got some reading from the council to do if no one comes.

I offer a Skype surgery service too and some people have taken that up, not many, though – I don't mind the fist waving so much then.

Added to this, a Conservative county councillor commented:

County Hall is County Hall: I'm there for meetings, council meetings, meetings with officers, meetings with others, lots of meetings, and although the public can observe the council meetings – the public ones – there is very much a distance. We have a public question time – which I'm not against, but it doesn't work, it's just like councillor's question time: question 3 weeks in advance, some one reads it out, the leader or whoever answers, that's it – they could have emailed, to be honest, but it's a bit of the public theatre of council now and it's very formal. There's no debate on the questions. We don't debate petitions – they disappear somewhere, not sure where. to be honest. But that part of things, the meetings are formal, they have to be really, we are elected and part of the job is to go through the formal decision-making and taking processes.

I don't get a lot of casework, but I make myself available. Sometimes I'm contacted about something that's from one of the districts, so I refer people to the district councillors – even if he isn't one of ours. I run a surgery 1st and 3rd Saturday of the month and it's never very busy, but you have to do it – I get more contact through phone calls and emails and people coming to the house.

In the last part of the comment we see the beginnings of a blurring of boundaries between council life and home life, and this is something that councillors across the political spectrum readily recognised as going with the territory. The proximity of the councillor to those they represent and serve will inevitably mean the blurring of boundaries, either social, private or locational. What is meant by the last of these is that the very location of the councillor within a community means that when they are visible they are fair game for an approach by the public. It is abundantly clear that those who interact with the councillor are no respecters of boundaries between the councillor's home, private or social life, and, as we will see, no respecters of work life either. Also, as we shall see, it is not just interaction with the public that blurs the boundaries: council decision-making also crosses from the formal theatres into the social, private and work life of the councillor.

Blurring the boundaries

Contact with the council

There is a point for all councillors where one part of their life – being a council-lor – spills over into over aspects, and in this section we explore the nature of that spillover and its implications for councillors. To make the assessment easier, the political decision-making and policy-development features of councillors' roles and the casework and support to constituents that they provide are treated as a bloc of activity: the political and the pastoral. That does not, however, deny the multi-faceted nature of the activity in that bloc, which has been explored in depth by writ-ers such as Heclo (1969), Corina (1974), Jones (1975), Newton (1976), Jennings (1982), Rao (1994, 2000), Heinelt (2013a, b) and Klok and Denters (2013). But, for the purposes of this analysis, the spillage from that bloc (not within it) into other facets of the life of the councillor is the focus of examination. In addition, and again to ease the analysis, the work and social life of the councillor is considered as a bloc of time and activity. Examples are given from all aspects of these blocs, but the blocs are not separated into their constituent parts, as that would result in *reductio ad absurdum*. To avoid that, examples are given from areas, such as family, friends, holiday or entertainment that would comprise the work and social bloc, as is necessary to discuss and illuminate aspects of councillors' experiences.

First to be considered is the spillage point from the formal political/policy role of the councillor into other facets of their life. While such political and policy work may be formally seen to take place in council settings and in the party group, it is clear from councillors across the political spectrum (including Green and UKIP councillors) and from Independent councillors that political decision-making and discussions and negotiations about policy and action do not take place solely in the theatres of representation – open or closed. Rather, what occurs is a continual process of deliberation and alliance building between councillors – normally but not exclusively from the same group. But there is no switch-off from this activity, and councillors report, almost as one, that there is no part of their life that such processes do not touch, especially where long-term policy or controversial deci-sions are involved that are likely to generate public interest or protest. Indeed, the same can be said for issues that touch upon ideological cleavages or personality differences within the same group.

Councillors report that the political aspects of their role spill over far beyond the confines of clearly identifiable 'political theatre', and that personal discus-sions, phone calls, email, Twitter and Facebook conversations take place almost anywhere, such as at home, or while travelling or at work. Councillors see such ongoing deliberation with their colleagues as a vital part of the process of policy- or decision-making that will eventually be finalised in some more formal council setting. One councillor expressed the view of many of her colleagues when she reported:

We had been working on the extension of a waste disposal site and it was really controversial – the group were split and there was public anger at what could happen and a lot of rumours flying around. Now, with the best will in the world – and that's lacking in some anyway – you can't just stop discussing that. My phone was ringing all hours of the day and well into the morning with councillors from my group and others and you take the calls; in fact, you make the calls too, because I was doing the same. You don't and can't switch off. I was out with my family for lunch on Mother's Day – the kids were treating me – I had three phone calls on the mobile and answered a couple of emails. I feel awful telling you about it, but the kids know I have to do this and they say: 'mum's off again' – the youngest ate my desert while I was outside on the phone – hot chocolate fudge cake if I remember. Well, serves me right, I suppose.

Councillors often referred to being phoned by other councillors or officers while on holiday abroad, even when those people knew they were on holiday or were not put off by the different dialling tone. A Conservative district councillor said:

I answered and the officer said – 'sorry: I didn't know you were abroad until I heard the tone – are you on holiday?' I said, 'yes, Corsica, but what is it?' Then I had this long discussion about the possibility of the scrapping of a parking permit scheme we have, which has caused a stink, while I was sitting round the pool as a nice waitress brought me cocktails.

The intrusiveness of mobile phones or email via smartphones adds to the 24-hour-a-day nature of all councillors' experiences. Answering, of course, is in the hands of the councillor, but not one councillor reported ever refusing to answer the phone or take a council-related call from an officer or member, whatever their own location or circumstances at the time. One councillor said: 'if it's on, it's answered; if I don't want to take a call, I switch it off – and that's normally when I go to bed.'

Such an attitude reflects a common theme raised by all councillors – that their accessibility, while to a degree under their control, is given willingly. A Labour councillor added in a similar vein:

If I'm away on holiday, I will relax only if I know that other members or officers will phone if they need to – then no news really is good news. But if something happened, anything, then I'd want to know and the fact I was on holiday would make no difference to that.

When pressed about what he would want to know, he replied:

Well certainly anything that was an emergency: fire, flood, bomb, earthquake – you know what I mean. But also if some policy had gone belly up or any major issue – it's difficult to specify until it happens, but I think the officers know me well enough to know I'd want to know, if I was on holiday abroad. I wouldn't be able to get back, but I could prepare – make phone calls, Skype, check the news, look at the council website. When we book our holiday there has to be good wifi and no huge time difference; it's no good to me if I'm 9 hours ahead or behind.

That very telling comment about wifi and time differences was a constant theme from councillors, and wifi while on holiday was considered a must by councillors, not for social purposes, but so they could keep in contact with council affairs. It shows that councillors think ahead and even when legitimately and acceptably uncontactable – such as when on holiday – council business is at the forefront of their minds, coupled with the desire not to be too out of reach. Indeed, councillors report that holidays are often a worrisome period because they might be uncontactable at a time when they would really like to be contacted. It is not just the council and its requirements that interrupt this aspect of the councillor's life, councillors are also contacted by the local media – newspaper or radio – and have provided press comments and recorded and live radio interviews while on holiday. As one Liberal Democrat councillor reported:

My partner gets a bit fed up if I'm on the phone when we're on holiday, but I said to him: look what does it matter if I sit here, in the sun, while you're reading and I'm talking to the radio – we're still on holiday; it's hot and all inclusive. He doesn't see it that way, though.

Councillors voluntarily make themselves available even when most of us would fully understand if they had shut up shop for a fortnight.

A Labour councillor made a very telling point: 'At least officers work office hours: thank heavens. They do work long hours, but I've not been phoned after about 8pm by an officer. Emailed, yes, but not phoned'. A Conservative executive member summed up a different set of experiences when he said: 'The Chief Executive or senior officers will phone any time of the evening or night – 10pm, 11pm, midnight, and I phone them. Some things just have to be discussed when they have to be discussed – no point worrying about the time or what the person you're phoning might be doing'.

It is not just the social aspect of the councillor's personal bloc of time that is interrupted by the demands of council business and decision-making or the intrigues of party politics, it is also working hours. The LGA councillor census (NFER, 2011: 18) found that just over 45 per cent of councillors were either in full- or part-time employment or self-employed. In the sample of councillors interviewed specifically for this research, just under half (49.7 per cent) were in employment of one sort or another. So the population of councillors in employment is slightly over-represented in this research, but in turn that provided valuable data from which to assess the way in which council business spills into the working life of the councillor.

It is noteworthy that there were no differences in the experiences of councillors working full or part time or self-employed when it came to council work seeping into employed work. What did differ was the way in which councillors in different occupational types were able to manage the process. Full- and part-time employed councillors reported that officers had no reservations when it came to contacting them in the office, either on an office number or a mobile number. Surprisingly, only one councillor reported having told officers specifically not to contact him at work, but as his office number was now known at the council, it was circulating among officers and an email sent round by the Chief Executive requesting that he not be contacted during working hours had yet to have full effect. But that was the only case found where such a request had been made.

The general view of councillors working in offices was summed up by a Labour councillor, thus:

> It can be inconvenient, but if I'm at a meeting, or something and my mobile's off then they can't get hold of me – if I'm sitting at my desk and it's convenient to talk, then fine; if, not I phone back when it is. You just have to be sensible about this. I'll even phone officers and if they're not in their office I'll ask them to ring back. The boss and my colleagues are OK with this – what I have to do at work gets done on time and well and that's what matters. You just have to come to a happy medium. Sometimes, when there's a big thing on at the council, it can get a bit much, and on a couple of occasions the boss has had a quiet word – nothing too heavy, but basically he understands.

Most office workers, however, manage the issue of spillage into the work environment through the use of email, a far less intrusive and obvious way in which communication can be kept with the council during the course of a working day. A Conservative councillor commented: 'I have very long email conversations that are more or less instant – I send an email, get a reply, reply, get a reply and so on – with council officers – and I can do that without disturbing colleagues or it being too intrusive generally.'

Those councillors in employment in manual or non-office-based jobs have another way of dealing with things: as one Labour councillor said: 'when I'm driving the bus not even the passengers are supposed to talk to me, so officers have to step back beyond the line'. Manual work could involve long periods when the councillor was not contactable by anyone, let alone the council. A Liberal Democrat councillor said: 'I'm a flight attendant; no one is supposed to use any electronic equipment while the plane is airborne! (although, unfortunately, that has changed a bit now).'

It was evident from the data that, for councillors who were manual workers or in occupations where contact by anyone was difficult if not impossible, lunch and tea breaks were an opportunity to check messages, make a few quick replies and try and keep on top of things. But it was often the case that the contact that office workers were able to manage during the day had to be completed in the evening for those in manual work, and that was not always possible, as one Labour councillor said: 'when I'm at home from work, so too are officers; there's always a time lapse in us making contact during the day, which could take days to come together.'

Breaks during the day are obviously woefully inadequate to enable councillors in manual occupations to respond to messages, and the evenings, as pointed out, made telephone contact with officers difficult. The strategy that emerged among workers in this category to manage council work involved finding blocks of time to deal with council communication in three ways: first, use holiday entitlement by taking regular days off from work and spending a day at the council or at home dealing with council communication; second, identify, or have identified for them by senior officers, a single contact officer willing to be telephoned during the evening and weekends and who would channel communication to other officers (this was not a widespread tactic, but is certainly one that exists); and third, use a long-term strategy of striking up a working relationship with those officers they had most regular contact with, which would eventually end in officers providing the member with home or mobile details and being willing to be contacted after hours and at weekends – much like councillors themselves. The third tactic was not available to new members and took time to develop.

What also emerged here was the difficulty, though not impossibility, of councillors in certain occupations staying in those occupations while taking on greater responsibility at the council, such as a cabinet place or a scrutiny chair. Movement up the political career ladder involves a real and stark choice for many of our councillors working in manual jobs or occupations in which contact during the day is difficult.

Paperwork

So far, we have only considered physical communication, but the issue of paperwork and the reading required in being a councillor places yet another strain on councillors in both their social and work life. Taking the impact on the social world first, councillors overwhelmingly stressed the growing demands of paperwork and, in particular, the amount of reading material that was presented to them. A newly elected UKIP councillor commented: 'I wasn't expecting the deluge of paperwork; it started in the first few days and just continues; but it's odd because there doesn't seem to be any recognition that you've only just got on; they treat you with paperwork like you've always been there.'

The undifferentiated approach by councils to new councillors was a constant theme from councillors and was reflected across parties. While new councillors knew they had to brace themselves for paperwork, it was not just the amount and the regularity that was an issue, but also the way it failed to recognise the existence of new councillors who were confronted with material that was a product of an ongoing cycle – it appears scrutiny, for example, has not broken the cyclical approach to council work. Once that shock was dealt with, all councillors – however long they had served – were acutely aware that paperwork had a tendency to spill into social and work life. Some vociferous complaints were made that indicated the resentment that exists for many at what is seen to be an excessive amount of paperwork and reading that is required of the councillor. In some cases, this view of the excessive nature of paperwork became transformed into a conspiracy theory, as demonstrated by the following comments:

> I'm sure officers do this to keep us in the dark; the really important stuff is buried under tonnes of verbiage. (Labour councillor)

> It's a defence mechanism, giving us all this paperwork and reports; that way officers can say – 'well, it was in the report' and they'd be right: it was. But hidden away where you couldn't spot it. (Conservative councillor)

> It beggars belief the reading we have to do and the material we are given – the problem is, yes, there are executive summaries, but then you have to look through the reports to check you haven't missed anything. Even then, you still could miss something and it's almost as though it's done on purpose to make sure you miss something. I'm not sure what the solution is, to be truthful. (Independent councillor)

However, councillors are also clear that reading reports is a vital part of the job. Indeed, despite the regularity of complaints about the weight of reading, there was also a general reluctance to see any diminution of the material they received. Rather, a desire was generally expressed to see material and information presented in different ways and using different media. Yet reports prepared by officers are still seen by councillors as a vital way in which they obtain the information they need on which to base their decisions or from which to develop policy.

Complaints from councillors about the weight of material they receive and their firmly held belief they want information may seem contradictory. But that contradiction can be reconciled. Councillors hold strongly to the view that as they are involved in making decisions, developing policy or constructing solutions to locally manifested problems, then they require information, data and research on which to do that properly. In addition, there is the need to be able to justify decisions or policy on the basis that it not only reflects a political preference but also the expert position of officers and the evidence they have collected, sifted and presented to members. While that material could be presented in seminars, workshops, using social media or in any number of different modes, councillors cling to the idea that an official report, which then becomes part of an official minute and documentation, must contain all that they need on which to act. Official documentation containing all the relevant data is a protective mechanism for councillors and means that the weight of paperwork is unlikely to reduce. As a Liberal Democrat councillor commented:

> We have discussed this in group, between the groups and with officers many times – we know there's a lot of reading to do and we know that information can be placed on websites, for example, But that means you have to go and find it and some might not, or might miss it. It's not being spoon-fed, more a fear of missing something.

The demands of reading, researching and dealing with council paperwork, of course, have an impact on the time councillors are able to commit to their role and naturally seeps over into other facets of their life. It is import to understand that effect if we are to understand the councillors' experiences of their office. As with contact by council officers, paperwork needs to be managed and controlled (see Barron et al., 1991), and councillors devise different strategies for doing that and for dealing with the spillover into social and working life. With these strategies, when considering councillors in employment, we see a similar difference between office and manual occupations that was evident when we explored contact from the council.

As might be expected, councillors that are office workers have an easier time than their manual counterparts in being able to read council material during a working day, and the overwhelming majority reported that most lunch breaks were taken up with this activity. A Labour councillor summed up the general situation when she said: 'I very rarely have a lunch break – I just work through – so if I have a particular piece of reading to do, for an evening meeting, then that day I make sure I do have lunch and read.' A Liberal Democrat councillor said, in a similar vein:

> I deliberately store up my lunch time – don't have one, basically – and then if I need to read something I have a long lunch break – as long as the office is covered. Normally, I'm in the office at lunch anyway and carry on answering the phones or emails and it's just the same if I have a lunch break to read council papers.

A Conservative councillor added:

> I'm normally in early and leave late and don't have a lunch break – that's what a lot of office life is like, so, if I find five minutes to read something, well, although we don't operate flexi time, I've stored up hours of unpaid overtime and I cash some of it in – as long as everything is done when it needs to be done, if I need to read council reports during the day, then I do.

Office-based workers admitted that as long as what they had to do was done, on time and properly, and given that many worked well over their contracted hours, then the flexibility that some office occupations provided enabled them to keep up with council reading. Office worker councillors argued that they were not taking time away from work, rather cashing in on hours they had banked and which they would have banked even if they had not been councillors. That banked time is used to deal with the constant spillage into the councillor's working life of the reading required of the councillor.

Manual workers fared less well, as they do with phone and email contact from the council during the working day. But, overwhelmingly, those in manual occupations were prepared to give up lunch breaks to read material and even to use short tea and 'smoke' breaks to skim over papers. One councillor went as far as to admit: 'yes, I have sat on the toilet and read a council report while at work – best place to read it too – it was rubbish'. While some office work can be as heavily regimented as manual work – none of the councillors interviewed worked in a call centre for example – manual worker councillors expressed that the lack of autonomy and independence they often experienced during a working day did not allow them to spend much, if any, time on reading council material, other than that described.

The strategy most mentioned was to minimise the reading required by being selective, skim reading and by focusing only on those issues of specific importance. Such a strategy was also employed by white-collar workers but it was driven more by choice than by necessity. In addition, manual workers often rejected overtime, or ensured that they finished work strictly on time to make sure they had time for council reading. Another tactic employed by many was to use public transport rather than drive. Several councillors stated that instead of driving to work, which they had done before being elected – they used the train or bus, because travelling time could then be used for reading. A Labour councillor stated: 'when I got elected I stopped driving and started using the train – waiting at the platform and on the train I can read – I'm probably more upset than most if I don't get a seat because standing and flicking through a report isn't easy on a crowded train'.

Social life was even more permeable than work life when it came to council reading, and it is when we look at the effect on the time councillors could potentially have away from council duties that we see the degree of sacrifice they make to commit the time required to reading and research for council duties. Allocating 'social' time to council duties was far easier than dealing with the need to assess written material in the workplace. Social or 'free' time simply merged with whatever demands were made of councillors to attend to council documentation. There were few, if any, barriers to reading, with one obvious exception, and that was if councillors were out socially and were undertaking activities that physically prevented them from dealing with material – of course, at those moments they were potentially accessible by phone. A Conservative councillor commented:

The reading required is astonishing, so, yes I'm obviously selective – very much so. But, sometimes I just take the dog for a walk or go to the town for a wander around for a break. While I'm anywhere at all where one could read – I usually end up doing just that.

Councillors consistently report that any time spent relaxing would be eaten into by the need to undertake some reading of council material. That time 'relaxing', however, was very limited and councillors often forego the usual family-orientated leisure time that may be simply watching television. As a Liberal Democrat councillor noted: 'even for the few moments I might get to plonk myself down in front of the telly with my husband, I'll be flicking through some paperwork – it's very rare that I'm not looking at something. If I want to see a film all the way through – we go to the cinema.'

Those councillors that were single and living alone were particularly caught by the spillage of council paperwork into what might be called their 'free time', to such an extent that they did not get much, if any, 'free time' at all. An Independent councillor, who was living alone, summed up the situation thus:

> I don't really have spare time as such. I mean I do go out, socially, with friends, but when I'm in the flat I'm normally doing something for the council. The radio or television might be on in the background but I don't really ever stop, stop, if you see what I mean. That's quite distressing now I come to think about it; I have to actually leave the flat to consciously do something else where I can't deal with council papers.

What we see here is that only the most careful and disciplined councillor can protect her or himself from council work seeping into their working or social life, but the overwhelming majority of those interviewed chose to accommodate that seepage as it goes with being a councillor and is one of the many sacrifices councillors make in their office. There are no clear barriers between the work and social life of the councillor and the time given over to duties and demands that flow from council business. Indeed, survey and diary-keeping studies of the time councillors spend on council duties cannot adequately capture the hours committed because of the lack of clear boundaries and councillors consequently failing to accurately report exactly how much time they give to the work they undertake. It is surprising that little resentment was expressed by councillors about the way the council, as an institution, reached into their work and social life. Rather, there was a positive acceptance that such demands were part and parcel of the role they had taken on – councillors do not have to be disciplined to fit council work into their everyday life, they have to be disciplined to fit everyday life into their council commitments.

A word about meetings

'Meetings', and what that term implies, are for many what being a councillor is all about and it is because meetings are so central to councillors' experiences that so little reference was made to the whole notion of 'meetings' by councillors in the research. Studies of councillors' allocation of time to their various duties show that meeting attendance is a core activity. But such studies leave us wondering why meetings are so vital a part of the councillor DNA? It is a given that there will be meetings not only of the council, but of the party, community groups, partnership bodies and a whole host of other organisations which were explored in Chapter 4. Councillors simply accept that meetings have to occur, and for some, the real feeling of being a councillor came through attendance at meetings – formal or informal. As one councillor summarised it for his colleagues: 'there are a lot, yes [meetings], but it's where you can get things done, there's an interaction, a debate, a movement towards a decision – it's the culmination of what could be months of other action in a single place where you can act as a politician'. The word 'politician' here could quite easily be replaced with 'governor'.

Overwhelmingly, this the one thing councillors expect: there will be meetings. And the one area of training and experience councillors do receive before being elected is how to attend and behave in meetings. One councillor commented: 'I attended over fifty meetings about flooding in the area and about the development of a 20-year flood action plan; fifty, then I stopped counting them'. Another councillor commented: 'yes, there are lots of meetings, but then what would you expect – none?' In a similar vein, a councillor stated:

> yeah, loads [meetings] but who doesn't go to loads of meetings – in any occupation or club or group – it's what we do as people to work things out and formalise decisions – sort of dictatorship by committee. Someone once said a camel is a horse designed by a committee meeting; yep and it's perfectly designed for what it does.

Thus, councillors accept meetings and, indeed, expect them to be a central part of their experience, in which they expect to invest the majority of their time and energy. It is interesting, therefore, that aspects such as paperwork, a vital support function to meeting attendance, loomed much larger in the reported experiences of councillors than meeting attendance. Indeed, councillors' strategies for dealing with meetings were similar whether they were in full-time paid occupations or retired or otherwise not working, or whether they displayed the characteristics of *corporate* or *associated* councillors (see Chapter 3): go to the ones that you can and avoid the ones you don't need to attend. But for many councillors, there are few meetings they feel they do not need to attend and so selectivity is replaced by the drug-like experience of meeting attendance – the more you have, the more you want to go. But while selectivity works for some, attendance at all possible meetings works for others. However, councillors do question aspects of the meetings they attend (not just council meetings): their value; the effectiveness of meetings as a way of ensuring outcomes in practical terms; the uncontrolled energy that seems to develop behind the calling and holding of meetings; the difficulties of seeing action occur as a result of meeting attendance; the behaviour of some of their councillor colleagues or others, in various meeting settings; and that some meetings are chaotic, fruitless, time-consuming or just boring.

Yet meetings – of whatever kind – serve the purpose of providing a deliberative forum for the exchange of views, the exploration of competing demands, and the development of lines of thinking that lead to action, and they are where authoritative decisions can be taken and therefore provide councillors with a legitimised setting in which to take action. It is for these reasons that criticisms of the time councillors spend attending meetings is unlikely to result in changed behaviour, as the collective and reciprocal exchanges at meetings, formal and informal, is a reflection of the interactive nature of politics as a process.

People, patch and privacy

So far we have looked at how official council duties spill over into other aspects of the councillor's life. Now it remains to look at how being a 'public person' (Lee, 1963) rooted in and with great proximity to the community spills over into councillors' social and work life. Councillors face intrusion by their constituents into all facets of their private life, but it is an intrusion that they acknowledge comes with the nature of the office they hold and, if not welcomed, is certainly accepted. Indeed, councillors consider that easy access to them for their constituents is a positive part of their representative tasks, and while examples of over-intrusiveness were given, such occurrences were excused as induced by times of considerable stress for the constituent concerned. It is, however, when exploring with councillors the effects of their proximity to those they represent that the term '24-hour-a-day job' is the most used and repeated.

It is not that councillors cannot see the boundaries between a personal/private event and being an elected representative of a community; rather they are often placed in a position where they have to ignore such boundaries. In the research for this book, not a single councillor reported that if they were approached by a constituent while socialising or out on family or home-life activities they would ask that constituent to contact them at a more appropriate time. Indeed, such intrusions saw councillors ready to respond and spend time discussing the latest instalment of a constituent's problem while the councillor's family or friends went about the social activities concerned, to be re-joined by the councillor later. What is apparent is the difficulty councillors can experience in conducting what to the rest of us is the normal everyday activities associated with private life. By contrast, it is a standard strategy of councillors to use everyday social interactions to ensure they are contactable and have contact with their constituents.

One female councillor summed this up by saying:

> I make sure I walk the children to school every morning and, much to their annoyance, we are always a bit early. I like to get to the playground as early as possible and stay around after chatting for as long as possible. Sometimes folk will come up and ask about some problem I'm dealing with, or give me a new problem; or they'll discuss why the bins weren't emptied, or the traffic, or anything at all really. It's like an open-air surgery.

Similar comments were made by many councillors:

> I go to our local pub most Saturday lunch-times, sit there, have a beer and just wait till someone comes up for a chat. If I'm dealing with a specific problem for someone, they'll always approach me wherever I am.
>
> If I go to the local shop – it's about a 10-minute walk if I go the quick route – but I always go the long way round through the local estate and that should take about 25 minutes. But it never does – it'll take an hour, or even a couple of hours, because people will always stop me and want to talk about something. Look, if I didn't want to do that, I'd jump in the car, drive and be home in 30 seconds – unless I was stopped in the shop.
>
> I can't do the shopping in Sainsbury without someone coming up to talk about something – I don't mind, we just factor in 'surgery time' into the trip – in fact I factor in 'surgery time' into most of the things I do.
>
> The kids, when they were young, never quite got why strangers would come up and talk to daddy, but now they're used to it – I'm just waiting for the time when it's embarrassing for them – although I expect that'll be after they want to be seen in public with me at all anyway.
>
> I used to get up at 7am to go to work, but people realised they could get me on the phone at that time, so, now, I get up at six, just in case the phone goes.
>
> Our dog loves it – she must be the most walked dog in the ward. I just get her lead and off we go. See, she gives me an excuse to be walking round – looks a bit pompous if you just stride round the place offering people the opportunity to come and talk. So I take Logan out and can legitimately wander around, scooping poop as I go, and it never takes long for someone to come up to me about something – even with the poop scooping.

It was therefore a deliberate strategy of councillors to use what they would be doing anyway as part of their private life as a way of keeping both visible and contactable and being seen to be approachable. The only occasions when such proximity caused a problem was when tempers became frayed over a personal or policy issue and constituents overstepped the boundaries of normal interaction.

Councillors are public property and the public, it seems, are not always backwards in coming forwards with their views and expressions of anger – even when the councillor's family or friends are present. Such outbursts are not unusual occurrences. A Labour councillor reported:

> I've been sworn at, shouted at, fists shaken at me and insults yelled across the street. It's bad enough when that happens but when I'm with my partner, or the children, or friends it gets a bit much. Sometimes, though, I'm glad I've got company with me because if it really turned nasty at least I'd have help and witnesses!

What is worse for the councillor is when anger is not just expressed at a chance public encounter but arrives at the doorstep. It is not unusual for a knock on the front door to lead to an altercation with an enraged constituent. Or for the phone to ring and for the conversation to be largely a torrent of invective aimed at the councillor or the council. Phones can be put down, but doorstepping, especially of the aggressive type, is far more difficult to deal with and requires techniques in which councillors may not have received training or which they deal with by indulging in a stand-up row, or in threatening or actually calling the police. A Conservative councillor commented:

> It was a difficult planning case and I did what I could but it was never enough for [named individual]. He resorted to coming to my home – if I saw him coming up the drive, I sent the children out to the garden, or upstairs because I knew it would turn nasty and it always did. Not so I'd need to get an injunction, although I did call the police once.

Put simply, the proximity councillors have to the community and local people means there are no boundaries between the public person and the private person – yes, they can walk away from an interaction, but many choose not to, and even go further and use chance occurrences as a way of providing access to them as public representatives or as a way of gathering intelligence.

It is, however, not all negative, as a Liberal Democrat councillor commented:

> It was really nice of a resident to make a special journey to my flat and knock on the door – at the weekend – just so as to thank me for sorting out what was a very complex housing issue. I do get thank yous and even the odd thank-you card. It makes up for all the brickbats to get a few bouquets.

It is not unusual for councillor to receive thanks. Councillors report that satisfied constituents will often thank them, in person, over the phone or through email, and however the 'thank you' comes, it is appreciated but not expected.

The line for councillors is, however, well and truly crossed when constituents make contact with them at work. This does not appear to be a widespread problem, but in the interviews it was clear that when a councillor's work telephone number leaks into the public domain, some members of the public will have no restraint in using it to call during the day. For some, the need to speak to a councillor is an immediate one. Councillors deal with such intrusions in different ways: arranging to call back at lunch or a break; arranging to visit the caller or have them come to a surgery; and in most cases attempting to end the call quickly, firmly, but without leaving the caller feeling as though the councillor does not care. As one councillor commented: 'It's a special type of person that will phone you at work; the sort of person for whom I'm more a counsellor than councillor.'

The counsellor–councillor blurring was another recurring theme in the relationship that councillors found they had with some, but by no means all, of their constituents and those whom they might come across in their private life. It is clear that some cross the boundary from needing the services of a councillor to take up casework into territory that is more about finding support to resolve emotional problems or personal conflicts with which they are struggling. It is because of the councillor's proximity to the community and the ease with which they can be approached that those requiring such support will strike up a relationship with them. In some cases, councillors have referred such people to professional advisors of one sort or another. More often, though, the strategy is to listen, be sympathetic and give time, support and guidance that may assist an individual in resolving some personal issue.

Such intrusion into private space affects all those types of councillor we identified in Chapter 3: the *corporate* councillor – whose main preference is to give attention to the running of the council; the *associated* councillor – whose main interest is in interaction with the complexity of politics outside the council and in mediating interests and arbitrating between conflicting causes, and councillors of the *lay* and *professional* genre. No councillor can choose to isolate themselves completely from such spillage between their public and private life, and it would appear that none wish to do so – despite different preferences for aspects of their work as councillor. Indeed, even corporate councillors of the most professional turn seem to relish the accidental interaction they have with constituents because for them it fulfils a policy research role as well as a pastoral one.

The general experience for the councillor, then, is one of, at the very least, a blurring of boundaries between council affairs and life beyond the council. And very often there is a complete breakdown of any boundaries between the office of councillor and the private life of the holder. Councillors are public property, and if any constituent has a problem and no one else can help, even those citizens who do not know their councillor think maybe they could use her or him. Experience shows that they will; councillors become the 'A' Team.

Conclusion

The chapter started by declaring that the proximity of the councillor to their constituents and their physical location within the communities they represent was a unique feature of their particular representative office. What is clear is that such proximity brings with it a blurring of the boundaries between the political, personal and private life of the councillor and which can see one facet or another of council duties and responsibilities spill into the councillor's work and social life. Indeed, what we see is that the work and social life of the councillor is as much a theatre of representation as formal council meetings themselves or their political parties. While it is difficult to compartmentalise councillors' work, family and social life, it is even more difficult to maintain strict boundaries between any aspect of non-council activity and the duties of the councillor.

Councillors do develop strategies to deal with the spillage of council work into other areas of their life, but those strategies, as we have seen, are about managing, not avoiding, those spillages. Councillors operate on an assumption that there is little, if any, private space for them to inhabit, so council and constituent interference with work, family and social life requires the sacrifice of time from each of those personal arenas. Interference with paid employment requires specific tactics, such as allocating time during the working day to council activity, and interference with social life requires the sacrificing of social time, such as periods on holiday, to deal with council work. What we have seen in this chapter is that councillors rarely say 'No' to contact from the council or constituents, whatever their location or activity at the time the contact is made. The sacrifice of their time is one aspect of the councillor's role that is inadequately accounted for in assessments of their time allocation to council duties or in the recognition given to councillors for their work.

Councillors warmly embrace the chaos that goes with the permeable boundaries of their public and private life, and indeed they use the flow from one area into another, sometimes even encouraging it, as a way of strengthening their work as councillors. Work and social life and normal everyday action and interaction can be used as intelligence gathering and as a way of integrating even further into a community. Fuzzy and fluid boundaries between the holder of the office of councillor and the duties of the office are a vital part of its functioning. Proximity to place and people, and being from and embedded in their communities, is not only a special feature of being a councillor but also makes demands on the non-public aspects of the councillor that few fully recognise.

Councillors give willingly of time that would normally be allocated to other aspects of their lives and do so from a sense of commitment to public service or from a democratic spirit, as we saw in Chapter 5. Given the commitment and sense of duty that councillors express and their experiences of intrusion and spillover into their non-council lives, we are left wondering how far these are recognised or contrasted in the Government's view of what councillors do – the official mind – and in the public image of the councillor shaped by the media. It is therefore to this official mind and public image that the next chapter turns.

7

Official mind and public image

Introduction

In this chapter, two separate but linked understandings of the office of councillor are examined for what they tell us about the perceptions that are held about councillors. The justification for this is that the two sources of those perceptions under investigation – central policy-makers (termed here 'the official mind') and the press – shape not only the reality of what councillors can and cannot do, but also public perceptions about councillors. Chapter 2 highlighted the way that the various roles of the councillor and the office of councillor have been conceptualised and how contemporary policy interest never shifts its attention too far from councils and councillors in an effort to shape and reshape the office. Taking this policy focus alongside the way the responsibilities of councillors flow into all facets of their life, which was examined in the previous chapter, it is necessary now to contrast the realities and experiences of being a councillor with what 'the official mind' perceives about that office. It is necessary to do this because the views held by central policy-makers and the media are more likely than anything to determine the ultimate direction that ideas about, and developments in, local democracy and local representative office will take. And it is these views that will decide issues such as the number of councillors there should be sitting on what types of councils.

In the early 1980s, Page (1982) and Jones and Stewart (1982) referred to a 'culture of disdain' that the centre held for local government and, by extension, that disdain stretched to councillors. Jones and Stewart (1982: 12) saw such disdain not as part of a political culture expressing widespread public contempt for local government, but rather as emanating from political and policy elites. The intention in this chapter is to track whether the official mind has indeed displayed a long-term disdain and disregard for councillors and whether this perception has altered over time. In so doing, the chapter will explore policy documents and pronouncements to assess the veracity of the claim that there is a centrally held disrespect and disregard for councillors as local politicians. By necessity, and where necessary, the exploration will extrapolate examples of general disdain for local government, its position in the constitutional framework of the country and views about its role, efficiency and effectiveness to also include councillors.

In addition to understanding what the centre thinks about councillors, the chapter will also explore the way the media – the press in particular – report the activities of councillors. It does this to understand how media reporting can contribute to wider public perceptions about councillors and the consequences for local democracy of such perceptions. Councillors are most certainly in the public eye and are public property – as we saw in the last chapter – and as they make authoritative decisions which affect the future of their communities and the lives of local citizens, they are rightfully open to media scrutiny. The chapter does not set out to blame the media for the nature of its reporting, rather simply to understand whether councillors get a good or bad press or a mixed (balanced) press and whether what is reported about councillors undermines or supports local representative democracy.

We saw in Chapter 5 the various motivations and factors that lead councillors to stand for office, and in Chapter 6 we saw the consequences of their election and the duties they have to carry out as councillors on various facets of their non-political life. So, by moving on to explore and bring together the official mind and press reporting of councillors we can unlock another insight into why so many are prepared to serve as councillors. Are they encouraged to seek office by the high regard, esteem and status with which they are held in the mind of central government and the press? Or do they place themselves before the local electorate and suffer the highs and lows of election campaigning and the demands made upon them once they are elected despite, and not because of, what government and the media think about them and the office they hold?

The chapter is presented in two parts: the first gives a brief historical overview of central attitudes towards local government and of what thinkers important to the development of local government in England have had to say about its role. It highlights that the tension between localisers and centralisers is a long-standing one and not just a product of contemporary thinking. The chapter then explores the most prominent official commissions and inquiries into local government for what they reveal about the developing official mind about councillors and to examine the trajectory in elite views that have converged into a shared vision that has done so much to shape the nature of the office of councillor. It examines the consequences of those views for the office of councillor.

The second part of the chapter moves on to explore how councillors are reported in the media. It focuses on the press rather than electronic media because the press leaves a permanent written record. This part of the chapter does not employ content analysis to explore meaning and authenticity or the frequency of certain key words in reporting, as such an approach is appropriate to a major study of the relationship between councillors and the press as a separate project. Rather, the chapter presents the findings of a randomly selected forty local newspapers from across England, and uses a selection of individual press stories from those papers to construct a picture of how the press report the activities of councillors. Rather than taking these newspapers and tracking them over a period of time, I took one or two issues and identified common themes that had emerged across all forty to construct an understanding of the broad nature of reporting and to identify the framework within which press debate about councillors is conducted.

PART ONE: UNLOCKING THE OFFICIAL MIND

Journey to the centre

In exploring the development of thinking about councillors and local government that rests at the centre, it is worth noting that Chandler (2007: 109–10) reminds us that Palmerston and Gladstone both expressed sympathy with the view that local government should be left alone, as far as possible. Yet they did so in the firm understanding that while local government could be left alone, it could not compete with the centre as a source of political authority and that councils would not pursue policies or espouse values that were at considerable variance to those of the centre. Indeed, the public service role of local government, as opposed to a more broadly political governing role, developed with the burgeoning public sector responsibilities that emerged during the Victorian period, which in turn saw the development of a wide range of bodies charged with public duties. Improvement Boards, Poor Law Guardians, or Local Boards of Health, to mention a few, alongside municipal corporations, all shared some form of responsibility for ensuring what today would be called the 'well-being' of local communities. That disparate source of service responsibility was to eventually, over a long process, converge in the local corporation (Keith-Lucas and Richards, 1978; Byrne, 1994; Chandler, 2007).

John Stuart Mill in *On Liberty and Considerations on Representative Government* devotes a chapter to 'Local representative bodies' in which local government is clearly seen as underpinning a liberal state but also as a clearly subservient, if important, element of the overall governing set-up. Indeed, for Mill, one of local government's important roles was to ensure efficient administration of local business. Mill sets out the importance of local representative bodies as places where the citizen can gain experience of governing and of acting for the wider public interest, rather than being motivated by self-interest alone. There is a note of caution, however, that minority, or rather property, interests must be protected by plural voting, and he clearly links local representative bodies to the spending of public money thus:

> For the honest and frugal dispensation of money forms so much a larger part of the business of the local than of the national body, that there is more justice as well as policy in allowing a greater proportional influence to those who have a larger money interest at stake.

He stresses the need for local control of local affairs, however:

> It is but a small proportion of the public business of a country which can be
> done well, or safely attempted, by the central authorities; and even in our own
> government, the least centralised in Europe, the legislative portion at least of the
> governing body busies itself far too much with local affairs.
>
> (Mill, 1948: 278)

Mill advocates locating all the business that affects a locality within one body: the
local authority. But it is clear from *On Representative Government* that while local
authorities are valuable schools for socialising individuals into politics and are
an effective way of dispensing local business, they are not competitors to central
government. Rather, as Chandler (2010: 7) points out, the purpose of local government is to support the overall governance of the nation.

The English political theorist Joshua Toulmin Smith poses a different view of
local government, or rather local self-government – one which sees it as part of
the struggle against centralisation and the undermining of English common law
practices. He poses the two competing factors, thus:

> Local self-government is that system of government under which the greatest
> number of minds, knowing the most, and having the fullest opportunities of
> knowing it, about the special matter in hand, and having the greatest interest in
> its well-working, have management of it, or control over it.
>
> (Toulmin Smith, 2005: 17)

Contrast that to his definition of centralisation:

> Centralisation is that system of government under which the smallest number
> of minds, and those knowing the least, and having the fewest opportunities of
> knowing it, about the special matter in hand, and having the smallest interest in
> its well-working, have the management of it, or control over it.
>
> (Toulmin Smith, 2005: 17)

But for Toulmin Smith there was also a distinction between representative government and local self-government. The latter does not derive its legitimacy from
Parliament, which Toulmin Smith saw as usurping local self-government and as

> [h]aving no original authority of its own. It is a result, not a source. Its authority
> is not, like that of the folk and people, self-derived and inherent. No doctrine
> can be more self-evidently absurd than that of such original authority; while the
> implication of it is the true ground-work of centralisation.
>
> (Toulmin Smith, 2005: 29)

In Toulmin Smith's view, local self-government did

> [n]ot then consist, as many imagine, in having local bodies, elected or otherwise, and leaving the exclusive management of everything in their hands. Its essence consists in this: – that, while these local representative assemblies exist, like the national one, for the more convenient administration of affairs, arrangements also exist by which regular, fixed, frequent and accessible meetings together of the freemen themselves shall take place; at which all matters done by the representative body, local and general, shall be laid before the folk and people, discussed and approved or disapproved; and, at which all matters of common interest to the respective communities, either as separate bodies, or as parts of the great national whole, shall be brought forward, and fully canvassed and considered; and, having undergone this process, the public opinion thereupon shall be truly, peaceably, and healthy expressed.
>
> (Toulmin Smith, 2005: 42)

His 'regular, fixed, frequent and accessible meetings' and the bringing together of folk and people was a defence against centralisation and a recipe for a form of public participation that contrasts local self-government with local representative government.

But it was not Toulmin Smith's vision that won out, and what we see throughout the period from the 1835 Municipal Corporations Act is successive pieces of legislation that alter the nature of local government or its services and responsibilities and which gradually introduce greater and greater central oversight and control. Local government is firmly established in the governing framework of the country, but as a creature of statute, owing its very existence to Parliament. It was the formation of the Poor Law Board in 1847 that cumulated in a minister being given detailed control of a large slice of local government functioning and over rates and expenditure (Chandler, 2007: 63).

During the Victorian period, this battle was played out between centralisers, such as the English social reformers Chadwick and Bentham, with a focus on public service provision by authorities which needed central oversight and control, and anti-centralisers (localisers), such as Toulmin Smith, with a different conception of local control and autonomy. As services and expenditure developed, especially around poverty, health and sanitation, central oversight and control was exerted through various government ministries. The tendency for central government to micro-manage was evident from the earliest beginnings of the welfare state, but as Toulmin Smith eloquently put it:

> In the preamble to the laws promulgated by King Alfred, by Authority of his Witena-germote, it is said: – 'I dare not be so bold as set down for law aught much of my own; for this it is unknown to me what of it would be liked by those who shall live after us.' That is the true spirit of the law-maker of a free country,

and the result of his law-making. Exactly the reverse are the spirit and result of
the law-making of our day.

(Toulmin Smith, 2005: 155)

Indeed, Toulmin Smith's *Local Self-Government and Centralisation* can be seen as
an essentially English antidote to the centralising tendencies of the British state,
but it was an antidote which ultimately failed to offer a cure. Together, the thinking
of Chadwick and Jeremy Bentham was part of the foundation of a centralist view
that local government should be subservient to the wishes of the central legislature
(Parekh, 1973: 224), and it was a view that was ultimately triumphant. Indeed, in
1871, we see the first real steps to provide a central point of government oversight
and monitoring of local government with the formation of the Local Government
Board, which took over the responsibility for local government from the various
ministries existing at the time. As Chandler (2007: 65) shows, the centralising
tendencies of the Poor Law Board came to dominate the activities of the Local
Government Board, which in turn saw the gradual process of erosion and ultimate
termination of the 'relative independence' of local government.

While there had long been a tussle between centralisers and anti-centralisers,
which came to a head in the 1800s, it was a tussle with much greater anteced-
ents, as the centralising tendencies of British government have their roots in the
Norman despotism and the need of a foreign political elite to control a conquered
nation (England) from the centre (Redlich and Hirst, 1958; Copus, 2011). The
centralisation of England today is not a new phenomenon, rather it represents the
culmination of the long process of development of central control of the localities
that could be said to reflect the 'disdain' for local government and local politicians
that has already been noted.

The development of the contemporary official mind

The deliberately brief review of the historical context to the contemporary official mind was meant to provide no more than background to the following
debate, which now focuses on the modern display of thinking about councils
and councillors. It also enables us to understand the limitations of current day
localisers' conceptions of localism when compared to Toulmin Smith's radical
approach to local self-government. Thus, the chapter now explores what certain
seminal investigations have had to say about the office of councillor and how
they have shaped contemporary thinking about councillors and their roles in
order to highlight where such investigations have influenced or failed to influence official thinking.

The discussion focuses mainly, but not exclusively, on two cornerstone investigations of local government: the Committee on the Management of Local

Government, 1967 (the Maud Committee) and the Committee of Inquiry into the Conduct of Local Authority Business, 1986 (the Widdicombe Committee). It does this because these two investigations not only summarised contemporary thinking but gave a sharp stimulus to the development of particular views about councillors and the office of councillor that are still being refined today.

The Committee on the Management of Local Government

The research conducted for the Committee on the Management of Local Government, which reported in 1967, was not the first investigation of local government, by any means, but it provides a valuable insight into the way thinking has developed about councillors and the purpose of their office. In the research volume about councillors (1967b) and the committee's report, we see an emerging concern about the 'representativeness' of the councillor population, thus:

> In some respects, councillors differ widely from the general population. They are much older on average. Only one-fifth of male councillors are under the age of 45. More than half are over 55. Only 12% are women. The proportion of councillors who are employers and managers of small businesses or farmers is four times that of these groups in the general population. On the other hand, manual workers, who form more than half of the male population over 25 are numerically very under-represented on councils.
>
> (1967b, para 1: 7)

> Councillors are somewhat better educated than the general population. Forty-four per cent had only elementary education and no formal qualifications, compared with about 70% of the general population.
>
> (HMSO, 1967b, para 2: 7)

The report also noted that the 12 per cent of councillors that were women contrasted with 50 per cent of the general population being female (HMSO, 1967b: 16).
Similarly, a recent LGA census of councillors found that:

- Most councillors (68.5 per cent) were male; 30.6 per cent were female in 2010.
- The proportion of female councillors had increased from 27.8 per cent in 1997, although the proportion is still considerably lower than in the adult population (51.2 per cent).
- The average age of councillors has increased from 55.4 years in 1997 to 59.7 years in 2010. In 2010, 88.3 per cent of councillors were aged 45 and over, compared to 52.6 per cent of the adult population.

- The proportion of councillors who were retired has increased from 34.1 per cent in 1997 to 47.2 per cent in 2010, compared to 19.1 per cent of the adult population.
- 55.9 per cent of councillors in 2010 held a qualification equivalent to NVQ level 4 and above, compared to 31.2 per cent of the adult population (NFER, 2011: 5).

Here we see two things in Maud's reporting: first, the recognition that the councillor population is sociologically different from the rest of the population, and second, the employment of a particular interpretation of 'representative' that focuses not on political values, but resemblance to a wider population and one which stresses that the councillor population should be a microcosm of the wider society. But Maud did conclude the following:

> Some witnesses argue in written evidence that councils should be more representative of the electorates they serve. It is neither possible, nor in our opinion is it desirable, that councils should is some way be representative of all the varying interest, economic groups, income or education levels in the community ... The overriding aim must be to recruit people of integrity for without this the work of local government will be discredited.
>
> (1967a, para 508–10: 143)

As we shall see later, a focus on 'representativeness' still exists in debates about councillors, but it has shifted away from Maud's mere recognition of the differences between councillors and the general population to one which stresses resemblance of council chambers to local populations as a virtue in its own right.

Maud presented many useful insights into the attitudes of councillors towards the satisfaction that they get from council work, particularly in contrast to their paid employment. Councillors in more urban authorities and middle-aged and younger members found council work more satisfying than their paid work. As the report went on to note, 'for members whose jobs are more routine and offer less scope, council work is clearly more often a means of obtaining satisfactions not offered by their occupations' (HMSO, 1967a, para 491: 139). It went further to stress that, for councillors, almost:

> two-thirds of the main satisfactions of local authority work relate to some particular council activity; housing and old people's welfare account for over half these particular activities; education matters are a sizeable source of satisfaction ... over a third of all members prefer work which relates to individual people rather than broad policy matters, and about half of the women members feel this way.
>
> (HMSO, 1967a, para 492: 139)

It would appear that the councillor, at least in Maud's findings, prefers to be a specialist rather than a generalist, and there begins a gradual separating out of the policy councillor from the pastorally focused councillor (acknowledged in the discussion of councillor roles in Chapter 2) – a process reflected in later reports and finally in government legislation in 2000. Indeed, Maud laid specific ground-work for the shift to cabinet-based local government with its recommendation that councils should establish a management board of five to nine councillors (HMSO 1967a, para 158: 41). The roles Maud envisaged for this board, formulat-ing objectives, reviewing progress, oversight of the organisation of the council, a decision-making role and presenting business to the council, shows it as a nascent cabinet (HMSO, 1967a, para 162: 42).

We also see in Maud that the frustrations for councillors of council work often resulted from administration rather than specific council activities and that many of these frustrations arose from relationships with other tiers of government, nor-mally central government (HMSO, 1967a, para 494: 139). In a powerful statement arising from the research presented in Volume V of the Maud research, what was stressed was how little control of council activity elected members had, and the committee concluded in its report:

> The research report [Volume 5] emphasises the consuming interest of members in matters of detail and in matters affecting individuals and refers to the 'illusion' which many members have that they are contributing to the work of the author-ity when in fact they are 'doing nothing'. We believe, however, that there are a small minority who like to reach decisions quickly and who think in terms of broad policy development rather than personalities, and to these council work as at present organised can be frustrating.
>
> (1967a, para 496: 140)

One other aspect of the committee's consideration that throws light on the development of official thinking is Maud's refusal to be drawn too far into a wider debate about the calibre of councillors – which has been a concern, for some, almost since the inception of democratic local government. Remarkably, Jones (1969: 149) reports *The Times* newspaper in 1880 bemoaning the calibre of coun-cillors and laying the blame for the poor state of affairs that it observed at the feet of party politics. The terms of reference for Maud stated that the committee was to:

> [c]onsider in the light of modern conditions how local government might best continue to attract and retain people (both elected representatives and principal officers) of the calibre necessary to ensure its maximum effectiveness.
>
> (HMSO, 1967a, para 1: 1)

But, as Maud argues, the term 'calibre' can only mean the

> [d]egree to which councillors have qualities which ensure the successful con-duct of local government work. An operational definition of the term 'calibre'

would require a statement of all the qualities needed for the efficient performance of all the functions of a public representative and acceptable ways of meas-
uring these qualities.

(HMSO, 1967b: 3)

The committee noted, rightly, the difficulties and dangers of addressing and mea-
suring 'calibre' of councillors in circumstances of political, technological, economic and sociological change and at times of increasing complexity of the issues
and functions with which they were required to come to terms. Indeed, the committee stated bluntly and admirably that: 'we have, then, nothing to say on the
subject of the calibre of councillors' (HMSO, 1967b: 3).

Maud did not entirely duck the issue, however. The report did draw attention to a considerable amount of opinion that was critical of the existing crop of
councillors and their ability to run efficient and effective local government (see
HMSO, 1967a: 142–4). Maud rejected the need to assess whether there had been
a decline in quality of members but rather stressed the increasing demands made
upon them and the increasing complexity of their responsibilities. In this regard,
Maud defended the councillor against unreasonable and impressionistic attitudes.
In addition, Maud noted that there was little to be gained from producing a list of
human virtues and trying to match councillors against it or to ensure those elected
were in possession of such qualities. Instead it stressed the importance of what
members were expected to undertake as a guideline to the qualities that might
be required. Maud also quoted the Royal Commission on Local Government in
Greater London (Cmnd 1164: para 235) thus: 'a high degree of intelligence, experience, personality and character should be aimed at and can legitimately be hoped
for' (HMSO, 1967b: 143). To this, Maud added:

a. the capacity to understand sympathetically the problems and points of view
   of constituents and to convey them to the authority and, at the same time, to
   interpret and explain the authority's policies and actions to those whom they
   represent (a representative capacity)
b. the capacity to understand technical, economic and sociological problems
   which are likely to increase in complexity (an organisational capacity)
c. the ability to innovate, to manage and direct; the personality to lead and guide
   opinion and other members; and a capacity to accept responsibility for the policies of the authority (a political leadership capacity).

Maud was right in refusing to be drawn into a popular debate about councillor
calibre and to indulge an already developed stereotype about councillor ability,
and by avoiding such discussions, Maud had the effect of not giving credence
to impressionistic and imbalanced views of councillors and their capabilities. In
the longer run, however, such avoidance and failure to tackle the debate head

on, as we shall see, may have proven fateful, especially in allowing such popular misinterpretations to permeate the official mind in regard to thinking about councillors.

While the above is a necessarily short and very selective overview of what was a comprehensive exploration of local government conducted for and by the Maud Committee, it is clear that Maud provided remarkable data and insight into local government. Moreover, it also defended not only local government but also councillors and the office of councillor from ill-informed public criticism while also highlighting that where problems existed they were endemic rather than epidemic. A theme running through the report – despite its numerous recommendations – was that local government, and the councillors who served upon it, should be *trusted* to manage and run their own affairs. Maud was concerned with the very nature of the office of councillor and its location within local communities of place and the interest that people obviously have for their immediate surroundings. In addition, it was concerned for the probity and reputation of local government and councillors.

While there are in Maud seventy-nine specific recommendations for change, there is little that can directly be blamed for creating or giving credence to reasons to hold councillors or local government in disdain. Except, of course, that any recommendations for change made as a result of a full inquiry can be held up generally as highlighting fundamental weaknesses and flaws in the subject under investigation and therefore provide a general starting point that assumes there are problems which must be resolved.

Committee of Inquiry into the Conduct of Local Authority Business

The Committee of Inquiry into the Conduct of Local Authority Business (the Widdicombe Committee) was set up in February 1985 and published its report in June 1986. The inquiry was conducted in rather more turbulent times for councillors than its predecessor and spanned the mid-years of the second government of Margaret Thatcher. It was a time of intense political conflict in which town halls controlled by the new urban Labour far-left were locked in an ideological struggle with the right-wing central government. It was a period that saw reductions in public expenditure, a reduction in the powers and responsibilities of local government and an increasing number of financial and legal controls imposed on local government (see Parkinson, 1987). Indeed, it was a time in which many councillors firmly rejected the idea of a *RealLokalPolitik* considered in Chapter 4 and saw themselves as engaged in a wholly party-political and ideologically driven set of interactions with the centre, and those councillors made decisions accordingly.

The early to mid 1980s saw two implacable opponents, the new urban far-left, concentrated in a number of Labour-controlled councils and the right-of-centre government of Margaret Thatcher (whose policies were also criticised by many Conservative councils and councillors at the time and since) facing off against each other. Left-wing Labour-controlled councils attempted to use their local mandate as a counterbalance to the mandate granted to central government in order to pursue polices diametrically opposed to the government. Those policies resulted in the rate-capping rebellion in 1985, where a number of English councils undertook not to set a budget for the 1985–86 financial year (see Blunkett and Jackson, 1987; Livingstone, 1987; Goss, 1988; Hatton, 1988; Taafe and Mulhearn, 1988). The political campaign ultimately ended in failure, but it was against this backdrop that the Widdicombe Committee conducted its inquiry and which undoubtedly shaped its outcome.

The terms of reference for the committee reflect this background:

> To inquire into practices and procedures governing the conduct of local authority business with particular reference to:
>
> a. The rights and responsibilities of elected members
> b. The respective roles of elected members and officers
> c. The need to clarify the limits and conditions governing discretionary spending by local authorities
>
> and to make any necessary recommendations for strengthening the democratic process.
>
> (HMSO, 1986a, para 1.1: 17)

In addition, the report of the committee noted that the Secretary of State for the Environment (Patrick Jenkin, who ceased to be Secretary of State in September 1985), in announcing the terms of reference for the inquiry, also set out a number of items he wished it to give particular attention:

- ensuring proper accountability of councillors
- strengthening local democracy
- clarifying the status and role of party groups in decision-taking
- ensuring participation and accountability of councillors in decision-taking
- examining problems that arise from councillors having a conflict of interest, particularly where councillors were employed by another council
- considering the merits of the development of full-time councillors
- members' allowance and remuneration
- the use of co-option to council committees
- studying officer member relationships
- clarifying the discretionary spending available to local government.

> (HMSO, 1986a, para 1.3: 17)

Further, the report of the committee also states that the Secretary of State commented:

> In view of the growing public concern about the use made by some local author-
> ities of their discretionary powers to engage in overt political campaigning at
> public expense, I am asking the committee to submit an early interim report on
> this question.
>
> (HMSO, 1986a: 18)

One thing the Widdicombe Committee did not do was to follow the lead set by Maud, as it came out against any form of executive body of councillors being created, a conclusion driven by a fear of party-political domination of council activities and parties with small majorities being able to fully control a council through executive powers. It did, however, support delegation of decision-making to committee chairmen. One of the more controversial recommendations made by the committee was that council officers on or above the rank of 'principal officer' should be disqualified from election to other authorities. It also recom-mended that the powers of the local ombudsman be strengthened, as should the ability of local citizens to challenge council decisions (see HMSO, 1986a: 235–48 for a full list of the committee's recommendations). In a significant nod to the political background against which the committee considered its evidence it rec-ommended that courts have the 'discretion' to disqualify councillors for a period of time in cases 'involving expenditure or otherwise, where they have author-ised an illegal decision or action and the court is not satisfied that the councillor acted reasonably or on the belief that the action was authorised by law' (HMSO, 1986a: 248).

If we take overall the eighty-eight recommendations made by the committee and place that against the turbulent political background of the ideological battle between sections of local government and the centre described above, we can see a remarkable restraint in the committee's recommendations – especially given its own terms of reference. Widdicombe largely followed the route set down by Maud in its research volume (HMSO, 1986b), which examined in detail aspects of coun-cillors' activity, including the socio-demographic characteristics of councillors, their working life, their views and attitudes about aspects of council work and the remuneration system. There was no hatchet job on councillors in this volume and it provided an overview of the working life of the councillor without pandering to the highly charged debate that was taking place publicly. It should be remembered that the committee conducted its investigation at a time when the media were reporting the activities of 'Looney Left' councils, and such reporting was being used not just to discredit a few councils and more generally Labour-controlled councils, but to discredit local government and councillors as a whole. The com-mittee's work, intentionally or otherwise, was powerful ammunition in the battle of attrition between local and central government.

Thus, from these two major inquiries into local government and the councillor – Maud and Widdicombe – we see that context and timing are important factors for the way in which government uses or responds to any findings and recommendations. It is not the results of the inquiries themselves that necessarily set the tone of a debate, rather it is what is selectively drawn from them that is an important part of the construction of the official mind. The next stage in the demonstration of the official mind in regard to councillors comes from a plethora of documents that can be said to represent the 'modernising agenda' of the Labour governments from 1997 to 2005.

Modernising local government

The thinking about councillors of the Labour governments in power from 1997 can be seen in a number of publications which set out the main principles of the 'modernisation project' (Labour Party, 1995; DETR, 1998a, b, 1999; DTLR, 2001; ODPM, 2005; DCLG, 2008). It was clear from the title 'modernising project' or 'agenda' that the Blair government operated on an assumption that local government and what councillors did, did indeed require modernising.

The first paper in the series, *Local Democracy and Community Leadership*, which was published in February 1998, was quickly followed in July 1998 by *Modern Local Government: In Touch with the People*.

Much of *Local Democracy and Community Leadership* concerned itself with democratic renewal and the need for councils to be open, transparent and to communicate more with their communities through participative democratic mechanisms. Chapter five (DETR, 1998a) set the themes that would be addressed again in *Modern Local Government: In Touch with the People* (DETR, 1998b). The general critique of the conduct of council affairs by councillors included: the number of meetings councillors attended, the time spent at the town hall, the need for more engagement and community-focused activity and leadership by councillors and the need for an executive and scrutiny distinction in councillor roles (even at this point the role of scrutiny in holding to account bodies beyond the council was recognised). There was also much exhortation about enhancing the power and responsibilities of councillors. Indeed, the role of the councillor was seen not only as a powerful one but also as a rewarding one, where the

> backbench councillor under such models could be less time-consuming, but more high profile, more effective and therefore more rewarding. This new role might encourage a wider cross-section of the community to stand for election as councillors, thereby strengthening local democracy.
>
> (DETR, 1998a: 32)

The analysis of the problem set out in the range of documents produced during the Blair administrations focuses mainly on leadership – or rather the lack of it provided by councillors operating in an opaque, cumbersome committee system which lacked transparency and accountability. Thus, three problems were at the centre of consideration: how to construct an open and transparent, but powerful local political leadership that could forge and pursue a democratically legitimised vision for the locality; second, how to hold it to account effectively and, oddly, how to restrain it from being too powerful; and, third, how to provide the remaining non-executive councillors with a valuable, fulfilling and influential role in the governance of the community.

These problems had arisen because the committee system made it difficult for the public to know who was responsible for various decisions and therefore to hold councillors to account. It also prevented councillors from providing external political leadership to their councils and communities as a whole and for councillors to be leaders within their wards or divisions. Indeed, the government was scathing about the length of time councillors spent in 'fruitless' committee meetings (DETR, 1998b: 11). The problem was that councillors spent too much time at the town hall at meetings dealing with internal council affairs, rather than looking outwards towards their communities, but they also had too few real influences over council decisions and too little say in what was agreed. In addition, councillors were failing to communicate the views of their voters into council decision-making procedures (DETR, 1998b, *passim*). As a result of this analysis, which was repeated throughout the various white papers produced during the time of the modernisation agenda, an enhanced role for all councillors was envisaged:

> Backbench councillors will spend less time in council meetings and more time in the local community, at residents' meetings or surgeries. They will be accountable, strong, local representatives for their area. They will bring their constituents' views, concerns and grievances to the council through their council's structures. Their role will be to represent the people to the council rather than defend the council to the people.
>
> Each councillor will become a champion of their community defending the public interest in the council and channelling the grievances, needs and aspirations of their electorate into the scrutiny process. In-touch local councillors, aware of and responsive to the needs of those they represent, will have a greater say in the formulation of policy and the solving of local problems than they could have within current committee structures.
>
> (DETR, 1998b: 23–4)

Councillors were to be powerful local politicians, expected to 'champion' their wards or divisions, but also to use the new scrutiny committees as a tool for wider governance activities. Indeed, scrutiny was to be the way through which the new powerful council executives (the solution to the problem of lack of leadership) were to be held to account. As far as council leadership was concerned, the analysis was straightforward:

There is little clear political leadership. This is not a reflection on the qualities of council leaders. It is caused by the structures in which they work. People often do not know who is really taking the decisions. They do not know who to praise, who to blame or who to contact with their problems. People identify most readily with an individual, yet there is rarely any identifiable figure leading the local community. This is no basis for modern, effective and responsive local government.

(DETR, 1998b: 15–16)

Directly elected mayors, or indirectly elected council leaders, would head powerful council cabinets (limited to ten councillors, whatever the size of the council area or the number of councillors) that would make decisions, within a policy framework, set down by the rest of the council. The executive would be held to account by councillors in scrutiny committees which would have the following responsibilities:

- reviewing and questioning decisions taken by the executive
- advising the executive on decisions and policy on local issues
- reviewing policy, formulating policy proposals and submitting proposals to the executive
- considering the budget proposed by the executive, proposing amendments and voting on the final budget
- taking responsibility, either with or without members of the executive, for those quasi-judicial functions, such as planning, licensing and appeals, which it would not normally be appropriate to delegate to an individual member of the executive.

(DETR, 1998b: 24)

It must be remembered that the context within which much of the Labour government's thinking was developed was the same as had resulted in the formation of the Widdicombe Committee by Margaret Thatcher's government. Part of the Labour DNA had been enthused with the idea that bad councils and councillors prevented the party from securing a general election win throughout the 1980s until 1997. Thus, behind much of the rhetoric of powerful councillors was a concern to ensure that such power was of a limited kind, overseen by regulations and inspections and set within a system in which any outburst of municipal radicalism could be constrained so as not to damage the party's general election chances. That fear was the spur to the modernisation of the Labour Party before the modernisation of local government.

The Blair government acted quickly on the ideas for changing the structure of political decision-making in local government which were introduced by the Local Government Act 2000. The Act gave to councillors a political decision-making structure that rested on an, albeit blurred, separation of powers, which mirrored the parliamentary system of a cabinet executive and a select committee system drawn from a wider body of representatives. It is hardly surprising that central reformers, convinced of the weakness of local government political decision-making and the apparent locking-up of councillors in the town hall, would see the solution in something close to home, at least for them. What is surprising is that from 1998 onwards, there was little deviation in government thinking from the original blueprint laid out in the white paper *Modern Local Government: In Touch with the People.* Each publication and subsequent piece of legislation followed the 1998 blueprint by addressing how to improve both the quality and effectiveness of local political leadership and how to refocus councillors on the representation of their wards or divisions and on scrutiny of the council executive and the outside world.

It is fair to say that this modernising agenda failed to convince all councillors that the committee system was a problem and the slow trickle of councils returning to that system, once it was made open to them again by the Localism Act 2011, indicates that failure (the next chapter explores this aspect further). The basis of the modernising agenda, however, was that local government was not modern, councillors were distant from those they represented and lacked strong and clear links to those communities, and they were internally and inwardly focused on committee agenda and the details of the business of the council and insufficiently concerned with strategy, long-term vision and broad political goals.

What we see here is a complete turnaround in central thinking from that of the 1980s and the Conservative government. But it was thinking which had developed from lessons learned the hard way, at least for the standing of the Labour Party. While it wanted councils to act quickly and effectively, it also wanted strong accountability and to control the activities of councillors through an inspection regime based on target setting and the achievement of centrally directed goals and standards. It was a government which had not come fully to trust councillors not to indulge a new wave of political battles with the centre. Yet it was a government that had seen its party languish in opposition in Parliament for eighteen years, when its only power had been through its councillors, who had, in many cases, led a far more robust and effective opposition to the centre than was possible in Parliament. But what if the tide turned and powerful councillors were now Conservatives locked in battle with the Labour government, and what if a few Labour councils also failed to behave themselves? It was the competing desires and fears behind the wish to see strong and effective local leadership and powerful councillors generally, mixed with the usual fear of the centre for loss of control over the localities, plus a strong dose of suspicion that some councillors might misbehave politically which was the backdrop against which the Councillors Commission was formed in 2007.

Councillors Commission

The Councillors Commission, chaired by Dame Jane Roberts, the former leader of Camden Council, was set up by the Secretary of State in February 2007 and reported in December of the same year. The Commission was very much a joint endeavour between the Department for Communities and Local Government and the Local Government Association and had as one of its primary aims an investigation of the incentives and barriers to becoming and staying a councillor – electoral fortunes to one side. It also looked at the support required for councillors, an issue very much connected to councillor retention, as well as exploring the remuneration system and the link between councillors and their communities.

Much of the focus for the work of the Commission was about what was needed to encourage wider sections of the community to stand for election and therefore it employed an interpretation of representation as resemblance. The Commission's report was, however, at pains to stress that it did not accept that only people of certain backgrounds could adequately 'represent' those of the same background. Rather, it sought the widest range of voices to be heard on councils for perceived practical and symbolic effects and to ensure that core issues of importance to different communities were fed into the democratic process (DCLG, 2007: 14). The latter point, of course, reflects the assumption of descriptive representation that such core interests are best presented and represented by people who are linked to a certain sectional interest within a wider community (Karlsson, 2013b).

The Commission was not formed in a turbulent time in the relationships between councillors and central government or in a time of intense ideological battles such as during the 1980s. It was formed, however, after councillors had experienced the changes brought about by the Local Government Act 2000 that introduced the executive and scrutiny distinction between councillors and which had been preceded by government promises of a brave new world of powerful and influential councillors shaping their localities. Indeed, the report of the Commission expressed the dissatisfaction and distancing that many councillors said they experienced from council decision-making as a result of the changes introduced by the Act. Moreover, it reported that councillors doubted the sincerity of central government claims of wishing to devolve power from the centre, and that they saw such power going not to local government but to bodies such as Local Strategic Partnerships (DCLG, 2007: 20).

The Commission saw no 'tension' between participatory and representative democracy. Indeed, the report urged councillors to: 'recognise and embrace the interface and act as a link between the two, recognising that representative democracy is informed and enriched by participatory democracy' (DCLG, 2007: 22). Yet this exhortation ignores the fact that many councillors have reported feeling challenged in their positions as representatives by the pressure to adopt the participatory approach championed by the then Labour government. It also ignored the doubt expressed by councillors about the effectiveness and desirability of the various participatory mechanisms favoured by the Blair government (see Copus, 2007, 2010b; Sweeting and Copus, 2013)

The sixty-one recommendations made by the Commission (DCLG, 2007: 69–113) were largely reflective of the government's own modernising agenda and the thinking behind that agenda, and it did not produce any radical suggestions for enhancing the power and influence of councillors or their ability to govern locally. Indeed, even the language of the report reflected government rhetoric, which was peppered throughout the document with terms like modern, open, transparent and responsive. The Commission presented a worthy, valuable, but highly functional set of suggestions that were more about changes to the existing system within a preconceived government agenda rather than a fundamental rethinking of the role, purpose and function of the office itself.

For example, the Commission suggested that the LGA should develop a clear set of role definitions for councillors, while accepting unchallenged that those roles should be very much as they existed and within the framework set down by the government (DCLG, 2007: 74). It made a number of recommendations: that the LGA and Improvement and Development Agency (IDeA) help political parties in determining best practice (another modernising agenda term) in candidate selection (*ibid.*: 95); that councils should adopt modern business and meeting processes which seek to remove potential barriers to participation (*ibid.*: 96); that support be provided for skill development and developing the IDeA charter for member development (*ibid.*: 101); and that the councillor census be continued and extended to parish councillors (*ibid.*: 108). This is not to say that the Commission was without a radical edge. Its suggestions for piloting the single transferable vote in local elections and the introduction of term limits for councillors, for example, displayed some challenging thinking (both these were rejected by the government). Largely, however, the report produced solid, worthy, workman-like and valuable recommendations, but little to shake the foundations of the office.

The government's response to the Councillors Commission was launched in July 2008, only six months after the Commission's report. The government, not unexpectedly, accepted the framework of representativeness as resembling sections within the community rather than the broad representation of political interests; the recommendations for stimulating greater diversity among the councillor population found particular favour. On many of the suggestions made by the Commission, the government promised action or reviews of the existing circumstances, indicating a positive response, or at least the willingness to think further about the issues raised. The government produced a warm response to the Commission's report and many of its recommendations, not least, the suggestion that councils should have a duty to promote local democracy – something which central government could do by removing many of the shackles that restrain local government and councillors and providing both with greater freedom. But, instead it chose to impose such a duty through the 2009 Local Democracy, Economic Development and Construction Act.

What we see in the government response is a willingness to engage in a debate about the role of the councillor but one conducted within an overall framework which matched the 'agenda for modernisation' constructed for local government at the outset of the Blair administration and before. There was, at least, a co-operative edge to the response, which itself recognised the importance of the LGA and the IDeA in ensuring further thought and action were given to many of the Commission's recommendations. Indeed, the Commission's report and government response were part of a collegial debate about the roles of the councillor and expectations of that office; they were, in effect, part of a coalescing of elite thinking about the functioning, but not the purpose, of the office. The closest the debate came to purpose was around the question of representativeness, but then, as we have seen, that was about giving voice to different sections of the community while at the same time expecting them not to pursue narrow sectional interests.

The co-operative relationship between the Commission, the government and the LGA and IDeA is apparent in this particular debate, as at more or less the same time as its response to the Commission, again in July 2008, the government also published a white paper on community empowerment entitled *Communities in Control: Real People, Real Power* (TSO, 2008). Three things are indicated here: that a growing elite consensus in thinking had developed which the Commission was unwilling to challenge; that the relationship between the Commission and government when it came to this investigation was so close as to be dangerously cosy; or that the government had already decided on its course of action and the Commission was therefore unlikely to influence affairs dramatically but instead was intended to provide the government with confirmation of its own thinking or an opportunity to challenge publicly ideas which did not integrate with that thinking. Whichever of these is the case, yet another opportunity to fundamentally rethink the role, purpose and powers of the office of councillor had been missed.

Councillors on the front line

So, we come to the most recent example of central exploration and thinking about what councillors should be doing, which came with the launch, in March 2012, of an inquiry into councillors and the community by the Communities and Local Government Committee of the House of Commons. In its call for evidence, the committee also expressed its focus on the 'representativeness' of councillors, again defining 'representativeness' as resemblance, and sought ways to enhance the socio-demographic diversity of the councillor population. The inquiry thus sought to explore very familiar territory for the centre, indicating thereby a continuing stream of thought about what troubles the centre about local elected representatives, but with some worthy and interesting developments in focus.

The committee sought evidence not only about skills, training and support for councillors and functional practicalities such as workloads, time commitment, time off work and remuneration, but also about ways to localise decision-making to divisions, wards and neighbourhoods, and local account-ability and the strategic leadership and governance responsibilities of council-lors. The call from the committee promised a reprise of much existing thinking, which is unsurprising given the length of time the centre, in one way or another, has expressed concern about or been interested in certain aspects of the office of councillor and its functioning. The committee's inquiry, however, held out the prospect that the debate would start to explore real changes in the role of the councillor.

In a very thorough and well-documented report (Communities and Local Government Committee, 2013), the committee attempted to re-establish a pow-erful role for councillors within the context of localism and particularly within the coalition government's version of localism. It did this by stressing that the government – any government – should not undermine councillors within their communities. In turn, it also stressed the need for councillors to be visible and active within their communities, thus recognising the responsibilities that rest with councillors in enhancing their own standing, locally. We have already seen in Chapter 6 that councillors not only recognise the need to do just that, but they also expect and tolerate the consequences that come from such a position – which is radically different from that experienced by MPs.

The Communities and Local Government Committee's report was particularly strong on suggesting that councils themselves provide sufficient and appropriate support to councillors and recognised that councils are often not structured to provide the type of support councillors require. The committee also recognised the increased demands that were being made on councillors and that such demands were likely to become greater over time, which in turn would result in a need for greater support from councils to councillors. Overall, the committee presented not only a positive report of the role and work of councillors, but also a set of recommendations designed to strengthen the office and provide a framework of support for councillors across the country. There was little that was negative in the document, and in some respects, it represented a 'manifesto' for councillors. Yet there was little that would suggest a radical overhaul of the office, a refocusing of role or that would treat councillors as governors of their communities and areas. Again, we see the continuation of a consistent line of thinking about councillors and the roles they undertake.

The government's response to the inquiry was based on a fundamental premise about councillors and the office they hold, namely that:

> the core principles of being a councillor are those of community service and volunteering … The government is quite clear that councillors are and should fundamentally be volunteers, and does not wish to see any move towards profes-sionalising the role through councillors becoming full time salaried staff.
>
> (TSO, 2013a: 1)

Now, there are two potential interpretations of such a conceptualisation of the councillor. First, if we think about the rhetorical thrust of a debate that casts councillors as lay volunteers who *should* give willingly of their time for little or no reward and certainly not for a pension, then we see a very clear image being created of something that is amateurish, unprofessional, part time and bordering on being unnecessary. The term 'volunteer' creates the image of councillors as individuals with the freedom to decide what they undertake, when, how long for and to what effect, and this is just not the case for the work councillors undertake. While councillors may not always be full time, or able and willing to give up work, that is not an indication of lack of commitment or professionalism in the role; rather, it was recognition of the structural and functional difference between councillors and MPs or MEPs. As one councillor commented in an interview: 'our former council leader gave up his job to become the leader and then two years later he was deposed by the group and he had nothing left'. A second added: 'I have never thought of being a councillor as being a volunteer; I do voluntary work and did before I became a councillor and being a councillor is far beyond being a volunteer.'

Second, however, we can think about volunteers as altruistic, careful, highly skilled, professional and dedicated and as individuals who increase the capacity of society by employing their own skills and resources to achieve an enhanced general well-being. Community service and responding to the needs of communities through voluntary effort has a long and proud tradition, and voluntary organisations and charities provide not only vital but highly professional services and resources. A councillor in interview, for example, proudly displayed a Community Service Volunteers (CSV) certificate of completion of a placement in supporting families; she was indeed a highly professional volunteer as well as a *professional* councillor.

Whichever of these two interpretations of volunteering one adheres to, the main premise remains the same: that the subject or purpose of volunteering activity is ancillary to other forms of provision and that it supplements and complements a more fundamental vehicle for provision. It is possible to argue this because contemporary welfare states have shifted from the idea that the voluntary and charity sector can be the sole provider of certain services of modern life to the view that the state is the central provider, and the debate is then more about the size, balance and nature of state or voluntary input. But with councillors we are not referring to a particular service or function, rather we are exploring the role that a type of elected representative has in the governance of not just local communities but also the wider governing framework. If an elected representative can be seen to fit either of the conceptualisations of 'volunteer' then their work is supplementary to and of a diminished purpose and necessity when compared to those non-volunteer, professional politicians. The question remains whether such a view of councillors is justifiable and sustainable and we will return to this question in the concluding chapter.

A second thrust of the government's response was to reject the idea of any sort of national framework within which the activities of councillors should be supported. Unsurprisingly, localism and decisions by individual councils on what they would provide formed the basis of the way forward. Indeed, leaving decisions to local councils was the response to many of the worthy recommendations of the committee. Such a response is not negative in that it does not disagree; rather, it can be seen as either true to the spirit of localism or as simply washing the hands of a troublesome issue – what to do about the current situation councillors find themselves in. Yet, despite the committee and government dancing around each other with suggestions and response, there is little that is dismissive or negative about councillors and their contribution. Indeed, the government paid tribute to councillors and the 'voluntary' contribution they make to their communities.

Conclusion

The inquiries and government responses that have been examined above do two crucial things at the same time. First, they recognise the value of councillors to the governance of their communities and the public service they provide and contribution they make to the overall governance of the country. A cynic might say 'well they would, wouldn't they?' because councillors are the backbone of the three main parties, and without them, or by diminishing the office and office-holders too much, the parties would lose key activists. Second, the inquiries, reports and responses conduct a struggle with developing an understanding of the role and the office of councillor so that it can be shaped into reflecting government thinking about local government and democracy and wider national policy objectives. Part of the second line of thought is how to alter the powers, roles, responsibilities and functions of councillors to match government thinking at any one time.

Despite the investigations and inquiries that have been conducted, some things are sure: more inquiries and investigations into the role of the councillor will follow; they will make a series of recommendations and exhortations for change from which the government of the day will cherry-pick the convenient and ignore the inconvenient; the centre will continue to see the office of councillor as wrongly formed, ill-focused and inclined to be fissiparous and will seek to rectify those inadequacies; and government-inspired change will remain a constant part of councillors' experiences. A recurrent theme of investigations has been that the office is somehow not right and must be mended – imagine if the role and office of MPs or MEPs was subject to such constant scrutiny and reshaping, yet we expect councillors to meekly accept this as their lot.

A second constant theme has been the question of representation by resemblance, that councillors should be drawn from all sections of the local community so as to look like those communities. While the consequences of this for traditional representative democracy and the role of councillors have been largely ignored or at least not fully recognised, it has now become a staple theme of inquiries. Thus, we can conclude that the centre conceptualises local elected representatives very differently from national elected representatives. By so doing, it indirectly recognises that the proximity of councillors to their communities brings with it different pressures and responsibilities from those experienced by national politicians, while the latter retain the right to reshape the office of councillor to fit their own thinking at any one time. There are perils in the conceptualisation and arguments for microcosmic representation which appear to assume that only those who are from a particular community can undertake the task of representing it. In this view, the role of the councillor is not to represent the interests of the whole community but that section of it from which he or she hails. That approach has serious implications for community cohesion as it displays a far more exclusive view of representation than has hitherto been the case. Indeed, a dangerous sectarianism could enter council chambers and party group meetings if diversity of recruitment is seen as an end in itself.

What we have not seen within the developing official mind, however, or at least in its public and official displays, is a view of councillors that expresses and articulates venomous disdain or, alternatively, insouciance about the role. Yes, there is a view that the office of councillor is somehow in need of constant exploration and change because the centre hasn't got it right yet, or because the centre keeps changing its mind about what it wants from councillors. Yes, there are times when the office of councillor has been held with less respect or understanding than others, and yes, on occasions ministers have made disparaging remarks about councillors (which will be explored in the next chapter) and yes, the constant increases in council size and consequent reductions in councillor numbers (see Copus, 2010a) could lead one to believe that there is a central plan to gradually reduce the number of councillors to a bare minimum, but it would appear that the source of disdain is more informal than formal when it comes to displays of the official mind (again, explored in the next chapter).

Government is neither overwhelmingly negative nor passionately positive about the office of councillor, and given the gradual transfer of council powers and functions to other bodies (see Dunleavy, 1991; Young and Rao, 1997; Stoker, 2004; Denters and Rose, 2005; Thoenig, 2011), we are left wondering: do we have local representative democracy as a quaint reminder of Victorian experiments with local democracy or do we have it as a powerful force for government of the country? Or is the official mind somewhere in between – meaning a toleration of this office until something better comes along. Time will tell. But in the meantime, government will continue to tinker with the office and concern itself with time spent, structure, make-up of the councillor population, its decision-making processes, relationships with the community and public and the balance in the office between developing strategy and overseeing services.

The final word in this part of the chapter must go to the Widdicombe Committee for articulating the centre's view of local government, one which has not been seriously challenged. While it endorsed Maud's statement that local government is 'an essential part of English democratic government' (HMSO, 1986a: 54), it also stated:

> In Great Britain Parliament is sovereign. Although local government has origins pre-dating the sovereignty of Parliament, all current local authorities are the statutory creations of Parliament and have no independent status or right to exist. The whole system of local government could be lawfully abolished by Act of Parliament.
>
> (HMSO, 1986a, para 3.3: 45)

And on that bombshell, we turn to explore another source of thinking about councillors: the press.

PART TWO: THE PUBLIC IMAGE

Media, message and manipulation

The purpose of the exploration in this section is to understand the nature of local press reporting of the activities of councillors and how the office of councillor is portrayed and to consider how this helps shape the public image of the office and the holder of the office. It also seeks to understand how a local media image shapes the relationship councillors have with the public and in turn adds to a wider popular conceptualisation of councillors and how that influences the standing and status of the councillor and the office. While it is important, conceptually, to distinguish the office itself from those that hold an office, such a distinction is difficult to sustain in the public mind and may become blurred into an 'all politicians are bad' view of the world. Yet such a view can be confirmed, challenged or changed in the public mind by the way in which the media continue to conduct their reporting, given, of course, that this is understood within the framework of selective exposure theory (see Zillmann and Bryant, 2008; Stroud, 2008).

If an individual either chooses news outlets because they confirm an existing viewpoint, or even goes as far as to only read reports in the same newspaper that coincide with those views, then there is little or no challenge to the original preconception. As people have choice in what they read, selective exposure theory tells us that they will choose only those aspects of reporting they find sit favourably with their past experiences, values, beliefs and assumptions. Such beliefs, of course, may not necessarily be negative ones, but where they are negative, then the avoidance of contrary views makes it all the more difficult to reshape attitudes through discourse and experience. But if people are actively selective about what they choose to read then it is new experiences, in this case with councillors, rather than reporting, that is the solution to changing views. Given councillors' proximity to those they represent and given that councillors set out to achieve political goals that are either ideologically shaped or set within the framework of what can be achieved (*RealLokalPolitik*), then there is a political and personal imperative for councillors to secure a good press and a positive public image.

The chapter now moves on to examine the nature of the stories that have been reported in the press and the sorts of newsworthy material they provide to local journalists, and what it is about councillors that is likely to be reported and how.

Councillors in the news

As mentioned in the introduction to this chapter, the analysis in this section is based on forty randomly selected local newspapers from across England. When examining the nature of the stories told about councillors, four main categories of local reporting were identified: *political, personal, financial* and *local*. Each of these categories could also be placed in a dimension that was either positive/supportive, negative/critical or sensationalist/objective. There is, however, considerable blurring of the boundaries between these categories, as we shall see. The *political* category of reporting focuses on inter- and intra-party interactions, policy problems and decisions, and political debate, and such reporting presents the reader with what could be seen as the normal cut and thrust of politics and political interaction. When presented with policy choices or with budgetary pressures and difficult financial decisions, the local press provide a source of information not only about the problems that have emerged but also the choices available to councillors and the logics of their positions. The press doesn't, of course, report verbatim the speeches of councillors in Hansard style, but what it does provide through condensing the issues and solutions forms the basis of how individuals will judge their councillors' decisions.

Political reporting covers campaigns councillors, individually or collectively, might be involved in, such as against library closures (a result of decisions made by their own or another council), hospital downgrades or closures, rail network inadequacies, policing priorities and actions, traffic speeds, town centre drinking (focused on pubs, clubs and the police) or local clean-up campaigns. As a councillor commented on her own local campaign to encourage shops to sell locally produced goods: 'They were a great ally in the campaign [local paper]; the editor was really enthusiastic and allocated a journalist to cover just my campaign. I couldn't have wanted better support.' The *political* category of reporting will expand into news of councillors' positions and comments on national and international matters, and both the local and national press reported widely on councillors' responses to the Israeli and Palestinian crisis that developed throughout July and August 2014. Particular attention was given to when councillors flew the Palestinian flag outside their town halls and one instance where a councillor had flown the Israeli flag from the town hall window in retaliation. Councillors are, after all, political activists and will express their wider political beliefs beyond those pertinent to council business and will use their elected office as a councillor to legitimise that expression from an authoritative position. It is therefore to be expected that the press will report public displays of political action, whether they are local or national.

A consistent finding of research among councillors is that when they were part of the ruling group, they almost exclusively perceived the local press to be in party-political opposition to them. Comments such as: 'they're all Tories' (meaning the reporters and editorial staff), 'it's a Labour rag' and even 'they can't stand Independents' were commonplace when talking to councillors about their local press. What we find here, however, is not so much a reflection of the local press's political stance and the use of opportunities to exploit its position; rather, it is more an expression of the press's role as observer, critic and vehicle for council accountability and of councillors' reactions to those roles.

Another constant focus of local press attention was on the reporting of the private and *personal* life of the councillor. Councillors are public persons (Lee, 1963), they are public property by virtue of the office they hold, and we have seen in Chapter 6 the kind of impact that membership of the council can have on the councillor's private life. It was this type of reporting that, when negative, councillors found the most intrusive. In a very candid interview, a councillor told the following story.

> I had an affair with another councillor and ended up leaving my wife and living with [named councillor] and this got into the press. It was the press that reported it before my wife knew anything – that's how she found out. I moved in with [named councillor] pretty soon after it came out in the paper and I suppose it's fair game – it didn't help, but well … The worst thing was a photo that was taken of me very early one morning as I was getting the milk in, still in my dressing gown and I knocked one of the bottles over, picked it up and went inside. Then this picture appeared of me in the paper and it made it look like I was a dirty old man poking around the wheelie bin and it had the headline something like: love rat councillor flees love nest in early morning lovers tiff, or some old **** like that.

The local media will report when councillors stray from the path of virtue or, of course, the law. A staple of local reporting was of incidences of councillors being charged or convicted of some offence or other and such reporting about councillors ranges from minor driving and parking offences through a gamut of illegality, including failure to pay council tax, animal cruelty, assault, theft (including data theft), drunken behaviour, sexual offences, firearms offences, domestic abuse, improper use of council facilities for party activities, use of council computers to access pornographic websites and, in one celebrated case from Guildford which reached the national news (as many such stories do), a councillor was charged with a range of offences including impersonating a barrister, fraud and offences under the Forgery and Counterfeiting Act.

One interpretation of this is that through this negative personal reporting the press constructs a public image of councillors as mendacious and dishonest and contributes greatly to a public view that they are 'just in it for themselves'. But such negative personal reporting is balanced by positive or sympathetic stories reflecting events in councillors' personal lives, which included stories covering: councillors' examination success at masters and PhD level, charity and voluntary activity, wedding ceremonies (and funerals of councillors' relatives), career promotions or new jobs, honours and awards to councillors (OBE, MBE, knighthoods and appointments to the House of Lords), coverage of incidents where councillors have been subject to physical assaults, burglaries or theft; stories reporting accidents, injuries, illness, hospitalisations and deaths, with the latter also including public tributes to councillors in newspaper obituaries or general stories. Indeed, some press tributes to recently deceased councillors were particularly touching and poignant. Thus, the local press do indeed provide a balance (though not necessarily equal balance) between negative and positive stories about councillors' personal lives.

The next category that was identified was that of *financial* reporting and this is a category which does blur with the political and the personal. The main focus of such reporting was, unsurprisingly, councillors' allowances and expenses, and here it was the tone rather than the nature of the reporting that needs consideration. Councillor allowance increases or, for that matter, decreases or no change is a matter of public interest and record and no councillor in any of the research complained that allowances should be secret. What did animate councillors was the tone of reporting, which included phrases such as: 'massive rise', 'pay hike', 'allowances sky-rocket', 'excessive pay', 'councillors vote own pay increase/rise', 'public fury over councillor allowance', 'councillors defend allowance storm', 'councillors justify allowances', 'U-turn on massive hike', 'record payouts to councillors', 'pay rises condemned', 'outrageous pay award' and 'lining their pockets'. In addition, there were reports of councillors making fraudulent expense claims and any consequences that might flow from such action – including examples of where councillors have repaid expenses either fraudulently or mistakenly claimed. Sensationalist language was, however, held alongside reporting such as: 'allowances frozen' (sometimes giving a successive number of years the freeze had occurred), 'councillors refuse pay increase', councillors reported as shunning an increase, individual councillors reported as donating an increase or all allowances to charity.

In addition to the reporting of allowances, there is a strain of reporting linked to other financial activities by councillors, whether that is council finances or the finances of other organisations. So we find the local press reporting councillors' alleged or actual financial misdeeds wherever they have occurred, such as in their employment. The implication of reporting any financial irregularities or fraudulent activities that relate to activities in other organisations, or even problems of personal debt, is that they are likely to act in a similar way in their council activities. Whether or not this is a reasonable conclusion to draw does not detract from the public position that a councillor holds and that they are therefore public property and of press interest when it comes to financial matters.

The category of *local* reporting focuses on those aspects of the councillor's activities and undertakings that reflect or reflect on the locality and, as we have seen with the other categories identified, there is, of course, some crossover between them. Here, though, we see recognition of the ambassadorial role of the councillor and of the councillor as a local public person or local notable (Lee, 1963; Bealey et al., 1965; Clements, 1969; Barker, 1983; Borraz and John, 2004; Getimis, 2013). A councillor who had attended a royal garden party, for example, commented in an interview:

> The garden party got a lot of interest. I was photographed holding the invitation and that appeared before the party. Then, I was asked to make sure I had a photograph taken at the party that I could give to the paper and they interviewed me about what had happened, had I met the queen, who else was there, that sort of thing – got very good coverage; I was surprised.

Attendance at any national event, such as a party conference or national local government event, and international events was also guaranteed to attract press attention, and here the reporting could, of course, be negative or sensationalist: 'councillor junket' was a favoured press headline, especially in cases where overseas travel was involved. Yet the reporting steered a careful line between what journalists thought was interesting and necessary and what was interesting but would feed a negative image of councillors. No such accusations of councillor junkets were levelled, for example, when a royal visit occurred or where a royal garden party invitation was secured by a councillor, as we have seen above. Reporting of the *local* type also covered remembrance parades, local weddings, meetings with private businesses and public bodies, attendance at major sporting events such as the World Cup or Commonwealth Games. Councillors are ambassadors at such events, whether attending in a personal or official capacity.

An overview

In the survey of the local press for this book, we do see a form of balance in reporting, but it is not necessarily an even balance of negative to positive stories or sensationalist to objective language. There is, understandably, a view among the local press that as the holder of an elected public office, all facets of the councillor's life are public property and open for investigation and reporting. That reporting may not always suit individual councillors, but what is evident is that as much as councillors will find something to complain about in the press reporting of their *political, personal, financial* and *local* activities, they are equally willing to develop an alliance with the local press within each of those categories. Thus, the relationship between councillors and local press can be mutually beneficial: councillors are a source of news and public interest and the local press can be used to promote issues the councillor wishes to pursue.

It is also clear that there is often a sensationalist style of reporting about the activities of councillors. This is the case across all categories of reporting and it is here that councillors find the most to object about in their relationship with the local press. Where the press report or run a series of reports that are critical and negative of an individual particularly, and the council or councillors generally, we find from councillors the feeling of being under siege and that they are subject, in their own often-repeated words, to a 'witch hunt'. The councillor under press scrutiny may feel subject to intense public glare and that such attention is unfair. But councillors are not passive recipients of unfair attention. A councillor commented that she had been called a 'liar and a coward' by the local press, but a referral to the Press Complaints Commission about the story had been upheld in her favour. She had subsequently approached the local radio station to publicise the fact and delivered leaflets in her ward with the judgment and made a speech in council about the outcome.

While this is an extreme example, it is not uncommon for councillors to feel unfairly treated, but they also need the press to report on their activities in a positive light. A councillor summed up the paradox nicely:

> I can't expect my own way all the time and if they [the local paper] criticise me for something, well they've used enough of my press releases and stories I've given them to make up for it – how I feel about the paper just depends on what they've said and when.

The difference between councillors' experience of press reporting and that of national politicians is that whereas the latter will find friendly and critical reports in different newspapers at the same time, councillors are normally subject to the attention of only one local paper, depending on their area coverage, and therefore lack the opportunity for papers to take a different view on the issues they are reporting.

A symbiotic relationship exists between councillors and local papers and this can add to a general view or public perspective of councillors within a given locality which may also flow into a wider view about councillors as politicians and individuals. Even though many localities have a single local newspaper – or have a regionally orientated paper – readers can still be selective in what they confront by either not reading a newspaper at all or only reading those aspects of it with which they agree or which accord with their preconceived political world view. But councillors are often very firm in their opinion that the local press shapes not only public debate but their own public image. It is likely that they are viewing local press reporting with their own reverse selective exposure and seeking out and highlighting those areas where the local press are critical, sensationalist or can be categorised as a political opponent.

In the research for this book not a single councillor was uncritical of the press or thought that the local paper was a solid and continuous coalition partner, rather than a single-issue ally; all councillors felt that they personally or a group of their colleagues or councillors generally had been unfairly treated or experienced unfair, objectionable press reporting. On the other hand, local journalists and editors that were interviewed claimed that they reported issues of public interest and that because councillors were public property, any and all of their activities were open to scrutiny. It is likely that the relationship between councillors and the local press will remain subject to the fortunes of local circumstances, but it also has the ability to, if not convince voters of either the honour or mendacity of councillors, then to shape local and national public discourse about the office.

Conclusion

Crucially important for the future development of the office of councillor is how those at the centre of government view the purpose of the office and judge the qualities and actions of councillors. There is little in the formal inquiries and reports reviewed in this chapter that displays a public and formal official contempt for councillors. While the inquiries considered recognise and accept the constitutionally lower status of local government compared to central government and therefore reflect that in thinking about councillors, and that is more or less forcibly expressed depending on the inquiry, the formal expression is not one of disdain. What does indicate a form of disdain, however, is the centre's willingness to explore and reshape the office of councillor, which takes place through the prism of central objectives across a range of policy areas. Moreover, it shows that the thinking of the centre is that the office of councillor is inadequately formed to meet changing circumstances, new problems and demands or to fit government thinking on the nature of local democracy. In addition, changes to allowances and payment schemes or removal from pension schemes (a policy of the coalition government 2010–15 was to end councillors' local government pension scheme policies at the end of their term of office and for new councillors not to be included in the scheme) or any unseemly argument about the financial worth of councillors downgrades the office. Such desire to conduct surgery on the office of councillor is indeed a form of disdain in itself.

Another form of disdain, outside of official reports and inquiries, is the comments that are made by ministers or members of Parliament about the office of councillor, and it is here that we see the centre much more willing to express public negativity. The Conservative Party Chairman, Grant Shapps, angered councillors, including Conservatives, with his comparison of councillors to volunteer scout-troop leaders (www.conservativehome.com), although at the time he was attempting to emphasise the government's view, discussed above, that councillors were volunteers and should not be seen as professional politicians. In an interview, an MP admitted that the Secretary of State had 'sat on Grant, for that comment', no mean punishment given the stature of the current Secretary of State, Eric Pickles. The same Secretary of State expressed a less than favourable view of councillors when he accused them of acting as though they were in 'Putin's Russia' (*Independent*, 20 August 2014). And where ministers engage in battles with councils and councillors over local allowance rates or policy issues, this also displays a disdain for both the office and the holder of the office of councillor. Although it is not wrong for ministers to express views about issues which generate public concern and interest, it is how that debate is engaged and the rhetoric deployed that can undermine the office of councillor generally.

The press also have their role to play in shaping the office of councillor and in the formation of public perceptions of the office and the individuals that hold it. As we have seen, there is a mutually beneficial relationship between councillors and the press, but it is subject to the needs of the local press to attract and retain readers and to reflect and indeed be part of shaping local debate, coupled with the needs of the councillor to be accurately and fairly reported and portrayed. Given the differing requirements of media and councillors, there is plenty of space for disagreement, and it is likely that such a tempestuous relationship will continue to exist despite the best efforts of individual councillors and journalists. But the crucial battleground is not so much what is reported and more how it is reported and the language used; an objective, unemotive and unexciting style of reporting may be better for the office of councillor, but it may not sell many papers.

The consideration of how the official mind of the centre views councillors and also how they are presented in both local press and national media is part of an assessment of the health of democracy, locally and nationally. It is more than that, however, as the view of the centre and the media, alongside generally held public perceptions, is important for the future development of the office. With this in mind, it is now possible to consider, in the next chapter, how the future of the office of councillor could develop.

8

New directions and new purposes

Introduction

A major theme of this book has been the need to understand and account for the constancy of change to which the office of councillor is subject and how government, changing public perceptions, social change and developing political priorities locally, nationally and internationally act to reshape and reform that office. Change is the one feature that councillors can expect throughout their term of office, and even those serving just one four-year term will be lucky not to have to deal with some alteration to what they can do and how they can do it imposed by external sources. It is in response to this need to deal with constant external pressure that the idea of *RealLokalPolitik* was introduced in Chapter 4. It also enabled us to understand the difference between councillors whose focus was primarily ideological and those who, while having an ideological base to their politics, displayed through their membership of a party, acted pragmatically and incrementally to achieve the maximum the office would allow.

Not only is change a constant theme for councillors but complaints about the amount, nature and speed of change they experience are a consistent aspect of councillors' own explorations of the office they hold. Moreover, as we have seen throughout the book, councillors are acutely aware of the limitations on their office and the implications and consequences of those limitations for what they are able to achieve (see also Cole, 2002; Klok and Denters, 2013). Moreover, the structure of the council as an administrative and managerial organisation is not necessarily shaped to support councillors in what they do; rather, it is organised with the core purpose of administering and managing the provision of public services more so than supporting a distinctly political set of responsibilities and functions.

While councillors do receive varying levels of support across local government for their varied roles, that organisational support is focused on what councillors do in relation to the council and not on the consequences of them being elected representatives. On the one hand, this may seem an obvious conclusion, but the outcome is that councillors are forced to look inwards towards the council and to focus on its needs and requirements rather than on a wider political set of activities or the securing of a wider political vision. Since the Blair modernising agenda explored in the last chapter, councillors have been exhorted and encouraged to focus much more on being community leaders and this role is premised on an externally facing, semi-governing process (DETR, 1998a, b, 1999).

Another constant theme that has emerged is that the major government-inspired inquiries that have explored the roles, tasks and functions of councillors have done so from the perspective that the most vital attributes and responsibilities of the office have already been set and that what is required is, to one degree or another, a reshaping of the office to meet new circumstances. Given the successive inquiries, commissions, reports and explorations of what the office of councillor is about, what it does and how that could be changed, it is surprising that there has not been a fundamental rethinking of the office and of its purpose. The lack of such radical or fundamental thinking about the office of councillor comes from a view that the governing system and constitutional settlement in England is, while not perfect, in no need of major reform, at least when it comes to the relationships between central and local government. Such a view, as we will see later, has been challenged, and such challenge provides opportunity to rethink the office of councillor and its role in the overall governing system.

It is not just the government, press and public that has a range of views about the way the office of councillor should develop. Councillors themselves have views about the powers and purpose of their office and about how it should develop over time. Those views are valuable because they reflect the frustrations and experiences of the councillor population and as such provide an insight into the limitations of the office and what can and should be done to overcome those limitations. What follows in the next section is a rethinking of the role of the councillor that, while recognising the constitutional constraints that bind local government, provides a framework within which the governing purpose of local government and the councillor can be strengthened. The second section, by contrast, provides a deliberately radical and fundamental rethinking of the office of councillor, one which is not constrained by the existing governmental system. The section also sets out what a new role for local government and councillors might be in a newly shaped relationship between the British central state and the English nation and its localities.

Councillors: getting the best from executives and overview and scrutiny

The previous chapter examined the changes introduced into local government political decision-making by the Local Government Act 2000, which formalised the already existing informal distinction that existed between council leaders and committee chairs and backbench councillors. By formalising the council cabinet of the leader and up to nine other councillors, the Act sought to speed up decision-making, place responsibility in the hands of individual councillors and make that leadership publicly identifiable and, as a result, easier to hold to account. A side effect was to give councils at least a feeling that their shape, if not their powers, reflected that of government, albeit one based at Westminster.

A major assumption behind the changes brought in by the 2000 Act was that the governing capacity of councillors would be enhanced by formalising a cabinet system in local government and that cabinet members would develop the characteristics of ministers in central government. In Chapter 1 we described the governing capacity of councils and councillors as the focusing of resources and activity: to bring about political action; to forge coalitions and partnerships and create alliances to pursue policy objectives; to contain or exploit conflict; to process and conceptualise policy problems and to construct solutions; and to generate additional resources to take action that will influence or bring about change in the policies or behaviours of citizens, communities or private and public bodies. Thus, enhancing councillors' ability to make things happen and to take political action should be a logical consequence of any structural change introduced by central government to the way councillors make decisions.

But cabinets were only one part of the blurred separation of the executive group from the council; the other part is overview and scrutiny. As we saw in the last chapter, overview and scrutiny has two main functions: first, internally, holding the executive to account and reviewing the policy and effectiveness of the council, and second, as a resource to explore the functions, policies and processes of other organisations to which it wished to turn its attention and by so doing to govern through influence (Pluss and Kubler, 2013; Klok and Denters, 2013). The full council is therefore a resource for overview and scrutiny and a forum within which to give wider publicity and public airing of its findings and policy suggestions. Together, these two bodies provide a potentially powerful tool for councillors not only to ensure that the executive accounts for its activities and is held to account, but also that the world beyond the council can also be subject to the same accountability. Overview and scrutiny extended the reach of the councillor beyond what the council did and, while it has no powers to enforce its views or to subpoena witnesses, councillors' governing capacity was given a useful ally. In addition, the ability of councillors to take political action and to act in a politically innovative way to solve problems and govern in a broad sense was strengthened, albeit through soft political powers of influence and negotiation, rather than through harder powers of legal compulsion.

What we do know is that many councillors are having difficulty in coming to terms with scrutiny as a process. Complaints among councillors centre around feelings of disconnection from council policy- and decision-making, a disquiet at what is seen as the focusing of power in a ten-member cabinet and, most pointedly, a feeling of loss of influence and power as overview and scrutiny can only make recommendations, not decisions (DETR, 1998a, b, 1999; Ashworth, 2003; Ashworth et al., 2007; Coulson and Whiteman, 2012). Indeed, over a decade after the Act which introduced the scrutiny function, some councils have taken advantage of powers granted by the 2011 Localism Act to return to the committee system. Councils such as Cambridgeshire, Nottinghamshire and Norfolk Counties, Hartlepool (which moved from an elected mayor to a committee system after a referendum in 2012), the London Borough of Barnet, Newark District Council, Reading, and Brighton and Hove have rejected executive decision-making and returned to a committee decision-making structure (CfPS, 2014).

In the research for this book, the following comments from councillors sum up the feelings expressed by those that want to see a return to the good old days of the committee system:

> It's the best form of democracy. You have a debate, a vote and a decision is made. (Labour councillor)

> Councillors get the chance to specialise, become expert in a particular area and get to know the officers who deal with it. It's much more democratic and councillors are in control of what is happening. (Liberal Democrat councillor)

> Committees enable all councillors to take part in decisions and not just the cabinet – we were all elected the same way and should all be able to make decisions – committees enable that to happen. (Conservative councillor)

> Everything is done by the cabinet and as a result scrutiny is useless, it can't do anything and we just note officers' reports. (Independent councillor)

Interestingly, many pro-committee expressions were made by councillors who had never served on a committee as they had been elected in the post-2000 Act era. It would appear that the experiences and rhetoric of those that served on committees have a powerful resonance for newer members. Yet there has been a trickle rather than a flood of councils returning to committees, and although committees may give councillors a feeling of power and the ability to make decisions, they lack the ability and flexibility of the overview and scrutiny approach when it comes to the policy process, rather than decision-making. A fixation on decisions rather than policy is what draws councillors' attention away from the strategic governing potential that scrutiny provides but committees do not.

But let's deal with three consistent myths about committees as a way of making decisions. First, they enable all councillors to take part in decision-making. That might be the case in the absence of the party group system that is now the standard operating procedure across local government (see Bulpitt, 1967; Copus, 2004; Leach, 2006; Leach and Wilson, 2008) and where, in single-party settings, the groups decide their line and voting intentions on agenda items before each meeting. Even if groups do not meet before each committee meeting, the majority group's position would be obvious in that a committee chair would not permit recommendations to go forward that fundamentally opposed the ruling group's policy direction. Moreover, not all councillors are members of all committees, so clearly not all councillors can be involved in all decisions. While committees may provide a bit of theatre and the opportunity for political knock-about, the outcome has been predetermined and few councillors walk into a committee not already knowing the outcome – the odd reference back for more information or tinkering at the margins of a decision with some amendment is not a power to determine outcomes.

Only where a council has no one single party in overall control can committees give all councillors the chance take part in decision-making. In those circumstances, committees have the potential to make decisions, and while party group lines will be predetermined, the outcome of any vote will be uncertain. Even in such circumstances, committees can be adjourned while groups go into private negotiations. To bring about the desired and perceived involvement of all councillors in decisions would also require shifting to a voting system which ensured that few, if any, councils with a committee system had a single-party majority. Then, and only then, might all councillors be involved in decisions through committees.

The second myth is that the committee system is somehow more democratic than a system of political decision-making based on a separate executive and overview and scrutiny. That myth is closely related to the first and conflates democracy with the idea that all councillors must be involved in all decisions. This myth is based on a notion of democracy that has echoes of Athenian direct democracy, with the difference that it is all elected representatives that should be involved in all decisions and debates, not all citizens. Claims that the cabinet system is somehow 'undemocratic' fail to acknowledge a separation between the principle of democratic elections and representative democracy and that of democratic government. Representative democracy is the process by which councillors come to their office, whereas representative government is about leadership and political decision-making as a result of that framework (Pitkin, 1972; Manin, 1997; Judge, 1999).

What councillors who claim that an executive system of local government is undemocratic are really saying is: 'I was not involved in the decision or process and therefore it is not democratic'. Such charges are rarely, if ever, levelled by councillors at the parliamentary system. It is a view that propagates the fallacy that all councillors are equal – and forgets that some are more equal than others, whatever the system of decision-making and policy development. Government is about leadership and that is an exclusive process which demands that a wider body of councillors place trust in a smaller body, which they themselves might select (or not, as in the case of an elected mayor). A semi-presidential system of local government political functioning is no less democratic than a parliamentary system, and a semi-presidential system recognises that government is a process for selecting political leaders and enabling them to lead (see Haus et al., 2005; Heinelt, 2013a; Karlsson, 2013b).

The third myth is that those councillors who are not members of the executive are excluded from input to decisions and devoid of information, influence or the ability to be politically innovative within the system. This is a fatalistic and inaccurate view of the world the councillor inhabits, which has not recognised the potential that exists for governing by having in place the right mechanisms and processes through which to act as a vehicle of both executive accountability (Copus, 2008) and the accountability of others outside of the council. It is a myth developed by too much focus on the councillors that sit on the executive and their role and position and not enough attention on developing alternative avenues for political action, bringing about political change and on shaping the political environment beyond the council. It is a view, like the committee system itself, that is inwardly focused and concerned with the details of administration, not the development of policy and political influence.

When we look at each of the myths above, we can see that such complaints can also be levelled at the committee system itself, indeed, the 2000 Act merely formalised the system of committee chairs operating as a nascent cabinet. This too was a system of representative government, one which gave councillors a platform for debate – committees – but which separated from the main body of councillors the committee chairs, albeit informally, to form a leadership group of influential and powerful councillors. That group was closely located to and supported by the senior officers of the council. That they chaired committees rather than sat on an executive made this leadership separation no less real.

This book is entitled 'In defence of councillors', not 'In defence of everything councillors do or want', and therefore must have a critical edge about those councillors it also seeks to defend. Councillors that pine after the committee system are ignoring the fact that council political decision-making is not there to be structured for their benefit alone. Rather, it is to be structured to provide local citizens with a form of local democratic representation and government that is meaningful and relevant to their local needs and which is understandable and accessible. Moreover, it must, from a normative perspective, be able to effectively govern the locality and it is here that councillors require a system which enables them to do just that.

What follows now, then, is a series of suggestions for how to improve the current system made in the spirit of the 'tinkering' that is popular with central government, but going a bit further in its reach and in its trust in councillors. Yet what is suggested does not fail to recognise the tremendous steps taken in governing and shaping their localities by councils like Birmingham, Manchester, Liverpool, Leicester, the Borough of Newham and many others (there is danger in listing some, as it may annoy those not listed; apologies but space is short). Such councils are a testament to overcoming the limitations experienced not only by councillors but by local government in England as a whole. The success of such councils is a remarkable lesson in governing in times of austerity and constraint, in political innovation and in dealing heavily in *RealLokalPolitik*; the success stories, however, are also success stories in the skills and abilities of local political leadership – leaders, mayors and cabinets and councillors. What follows moves beyond political leaders to provide all councillors with an input to government but an input that sits within the constitutional and political realities of the existing system.

Revisiting councillors bringing order to chaos

Chapter 4 explored the complex world of agencies, organisations and public and private sector bodies with which councillors must interact and the array of inter-connecting networks within which they must operate. It also explored the strategies councillors developed to connect the players in governance networks, individually and collectively, to the democratically legitimised representative institution that is the council and by so doing to influence what happens in those networks. There is a need, then, to link the exploration in Chapter 4 with the organisational arrange-ments that councillors now inhabit (described in the last chapter), with a model that will strengthen the hand of those councillors not members of the executive as representative and local governors.

Those councillors that have yet to make an accommodation with overview and scrutiny and who seek to return to the committee system do so in the shrinking context of local government as a direct service provider. The trend for the grad-ual removal of direct service-provision responsibilities or the transfer of functions from local government to other agencies means that the days of the need for a political decision-making structure which enabled councillors to control vital public services have past. Yes, councils remain providers, and important ones at that, but such a role is now often shared with others. Today, it is partnerships, commissioning, inter-agency working, outsourcing, growth-focused activities, austerity management and supporting business and developing local infrastruc-ture that are the focus of political attention.

Yes, some services may, after a long and tortuous journey, find their way back to local government, such as public health's return in April 2013 as a result of the Health and Social Care Act 2012. But such a return of a partic-ular service responsibility does not mean a return to the idea of the coun-cil as provider. Rather, that transfer back emphasises, very neatly, the need for councillors to work with the huge, complex and powerful body that is the National Health Service in all its organisational guises, in an attempt to influence and shape the policies and decisions that emanate from it. Integrating health-care provision with public health, and then integrat-ing both with a whole range of other public services that impact on health and health inequalities to achieve not only effective service delivery but the long-term development of communities requires a very different political decision-making and influence-generating framework for councillors than that provided by committees. It requires not just a framework and struc-ture but a set of powers and resources for councillors acting collectively in an authoritative and electorally legitimised governing forum and also acting independently within their wards and divisions to take action and secure change as a local community leader. What follows is a way in which that can be achieved within councillors' wards and divisions and within governance networks.

Councillors as governors and leaders

Councillors face two community leadership competitors: local competitors, such as residents' groups, individual community leaders, pressure groups and community organisations, and competitors in governance networks, such as other public and private sector partners and policy-making organisations. We will look at these competitors separately. The main resources available for councillors when attempting to shape the direction of their wards or the direction of broader governing networks are soft political powers, such as influence, negotiation, pressure and compromise. As we saw in Chapter 4, the electoral mandate provides councillors with moral and political leverage to bring together diverse interests to focus on community problems, to seek local solutions and make decisions that can be expected to affect how a ward might develop as a community. To undertake the role of community leader as an authoritative decision-maker and politician, councillors require soft and hard powers and the enhanced status and recognition as politicians that the electoral mandate provides.

From a soft perspective, effective community leadership requires the councillor to embark on a co-operative process to deal with communities growing in assertiveness and less willing to acquiesce with decisions made by public authorities of any kind (Chamberlayne, 1978; Lowndes et al., 2001a, b; Pattie et al., 2003; Lowndes and Sullivan, 2008). Therefore effective community leadership relies on a councillor's ability to negotiate, compromise and build coalitions and alliances within and across communities located within the ward, to reconcile conflicting views across communities, to use a wide range of avenues for political communication, to make hard decisions about rationing and the use of scarce resources, and to place ideological concerns to one side when dealing with contentious local issues. All of which takes place within a framework of *RealLokalPolitik* and what the councillor can achieve within the ward.

The effectiveness of councillors as community leaders, however, cannot come from reliance on soft powers alone; soft powers are no powers at all, and the reference to them indicates a level of distrust towards councillors having ward-based decision-making ability. What is required for there to be 'powerful roles for all councillors' (DETR, 1999: 21) is for councillors to hold hard political and executive powers to make decisions at the ward level and to be able to direct the engagement of non-elected bodies with issues arising from communities so as to restore faith in representative local democracy (see Young and Rao, 1995). Restoring faith in local representative democracy means challenging the assumptions underlying the concept of co-governance, which enables citizens to take part in the business of the state in various policy areas and which relies on the engagement of citizens and citizen groups in decisions so as to share the decision-making process (see Ackerman, 2004; Head, 2005; Johnson and Osbourne, 2003; Somerville and Haines, 2008).

The problems with citizen participation or the deferring to neighbours and other groups as somehow more authentic than elected councillors have been discussed in Chapter 3. The model here is not to pursue even greater diminution of the office of councillor by indulging further co-governance paraphernalia; rather, it is to recognise that even with co-governance, someone has to make the final decision, and it is better to have those decisions made by councillors on whom all have the opportunity to cast a judgement through the electoral process. The approach required is a localisation of hard political powers by a statutory devolution of executive powers from councils and their leaders and cabinets to councillors representing wards and divisions. Such localised decision-making rejects the notion that neighbourhoods and community forums represent a more authentic process than that conducted by councillors as elected representatives and rejects the idea that political executive powers must themselves be centralised in the leader and cabinet.

Linked to this localisation of executive power is the enhancement of the status and standing of councillors and their office as legitimised decision-makers and the strengthening of their community leadership capacity through the transfer of executive decision-making ability to councillors in their wards or divisions. While recent research has shown that councillors adhere strongly to the principles of representative democracy and a Burkean interpretation of their role, there is also considerable support among councillors for people having opportunities to make their views known before decisions are made (Sweeting and Copus, 2012). Thus, the community leadership role of the councillor can be strengthened and informed by enhancing public engagement and participation in local decision-making at the same time as ensuring that councillors locally are the final decision-makers in the process.

It is when representing the ward or division that councillors often experience the most rewards from their office but also the most frustration (Drage, 2008; Karlsson, 2013b; Copus and Wingfield, 2014). Those frustrations arise from the low level of recognition and support often given by councils to the councillor as a ward/divisional representative. Again, that is not to say that some councils have not taken this role seriously, but the evidence from the research for this book shows that it is not standard across local government. When asked to assess the support they received from the council for their ward duties, the following comments summarise the two sets of experiences that councillors have in this regard:

> Excellent, I'd say. We have ward budgets to spend on projects that ward councillors can decide together to support; we have dedicated officers to deal with issues arising from my ward; and, we have secretarial support. Not much else I could ask for really. (Labour councillor)

Contrast that comment with the following statement:

> Nothing, absolutely nothing. As a councillor I have to do it all myself. There's no administrative support (other than basic secretarial stuff) specifically for

ward-based work and I feel more like a messenger than a councillor sometimes – just running backwards and forwards to different officers, more or less
begging for support. (Labour councillor)

The experience for many councillors is on a continuum represented by the
extreme points of the two comments above. Different councils providing varying
services to councillors may sound like the epitome of localism. But the effect is
to undermine the office of councillor and to hold the support and therefore the
effectiveness as a community leader that councillors will have up to the whim of
individual councils, senior officers, executives and changing party control. The
office of councillor as an elected politician in every council requires the same
ward-based support to make community leadership a reality. It is clear from
the research among councillors on which this book is based that devolution of
responsibility from the council as a whole to councillors in their wards is necessary to localise decision-making. What follows draws on that research as well as
on practices that some councils have already implemented to support councillors
as ward community leaders. Councillors in every English council should amend
their constitutions so that the following are a regular and institutionalised part of
the office of councillor:

- Devolved ward/divisional budgets to be available for spending decisions made
  by individual councillors, to be allocated equally between councillors within
  a ward.
- Discrete administrative and research support to be provided to all councillors
  for any ward and divisional activities. Such support must not be one officer
  for all councillors; rather, the support provided should be organised so that all
  councillors have direct access to a group of named officers as a unit within the
  council.
- All reports and decisions that affect specific wards/divisions to go to all ward
  councillors for comment *before* being sent to the cabinet, overview and scrutiny
  or council; councillors' comments to be reported to the cabinet, overview and
  scrutiny or council.
- All councillors to be able to place ward issues or any policy or decision that
  might impact on the ward on the agenda for cabinet and full council. Responses
  to the items placed on the agendas to be sent to all ward councillors.
- Each full council to have an agenda item for councillors to raise and debate
  ward issues – which need not be notified in advance.
- The council leader/mayor and cabinet to report annually (at full council) on
  how decisions and policy have affected individual wards.
- Ward councillors to have an executive decision-making power within their
  wards to be able to make decisions that are pertinent only to their ward.
- Every ward to constitute a ward committee that would have decision-making
  powers and budgets devolved to it from the council. The committee would

consist of the ward councillors and would meet regularly. Membership would be open to each ward committee to decide, but might include:

- representatives of local community groups
- local residents
- third-sector bodies active in the ward
- locally based business
- other public service bodies.

- Councillors to rotate on an annual basis as ward mayor. The ward mayor would:

  - chair the ward committee
  - oversee and co-ordinate the use of councillors' executive decision-making powers (see above)
  - negotiate with the council on the allocation of devolved ward budgets
  - co-ordinate the decisions of individual councillors in identifying projects to be funded and consequent funding decisions made by the ward councillors.

The above would need to be configured so as to suit the single-member county divisions by merging divisions and creating committees between them that are logically connected. The above may seem a recipe for more meetings, but those events will take place in, and be focused solely on, the ward or division represented by the councillor. In addition, they will involve others from the local community in a formalised and localised decision-making process.

The point here is to ensure that councillors are indeed community leaders for their wards or divisions, and they cannot become that without hard political powers, appropriate structures and processes and the right degree of officer support. Such arrangements, however, mean that councillors have nowhere to hide from the decision-making process. As one councillor from a council with budgets devolved to individual councils commented: 'I can't blame the administration or officers because I decided what to do and what not to spend it on.'

But councillors not only have responsibilities to their wards or divisions, they also have a role in the government of the area as a whole, and it is from the councillor as community leader to the councillor as governor that we now turn.

The councillor as local governor

The council leader and executive members may logically be seen as responsible for overseeing the strategic direction of the council and using their 'executive' status when engaging with partners singularly and as important players within collective governance networks. But such responsibilities are not limited to executive members alone. Through overview and scrutiny, councillors outside the executive are able to contribute to the strategic direction of the council and be influential players within governance networks. The latter, however, is often an under-developed aspect of the scrutiny function, but it is also a core function which requires strengthening and in a way that recognises the new reality of the separation between executive members and councillors. One of the implications of the separation between councillors with distinct roles and focuses is that councils should and must now be able to speak with more than one voice. While executive councillors and scrutiny are not in competition – after all, they reflect the majoritarian nature of English local government – they have very different contributions to make to the leadership and governance of the area, which may require the articulation of different priorities and policy options.

As we saw in Chapter 4, the concept of governance fundamentally alters local democracy and the role of the councillor, and such a shift requires councillors to focus externally on developing governing capacity to shape/direct/influence the activities of non-elected bodies so as to align them with the council's own vision. Moreover, councillors need to be able to inject a degree of 'government' into governance networks, not only to democratise the non-democratic, and not only to secure a linkage between the council as a representative body and the citizens they represent and the network members, but also to exert some control over those networks that extends beyond mere influence.

Councillors need to have the supporting institutional architecture that enables them to use the leverage provided by their democratic mandate to construct a shared vision for the development of the locality that is shared not just with those permanently based in the locality, but with larger-scale more transient businesses and organisations that impact on the life of the community. For instance, they need to work with Local Economic Partnerships (or whatever regional configurations the centre might create from time to time) and other supra-local (non-elected) bodies to develop infrastructure and design growth-orientated polices; to mediate between competing interests and views of how the locality should develop and to decide on the allocation of scarce resources; to be able to operate within governance networks that extend beyond the boundaries of a single council; and to hold to account every organisation, of whatever scale, that decides policy, spends public money and impacts on the council area. Overview and scrutiny needs to be designed to secure those political and governing objectives.

Since overview and scrutiny became a policy tool for councillors, experience has shown that it lacks the powers that would make it a far more formidable contributor to governance networks than is currently the case. It lacks the powers that are necessary for it to operate as a vehicle through which councillors could act as the governors of a locality (Leach and Copus, 2004; Ashworth and Snape, 2004; Ashworth et al., 2007; CfPS, 2014; also worthy of consulting are the many internal scrutiny reviews conducted for local government by Professor Steve Leach, which provide an extremely valuable source of information on the strengths and weaknesses of scrutiny within individual councils).

The main legislative framework for overview and scrutiny is set out by the following Acts of Parliament:

Local Government Act 2000
Local Government and Public Involvement in Health Act 2007
Health and Social Care Act 2012
Police and Justice Act 2006
Police Reform and Social Responsibility Act 2011
Flood and Water Management Act 2010

The framework provides the statutory relationship between scrutiny and a number of external bodies for which it has some responsibilities in scrutinising their work. Scrutiny may also come in the shape of Police and Crime Panels that have the task of ensuring the accountability of Police and Crime Commissioners (PCC). These panels are made up of councillors from each of the councils within the PCC area and are therefore a form of joint scrutiny between councils. But what we see here is what we see with all aspects of local government: a statutory duty or power which sets out what councils can do, with whom they can do it and how it must be done; in this case, overview and scrutiny.

So, how to strengthen scrutiny in its external activities and enhance its role, status and power within governance networks? Indeed, how can scrutiny inject a badly needed dose of government into governance? As with much of English local government, the solution rests with Parliament relinquishing control, regulation and over-prescription; it relies on Parliament seeing local government as a government. Moreover, the solution relies on a *general and unrestricted power to scrutinise* being given to local government and then for the centre to step aside and allow councils, individually and collectively, to work out how best to operate that power and to decide who needs scrutinising, how, when and over what issues. The *general and unrestricted power to scrutinise* must come with a full legal power to subpoena witnesses and evidence and for the creation of an offence of 'contempt of council' for those refusing or failing to attend scrutiny inquiries. If this were the case, scrutiny would not be limited in its reach and could launch inquiries into local, supra-local and national bodies from the public and private sector.

Scrutiny currently issues recommendations rather than compulsory instructions for change, and this needs to be strengthened. The scrutiny committee should be able to issue instructions for compliance with its recommendations that would require responses from those scrutinised that explored how best to implement the suggestions. Moreover, the chairs and vice-chairs of particular external inquiries would have the legal power, and officer support, to pursue with any organisation negotiations aimed at changing the policy and practice of that body. Should negotiations fail, then the recommendations of the scrutiny committee would carry legal weight.

By giving scrutiny councillors real power to conduct inquiries and ultimately enforce recommendations, a stronger governing role for councillors is structured which focuses on more than seeking influence within governance networks. Rather, what has been proposed will give councillors the resources to start to direct those networks, focus their activities and shape the policies and actions of organisations to suit the needs of local communities. Any scrutiny proposals will require careful integration with the council executive, but they will also require all councillors to recognise the different roles that exist for executive members and councillors. Moreover, it allows both sets of councillors – with their distinctive remits – to develop and promote different concepts of the common good or good governance. That difference, emanating from the same council, is no bad thing as it enables two sets of councillors to operate in different ways in the same networks.

Thus, executive members will be engaged in decisions within networks, while scrutiny will be holding that process to account and challenging practices and policies. What is required here is not only a recognition of the distinct roles of the executive member and the scrutiny/governor but a realisation that such roles are compatible with shared party-political allegiance. What has been discussed does not ignore the realities of party politics in local government; rather, it builds on the ability of councillors from the same party to hold and express different views of how the same issues should be approached and tackled. The purpose is to ensure that those with a democratic mandate can not only secure the accountability of the players in governance networks, but can use the legitimacy of their office to enhance their position and status so as to direct the shape and action resulting from governance interrelationships, so allowing councillors to bring coherence to complex networks. But that process is one of holding to account and legitimising governance networks, it is not government. It is to that aspect the chapter now turns.

Strengthening the government in local government

The use of the word government in local government has always had a different meaning from its use in regard to the centre. Local government (at least in England) is not government in the sense that it has an independent and continued right to exist and that it can directly control, through its own acts, the entire fabric of the locality: financially, economically, culturally, legally and morally. Although it can shape behaviour through nudge policies over issues such as obesity and alcohol consumption, for instance, that is not government, rather it is encouragement or public education (Jones et al., 2010; Selinger and Whyte, 2011; John et al., 2013). Indeed, central government itself can and does employ nudge tactics, but it also holds ultimate legislative authority which can be used to introduce compulsion and sanction, should nudge fail. What follows here will be fanciful for some, even dangerous, but it builds on a debate that is currently being conducted about devolution in England to compensate for the national devolution to Scotland, Wales and Northern Ireland. It is a debate partly driven by the great desperation of many politicians to ensure England does not have a parliament of its own and so seeks an alternative route for devolution – local government. It is a proposal that also builds on a serious debate being conducted by some to construct an independent and strong local government. The latter is explored in the final chapter.

The Blair government elected in 1997 moved quickly to introduce devolved political institutions to three of the four nations of the UK, a process from which England was excluded. Devolution to the Scottish, Welsh and Northern Ireland bodies is not and was never likely to be a one-time deal, as the referendum on Scottish separation from the Union showed. But, until Scotland does separate, there are three sub-UK governmental bodies created by the twofold asymmetrical devolution and constitutional programme of the Labour government from 1997; asymmetrical because of the imbalance in roles, powers and responsibilities between the three bodies and their relationships with the centre and because the largest nation of the UK – England – was deliberately excluded from the Celto-centric settlement.

By that Celto-centric devolution, the UK Parliament and central executive relinquished varying degrees of legislative and political control over the economic, cultural, political, moral, environmental, societal and structural direction of the three devolved chambers. It is a simple step and would right a democratic wrong to form an English parliament and to place the same level of powers and responsibilities with each of the parliaments. Moreover, the devolution process did little to provide localism with a certain future or to solve the confusion over the place of local government within the constitution (Bogdanor, 2009: 269).

What follows here seeks to end some constitutional confusion and can be implemented with or without an English parliament to create a strengthened and independent local government. It is a vision of a muscular localism with a powerful, politically independent local government with a constitutionally protected right to exist. To emphasise the politically representative role of local government, the maximum devolution of primary legislative power would be placed with elected councils and their councillors. The latter are to be seen as governors of their locality in their own right. It would therefore be councils and not central government which would set the legal framework that would exist within each council area. Decisions would need to be made about the nature of the legislative power to be devolved and what should remain at the centre, but this would be based on a localist and not a centralist presumption, in which the only matters that remained at the centre would be those that could be demonstrated as needing to do so, and even then, a heavy dose of local involvement would shape those policies. Indeed, it would be a federated England as a localised state where local government had what in effect would be 'states' rights'. Before an issue became one for national legislation it would need to pass a test. Such a test would ask:

- Does the issue require a response that extends beyond the boundaries of the country – international affairs, treaties, economic arrangements?

- Is national security involved?
- Is it a tax-raising power needed for central government to carry out its functions?
- Is it an issue that requires regulating between local government, such as currency, weights and measures, metric or imperial system usage?
- Does it affect national law-and-order issues and national policing? There is an assumption that some criminal offences and the sanctions imposed for them may vary across councils; indeed, municipal police forces may exist by decisions of local government.
- Is it an issue which clearly, demonstrably and unequivocally must be dealt with at a national level? (And, as will be seen below, in a localised state, there are few issues that elicit a yes answer to that question.)

Under a localised state, there would be a constitutionally protected primary legislative power and the ability to pass laws that would apply only within the boundaries of each council that enacted any law. Such a move would immediately refocus political attention away from the centre towards powerful local governing bodies – councils. Thus, a pressure group seeking to have some legal activity banned or abolished, or seeking changes in the law, would not have to fight one political battle aimed at Westminster and Whitehall – rather, it would have to fight 352 campaigns across each existing council area within England. If, for specific local reasons, or because it had been convinced by the arguments of local citizens or campaign groups, or because of its own political ideas – legitimised in a local election, a council wished to ban smoking in public, but to permit fox-hunting and another council wished to do the reverse, and at the same time, raise the age at which it was possible to drink alcohol to 25, or indeed to lower it from the current age, then so be it!

There is, of course, the question of unintended consequence spillover. So, if a council decided to set the age at which alcohol could be consumed at 25 years old, would not drinkers be inclined to travel to other areas where the age was lower? Experience shows that they might, but surrounding councils would have similar legislative powers and indeed may decide to tackle the issue of alcohol consumption in entirely different ways, preferring to focus on sale, cost and the licensing of premises because of a different set of local issues and priorities. But, unintended consequence spillover could also be solved by councillors carefully consulting with their neighbouring councillors and by scrutiny exploring all options and consequences in a pre-legislative phase. Councillors would have the power to construct a legislative, political, moral and economic policy framework within which policy responses to all issues of local concern would be addressed. Moreover, councils would no longer be subject to party-political duties imposed on them by central government, as the role of the centre would no longer be that of controlling the policy framework within which the localities operate. Councillors themselves, for example, would decide their environment, equalities and other policy and legal frameworks.

When it comes to the provision of public services, councils would decide how certain services were provided and could mix and match public, private, voluntary and charity provision and joint working provision with other councils. While central government might suggest the overall standards those councils should achieve – and those standards would be subject to independent monitoring – the delivery vehicles and models employed would be for councils to decide. What is envisioned here are councils and councillors operating as governing institutions with an emphasis on the governing, political and representational role they undertake, rather than on the provision of public services.

The muscular localism described here, which, to repeat, sees councils as states in much the same way as a federal system would, is only muscular if it rests on a finance regime that provides councillors with maximum choice and maximum freedom from central control. Councillors would have access to a taxation regime which would draw down powers from central government so as to support their new role as a form of English state government. Decisions on what could be taxed and what level of taxation could be imposed would rest not on the interests of central government but on the tolerance of local citizens and voters. Thus, a localised state would see the introduction of a radically reformed financing system, where councils had a far wider range of tax-raising (and spending) powers, which could not be limited or altered by central government – but may be subject to approval by local referendums, giving local citizens the final say. Councils could secure financial freedom by generating tax income not only from property taxes but also, for example, from:

- local income tax
- corporate income tax
- sales tax
- tourist tax
- car tax
- inheritance tax
- royalties from various extraction or business activities
- taxation of various advertisements and advertising activities
- property tax (including stamp duty)
- business tax
- pet ownership tax.

The menu above is, however, no flight of fantasy as each of these taxation powers exists for local government across a range of European countries. Indeed, in our muscular localised state, councils would be able to tax any range of matters and would be free to offer tax incentives, rebates or reductions as they saw fit. The basket of taxation powers available to local government could also be shared with central government on a percentage base as is also the practice in Europe (House of Commons Political and Constitutional Reform Committee,

2013). While this may sound to some like a recipe for tax and spend, in deciding which taxes to employ and at what level to set them, councillors would have to anticipate the reaction of their voters to any such suggestions. The base of the system is a trust in local government and councillors and a trust in the voters to respond accordingly to local government tax and spend decisions – but it is no more a matter to expect such trust in the localities than to expect it in regard to central government.

Imagine the following scenario: a council has within its area a major international airport with approximately 20 million passengers travelling through it each year. The economic and tourist activity generated by that airport already stimulates the local and regional economy. The council decides to levy a £10 tax on every passenger that travels in and out of that airport. It is highly unlikely that any passenger faced with such a charge will decline to travel, so passenger numbers will remain stable and only fluctuate with other market-driven factors. In addition, the council levies a small tourist tax which is collected and paid by tourists at any hotel at which they stay. Given the size of the main international airports in England, this power alone might see some councils secure almost complete financial freedom overnight.

Local government's financial independence from central government, and powerful councillors employing that freedom, is what would so worry the centralist. Although the central rhetoric in opposition to the general financial freedom of local government would be one that was critical of councillors, claiming that they would be unable to manage such responsibility or that they lack the calibre to oversee such activity, the real fear, however, is the loss of control for central government over the localities. And that is exactly the prize to be won. There can be no localism without independent financing and spending powers. The centre would have a financial equalisation role to play, but not to the extent of controlling the policy and decisions of councils through such financial mechanisms.

With great power comes great responsibility, and these new powers and freedoms in the hands of councillors bring scrutiny back into the picture. The Labour Party's Local Government Innovations Taskforce's final report (Labour Party, 2014: 32) has suggested the formation of Local Public Accounts Committees on the model of the House of Commons Public Accounts Committee, to scrutinise not only the accounts and financial activities of the council but also all public sector services within a locality. The council's own use and stewardship of its new powers suggested above would come under the scrutiny of such a new and powerful local select committee formed of councillors. Such committees would require a level of organisational support for their work parallel to that provided to a parliamentary committee, thus it would require the support of an independent unit within the council.

Given the distribution of powers and the shape of local government set out here, all of a sudden, councillors are local governors who are ever more meaningful, relevant, politically powerful and independent. Moreover, the voters would then have the ability to choose between competing policy options that would have dramatic implications for the locality. It is possible to hypothesise that under this model, local electoral turnout would match, if not extend beyond, current national turnout for general elections.

If we are to have powerful councillors that are able to govern an area from the basis of councils as local states (this does not refer to state in the Marxist analysis, see Cockburn, 1977, rather council states as a unit of government), then such power must be balanced by an equally powerful local citizenry. The strengthening of the local citizenry could come with a few simple changes to the architecture of local politics, with recall rights granted to citizens, changes to councillors' terms of office and the use of local referendums. Local citizens would have the right to recall:

- any individual councillor
- the council leader
- the directly elected mayor
- any executive member
- the cabinet collectively
- the entire council and for new elections to be held.

(Any of the above recalled by local citizens would be eligible to stand for re-election.)

The ability of citizens to remove councillors from office provides a powerful mechanism for ensuring accountability during the term of office and for allowing citizens to react to ongoing political problems or previously uncovered scandals or failures in office coming to light. It also reduces the avoidance of accountability by the decision not to stand for election again. Allowing citizens to recall the cabinet or leader specifically sharpens the weapon and enables the voter to distinguish where the source of responsibility may be for any malfeasance. Dismissing an entire council seen to be culpable in any wrongdoing may appear a nuclear option, but taken with the independent and governing status of local government in the new localised constitutional settlement proposed, it is a necessary safeguard for the local citizenry.

The term of office of councillor would be reduced to three years, with a limit of three successive terms of office, after which a break of at least a single term would be required of all councillors. Both these restrictions are required to provide the electorate with opportunities to cast a judgement on the policies and laws of the council and actions of individual councillors more often than they can at present. This will bind councillors more closely to the communities they represent and strengthen electoral accountability. Under this model, though, all councils would be organised on all-out three yearly elections.

Any council laws passed by our new primary state-based legislating councils would be subject to a binding referendum should local citizens call for such a public approval vote. This would not only create a cooling-off period before new laws were enacted, it would also stimulate lively political debate on the proposed local legislation. Moreover, citizen referendums would enable unpopular local law proposals to be overturned before they made the local statute book, and existing laws could be altered and new ones enforced by citizen referendum. In addition, citizens would have the power to call local referendums on propositions or initiatives emanating from communities and the result of these would be binding on the council.

Thus, any confusion about the nature of localism or the role of local government and councillors in the constitutional system is removed in our bottom-up localised state, where we see not only politically strong councils with governmental capacity and powers but a transfer of political powers to local citizens. The system is unashamedly representative in nature but with the injection of direct mechanisms as a safeguard for local citizens. It is not to say that councils within this system would not continue to engage in co-governance or embrace a range of participative mechanisms in the development of polices and the legislative framework. It is also not to say that they would not devolve to neighbourhoods or communities or construct neighbourhood forums or committees as they do at the moment. It is to say, however, that representative local democracy and those elected as councillors within it have the trump card when it comes to legitimacy, authenticity and accountability (Phillips, 1994).

Conclusion

Councillors are elected to office to provide a legitimacy from which they can take action to achieve some political objectives or secure a wider change to their localities that may be the product of a long-term vision. Equally, they may seek to serve the interest of a single ward and the communities within it. Further, they may also be placed in a position to act defensively in an attempt to protect their localities from what they see as undesirable polices emanating from central government of whatever political hue. The issue at question here has been to what degree should the system of local government provide them with the ability and opportunity to do just that? That question strikes at the heart of debates about the purpose of local government and councillors as elected officials within the current constitutional arrangement or within any constitutional developments that may occur over time.

In answering that question, the chapter looked at two possible ways in which councillors' position, office and powers could develop. The first followed on from contemporary policy debates and thinking and from the current direction of travel in local government. The second described and advocated a muscular localism with a powerful, politically independent local government. Both models firmly reject the traditional committee system of local government as an inadequate base from which to oversee and shape the complex governing networks within which local government must now operate. Moreover, committees encourage an inward focus for the councillor, drawing them towards a concentration on what the council does rather than its potential role as a governing institution which uses its electoral legitimacy to engage in and direct governance networks.

Councillors need to engage fully with the potential that scrutiny provides in order to take political action and to act as governors within the locality, and many have indeed done just that. The Centre for Public Scrutiny, a worthy organisation which researches and supports the scrutiny function in local government, provides countless examples of where scrutiny has been successful and innovative in its inquiries and in bringing about change (www.cfps.org.uk). The tools of scrutiny, as our model above has shown, provide a foundation from which councillors can influence the shifting organisational landscape they must both contribute to and hold to account as elected representatives. Indeed, given the government predilection for transferring responsibilities for public services in and out of local government, and given the decline in the council's role as direct provider, scrutiny is becoming a central platform from which the councillor can act politically. Moreover, given that many of the responsibilities that councils now have are becoming more governing orientated – economic development, partnership management, interacting with other agencies, commenting on national political issues and pursuing the further devolution of powers from the centre – then councillors require and deserve a structure of engagement that supports and enables them to take the political action they decide necessary.

The chapter also explored a model of local government that stressed the government and which saw councillors far more as authoritative politicians with powers to govern, not through influence, negotiation and compromise alone, but through hard political and governing powers. The model took as its premise that soft powers are no powers and what is required is for councils to be seen as state units within a system of political devolution in a localised form of federal structure. In that model, councillors become legislators and, as a consequence, legislative frameworks and policy priorities will vary widely across the country. But that variation will reflect local needs and issues and result from councillors as legislators having greater proximity to their communities than politicians at the national level. To many, the model will be fanciful, unworkable and even dangerous, but the notion of a free and independent local government is, as the final chapter will show, something which is part of a contemporary and ongoing political debate.

Alongside strengthening the governing role of the councillor – either as a logical extension to the existing contemporary setting or from a more radical perspective suggested in the chapter – councillors also require resources and support from their councils to enhance their community leadership role within their wards and divisions. Councillors as community leaders will remain an unfulfilled objective unless councils are organisationally structured to recognise and provide the support that they need in this role. It is not just a case of providing officer support but for councils to realise that, just as they organise in relation to the public services for which they are responsible, they must also organise to support political representation, community leadership and government, as these are as much outputs of the council as education, social care or traffic and highways management. Councils are political institutions and, while the organisational structure has come to terms, very rapidly, with the existence of council cabinets, a similar organisational reconfiguration is required to meet the needs of scrutiny as a governing facility and of the individual councillor as a ward or divisional leader.

We have seen throughout this book that the office of councillor and the individuals elected to that office have their own expectations of what they can achieve and that government and the communities they represent also have expectations of them. It is only right, then, that we debate how the organisational setting and the powers councillors hold can be designed to enable them to meet those expectations and to take the political action that they have been elected to pursue. We have also seen the impact on the non-political facets of the councillor's life that council membership entails and the sacrifices they are required to, and do, make, in the service of their communities. As part of the 'defence of councillors', the next and final chapter draws together the main threads and themes of the book and unashamedly goes on to celebrate the contribution of councillors to the governance of their communities and the country.

9

Conclusion: councillors, hope for the future?

Introduction

This book set out to explore and cast light on the complex world and experiences of the councillor. It has looked at the limitations and frustrations of the role and the nature of the work and life of the councillor as a local politician in close proximity to the community. This provided a basis on which a better understanding of the office could be developed that would contribute to a settlement about its purpose, powers and functions and thus put an end to constant centrally inspired or enforced reshaping. The book also aimed at a deliberate celebration and defence of councillors, those 18,000 or so individuals in England that make many personal sacrifices to represent, serve and govern their fellow citizens and by so doing strengthen the fabric of democracy, not only within those communities but nationally. In doing these things, the book also sought to strengthen the office of councillor and local democracy.

In these pages we have addressed the question: why do we have councillors? Is it merely because we are clinging to some romantic vision of a Victorian experiment with local democratisation, or is it because councillors provide a channel through which central government can implement its polices and have them tailored to local needs, or are councillors elected to provide opportunities for more citizens to be involved in elected politics? Do we have councillors so as to locate decision-makers in close proximity to those their decisions affect or do we have councillors as authoritative and legitimised governors of their communities with the freedom and power to act and innovate as they feel necessary? The answers to these and other questions posed in the book – especially in Chapter 7's exploration of the official mind – will decide what it is reasonable to expect councillors to achieve, individually and collectively, in their pastoral role in regard to their wards or divisions and in their broader policy-making and strategic role. In addition to this, of course, there are the expectations that councillors themselves have of what they can achieve pastorally and strategically and what they can reasonably hope to achieve in shaping the future visions of their localities.

In many respects, councillors are set up to fail to meet any set of expectations held by citizens, their communities, local businesses, the government and themselves, because these expectations are based on the needs of different groups and fail to account for the realities of the resources available to the office. In many other respects, councillors and their councils achieve stunning successes in governing their areas and in tackling the problems associated with austerity, economic growth, infrastructure development, innovative use of new technology and reshaping and reconfiguring the way in which they deal with the pressures of providing, or overseeing, the delivery and development of services essential to modern welfare states. There are, however, inherent tensions that councillors need to manage in overseeing service development and delivery, representing the needs of citizens and communities within wards or divisions and in taking a broader governing perspective to shape the long-term development of a community. In attempting to reconcile those tensions, councillors may appear to act in a contradictory fashion: demanding special treatment for a ward or an individual within it in a way that conflicts with council policy, or supporting a housing or business/infrastructural development that does not accord with the views and wishes of local people but which has a longer-term economic benefit and which at the same time places greater demands on hard-pressed local services, or complying with centrally imposed expenditure reductions while at the same time complaining about such reductions and thus appearing to lack any real strategy with which to provide a coherent and practical alternative.

In addition, councillors have to respond to or act within a framework set by the decisions of other bodies, where they themselves and their councils are only one among many contributors to a network of interacting organisations, exerting influence and in turn being influenced by others (Goss, 2001; Kersting and Vetter, 2003; Denters and Rose, 2005; Loughlin et al., 2011). Councillors, as we have seen in Chapter 4, bring some democratic legitimacy to such seemingly chaotic processes; they have an input to those networks legitimised by the public vote and can act as a vehicle through which network interactions and outputs can be challenged and held to account. They do this while at the same time operating in immediate proximity to those they represent and govern and in circumstances where there are few, if any, lines between the public office they hold and the private life that is left to the councillor.

Politics is a fluid business and does not respect time or boundaries, and this is particularly the case in local politics, as we have seen from Chapter 6. The accessibility of councillors means that they may be held to account or challenged in what they do not only through formal mechanisms or a future election but also in the street, the school playground, the pub, the shop, even at their own workplace. Accessibility may be a constant aspect of the councillor's life which, as we have seen, extends to officers, constituents and to party members. Accessibility or demands for access can also come in waves and be attached to specific local issues and incidences, but accessibility and proximity to the community is a special facet of the office.

It is partly this proximity of the councillor to the community that, as we saw in Chapter 5, acts as a stimulus to stand for election in the first place. Councillors are motivated by a sense of public duty and a desire to give something back to their communities, and that sense of duty is underpinned by a firmly held belief in the democratic system and the organisational architecture of representative democracy, in parties, candidates, electoral law and regulations, nomination procedures and election campaigns, and topped off, as one councillor put it, by: 'that wonderful moment when I heard the returning officer say the words "I hereby declare that [name] is duly elected councillor for [the ward]." Then it was real and that mattered.' That system is sustained by principles of debate, deliberation, discussion and then a vote and a winner and loser; it is a system which councillors cherish.

It is logical that, as elected representatives, councillors have a high regard for the mechanisms of the system which placed them in office, but it is a regard also born of the sense of duty councillors display, because that sense of duty also rests on wishing to take political action to secure either a very specific objective or improvement or from a broader and more general perspective. Thus, the election justifies the councillor's actions, and this is particularly important for councillors who stand to promote their party platform and to pursue a set of party-political objectives, and they do this based on the idea that those ideological objectives are ultimately in the best interests of the local community (see Rao, 1998; Copus, 2004; Brugue and Valles, 2005; Heinelt, 2013a, b). We saw from Chapter 3, however, that ideology alone is insufficient to sustain political action by councillors, it can also serve to isolate and insulate councillors from a broader range of approaches to solving the problems with which they are faced.

That is not to say that councillors are not party loyalists, or that party loyalty does not have its place in the set-piece exchanges of the council chamber, or in promoting the party as an election-winning machine and capable alternative to central government. But that party loyalty has to be tempered with the need to build coalitions and alliances in the complex networks within which councils and councillors operate, and therefore they must have a firm grasp of the *RealLokalPolitik*. Moreover, it requires councillors to recognise the *RealLokalPolitik* of their wards and divisions, the council as an institution, the entire council area and the supra-local dimension within which they operate. As a Labour councillor reported in an interview: 'If I'm working with Capita, or the health service or the police or the LEP, I can't go in and shout at them and demand they all become socialists. I have to influence, achieve what I can and change things that way.'

The tension councillors experienced between responsibility for those services the council provides or oversees and the need to engage with the complex policy world which they must attempt to shape and influence was made plain by one councillor, who, in exasperation, stated: 'people just think councillors are the saddos who have to decide when the bins are collected – there's a bit more to it than that.' Indeed, as we saw from Chapter 6, the public's relationship to the councillor is often that of caseworker and client, protestor and governor, or ambivalent citizen and close-at-hand politician. Indeed, councillors recognise that their office and role is not well understood by the public and that the public image does not reflect the reality. A councillor reported the following exchange:

Resident: So, what do you do for a living?
Councillor: Well, I'm a full-time councillor.
Resident: You must be on good money, then; I bet you're living the life of Riley.

The councillor then recalled that he spent some considerable time explaining the allowance system and the level of allowance received compared to his salary in the job he left to become a full-time councillor.

There are two reasons why it is necessary that the public understand fully what it is that councillors do, why and how they do it, and the limitations on what they can achieve. First, it would help to generally understand the sacrifices and dedication of councillors across the country, and second, local democracy in general would benefit from a local citizenry with a more realistic view of the life lived by those they elect to local office. Indeed, an enhanced image and status for councillors and the office of councillor, based on a clearer understanding of the office itself, would, in the long run, help to shape the official mind and the ideas for the future of the office. As we have seen in Chapter 7, that official mind has two dimensions. The first flows from a range of inquiries, commissions and subsequent reports which have explored the office of councillor and have been part of the way in which the office has be shaped, reshaped and reformulated over time, by central government. That dimension does not always display disdain for councillors but does reflect the sub-servient constitutional position of local government in England and therefore the view that councillors are a lower level of politician to those elected to Parliament. In turn, that view influences how policies towards the office of councillor are deter-mined in terms of functional aspects, such as allowances or pensions, and govern-ing aspects, such as the roles, powers and responsibilities councillors should have attached to their office. The second dimension of the official mind is a more insidi-ous aspect in that it springs from a public discourse and rhetoric about councillors and the office they hold. It is a message often sent through off-the-cuff remarks or, conversely, intended public statements made by senior national politicians that belittle the office and/or the individuals that hold it.

Throughout the book, constant reference has been made to councillors and the office of councillor, and that has been done to distinguish between two sep-arate and independent facets: the political position of councillor with the powers, functions and responsibilities that position brings and the status it holds and the individuals who hold that office at any one time. Given that in 2015 there are some 18,000 councillors in England, it is vital to recognise, in public debate, the vast array of character differences among those holding that office. Without the ability and willingness to make such distinctions and to recognise the realities faced by councillors, we feed a wider and damaging cynicism about local politics and local democracy which plays into the hands of those who wish to see fewer and fewer councillors and bigger and more remote local government. In turn, such cynicism means that national politicians, the press and public can overlook the contribution councillors make to their communities and to the governance of the country and may also fail to recognise the sacrifices councillors make in other facets of their life.

We have seen in Chapter 7 that the press do not exclusively and consistently produce negative stories about councillors; rather, press reporting is more mixed. The media see councillors for what they are: public figures, elected officials with decision-making ability and the power to allocate scarce resource and raise and spend local tax money (despite limitations that may be imposed on tax and spend powers by the government at any time). By virtue of placing themselves before the voters and seeking public office, through the public process of the election, councillors are public property. Therefore, their actions, of whatever sort, are open to reporting and to the public gaze. As we have seen, the councillor's private life becomes public property and negative press may flow from that, with stories appearing of criminal activity, convictions, fraud, violent conduct and drunkenness, all of which would appeal to the local press anyway, but more so if the perpetrator is a councillor. But, as we have seen, the positive aspects of councillors' lives are given rightly deserved media attention: weddings, funerals, exam success, health, sporting and charity achievements and a range of life accomplishments that involve councillors – even 'woman has baby' stories (so long as the woman is a councillor) have all appeared.

Coupled with personally focused reporting of councillors are, of course, the stories reporting the political decisions they make, and it is here more than anywhere that councillors often perceive that their local press is not balanced, or worse, supports the party in opposition. Such a view must be held against the role of the press in publishing and commenting on the activities and decisions of the council and in providing a forum for public debate about the information they present. Such reporting is, however, part of the framework within which local politics takes place and councillors are not, and neither should they be, immune from public critique of their political stance. Yet when criticism is about the direction of council policy or decisions, it is the majority group that is the subject. In turn, the criticising of a majority group or administration means that councillors in the minority groups may find their view is explicitly publicised and praised or implicitly supported. Thus, the press is part of an accountability process that will irritate a majority and please a minority group – it is not therefore in opposition to all political action taken by all councillors all the time.

This book is, however, 'In defence of councillors', not in defence of the local press, and in defending councillors, Chapter 8 argued for the strengthening of the powers attached to the office and for new ways of overcoming the limitations of the office, either within the context of the existing constitutional arrangements for local government, or in an entirely new constitutional system: a fantasy local government. The purpose behind the models suggested was to localise politics and to place real political power with local politicians in close proximity to those they govern and represent. Their purpose was also to recognise that executive members and scrutiny councillors all have a role to play, not only in overseeing the activities of the public bureaucracy that is the council, holding it to account and focusing the direction of its activities, but also in interacting with and giving shape and direction to governance networks and their participants. These roles require appropriate support features and resources, structures, process and powers so that councillors can govern through influence but also through enhanced structural and legal powers resting with their office.

Enhanced powers which enable councillors to take and direct political action to achieve their goals is one aspect to understanding how the office could develop. Secondly, but equally important, is the status that the office of councillor (and by reflection the office-holder) is accorded and the regard in which it is held by the public, those involved in governance activities from beyond the elected sphere, and politicians at other levels of government. An enhanced status comes with an increased perception and reality of public importance, the resources that surround an office and its holder and the ability to take political action and influence events; but it also comes with recognition of the qualities of individual holders of an office. It is no good simply to make a plea for an enhanced status as though what is being requested is a bit more respect for councillors; such a plea is useless at a time when notions of respect for authority are replaced by a more egalitarian mindset. Respect is to be earned, but by again separating the office from the individual, it is possible to enhance the status of councillors by enhancing the ability of the holders of that office to govern their localities or to be central to the life, development, defence and the future of their communities, towns and cities.

A long-standing councillor, first elected in the mid 1940s and to whom I have acted as election agent for the 1981 Greater London Council election, recounted the following in a quiet moment during the campaign:

> When I was first elected people would come to see me about things or come to my surgery and the men would always wear a suit and tie, be shaved and clean and tidy and the women always a smart dress, make-up; people would be polite, respectful, not deferential, but just decent. Now, it's dirty jeans, torn tee-shirts, dirty finger nails. It tells me how we [councillors] have just come down in the world.

If the reader wonders how I can remember, word for word, something that was said thirty-three years ago, it is because it was written down moments afterwards and has been rewritten as paper disintegrated and finally put on a personal computer. It was the first interview, of a sort, that ultimately led to this book. Can we (should we?) recapture a contemporary form of the status that was once accorded to the councillor reported above, a status and respect that was by no means unique to the individual or to that time and place but which was part of the recognition of the importance of the office of councillor and local democracy itself (see Rees and Smith, 1964; Hennock, 1973; Cutler, 1982; Owen, 1982; Goss, 1988)? It is not just subjective feelings of an individual's public standing and achievement or ability to take action that provides 'status', it is also the resources and powers open to an office that provides it and the holder with status. The next section addresses how some simple organisational changes to the office of councillor could enhance the holder's position and ability to effect political action; the third section explores a current debate about the status of local government and councillors which indicates that the fantasy model in Chapter 8 may have some merit to it; the chapter concludes by drawing together the main threads of the book and emphasising just why we should not only defend but also celebrate councillors.

Recognising a new reality

A search for status is not an end in itself. Rather, it is a search for a configuration of the office of councillor that matches current and developing requirements of that office and recognition of the demands that it now makes on its holder (Maud, 1967a, b; Widdicombe 1986a, b; Young and Davies, 1990; Bloch and John, 1991; Rao, 1993; Young and Rao, 1994; NFER, 2007, 2009 and 2011). The exploration in this book has studiously kept away from too much of a focus on the distinction between executive members and councillors for the reasons explained in Chapter 1, and that reasoning is all the more pointed when considering how to enhance the office's capability to take political action. Even without the executive and scrutiny distinction introduced by the Local Government Act 2000, personal and workload demands on the councillor are in an upward trajectory and councillors are currently faced with simply accepting those demands and accommodating them within their existing political and social life or retreating from council work and standing down from office (Bloch, 1992; Game et al., 1993; Erlingsson and Ohrvall, 2011; Allen, 2012). It is, however, a false assumption to suggest that the choice is one or the other. What follows must be taken alongside the changes suggested in the previous chapter when it comes to enhancing the scrutiny function within the existing constitutional framework.

   It is now time to finally grasp the nettle and introduce a number of full-time and salaried councillors across local government. It would be a simple move to make it a feature of local government that all executive members were required to be full-time councillors and were paid a salary. While many already are in effect full-time councillors, that is, they do not have a full- or part-time job (although the leader of Derby City Council elected in May 2014 announced he intended to keep his part-time employment in a bank), they are not salaried in the way that Members of Parliament or Members of the European Parliament are salaried. In addition to the cabinet members, all chairs of overview and scrutiny committees should also hold a full-time salaried position. With a full-time salary would also come full pension entitlement.

The salaries of the leader, cabinet members and overview and scrutiny chairs should continue to be set by an independent panel, but that panel would be expected to set salaries by reference to the existing salaries of appropriate officers within the authority. The council, as now, would be able to either accept or reject the panel recommendations but must provide reasons for any rejection and ask the panel to rethink. After a reconsideration, the panel would make a final set of recommendations that would be binding on the council until the next review, and the review cycle should be on a four-yearly basis to coincide with council elections. In addition, the appointment of leader, cabinet and scrutiny chairs should be subject to a special confirmation meeting of the full council at which the candidates would be expected to set out their reasons for selection and their visions for the office for which they are presenting themselves. It should be a legal requirement that the council confirmation meeting is not subject to any party whip. In councils with a committee system, the same expectation of a full-time salaried position would rest on the chairs of committees and the same approach should be taken to the salaries and appointment of those chairs as in executive-based councils.

In modern local government and with the role it is now expected to play within governance networks and wider government of the country, it is no longer acceptable to expect the leadership and other senior councillors to operate either on a part-time basis or through a system of allowances rather than salaries. It is also intolerable that a salary and pension scheme would be subject to the whims of any future government and, while that general issue is dealt with more fully in the next section, at this stage, suffice it to say that a constitutional lock would be required to protect the salaried nature of the office of senior councillor from change and a revision to a non-salaried basis by a future government.

To those who will argue that such a move will distance the councillor from those they represent and that it will lead to an even greater professionalisation of councillors, there are two responses. First, it is necessary to remember the crucial aspect of the office of councillor: its proximity to the voter and its location within a distinct area. It is the fact that councillors are part of the community they represent that will protect the office from becoming too distant. It is only with the advent of even larger councils than at present that we could start to see an intolerable distancing occur, and this issue is also considered in the next section. Second, the response to the accusation that salaried councillors would become more professionalised is: good. Professionalisation is not a wicked process and it is one that has, in any case, already occurred to the office of councillor across Europe (Aars et al., 2012; Verhelst and Kerrouche, 2012; Steyvers and Verhelst, 2012a, b) As we discussed in Chapter 7, professionalism is as much a state of mind as a state of fact, but for the councillor, it must be a state of fact, too.

A brief word needs to be said about the effect on salaried councillors of the loss of office at either an election or because of a decision by the group after an election. The councillors concerned would indeed lose their office and consequently their salary, but it is an individual's choice to take on such a role. The possible consequences of that choice will be known when the decision is made to take on the offices that would be categorised as full-time salaried councillor. The salary paid to full-time leaders, cabinets and scrutiny chairs recognises the role of a group of councillors as it now stands and as it will develop over time. But alongside these full-time councillors will remain councillors who are part time, or at least not paid a full salary in the way that has been described, but would continue to receive allowances as at present. So, what of those councillors? The main task such non-salaried, but not necessarily part-time, councillors would undertake would be that of overview and scrutiny and holding the executive to account, conducting inquiries into the activities of external bodies, influencing and shaping governance networks and identifying policy problems and solutions.

The scrutiny process undertaken by these councillors would occur within the framework of the enhanced scrutiny system that was described in the previous chapter. In addition, non-salaried councillors would be ward and divisional community leaders and representatives, also within the enhanced ward framework set out in Chapter 8. Councils would need to be structured not only to recognise the role that the non-salaried councillor undertook but also to support that role with the organisational resources necessary to enable councillors to interact with the widest possible range of organisations in the most effective fashion. Such support has to be provided as these councillors will, and must be, as much a part of the governing process as salaried councillors. It is, of course, this group of councillors that will appoint from their number the council leader and hold confirmation hearings for the cabinet – there is therefore no bar on these councillors becoming salaried as their political career develops.

Yes, there will be two types of councillor, and yes, the roles and responsibilities of the distinct and separate offices of councillor will differ, but that reflects the reality of the requirements on councillors; simply failing to formally recognise that does not make it go away. There have long been and will always be two types of councillor: the leadership group and councillors group. It is time our system of local government recognised something that has long been the case and accommodated it with more formal recognition than was granted by the 2000 Act and subsequent legislation. But also in need of formal recognition is the limited nature of the political and governing powers that rest with councillors, because a major reason behind government inquiries into the role of the councillor stems from a view that they are unable to ensure that local government operates effectively or can meet central government objectives and that they are incapable of responding quickly to a rapidly changing economic, political and social environment. In the last chapter, a 'fantasy local government' model was presented which emphasised the 'government' in local government. It is now time to see if fantasy can become reality.

Independent local government: a new settlement for councillors and councils

In November 2010, the Political and Constitutional Reform Committee of the House of Commons launched an inquiry that explored the desirability, possibility and opportunities for putting the relationship between central and local government on a statutory footing. Such a move would implicitly be based on a strengthening of the standing and status of local government and councillors, otherwise there would be no point to any codification of the constitutional status of local government. As part of the inquiry and after an initial call for evidence, the committee commissioned the production of a code which would set out the basis for that statutory relationship between central and local government, which was designed to vastly strengthen the level of local government independence from the centre. Throughout 2012, the committee consulted on the draft code and collected additional evidence and responses from local government, councillors, local government institutions and academics.

At the end of that consultation, the committee reported its findings and included in its report the draft code of relationships between central and local government (House of Commons Political and Constitutional Reform Committee, 2013: 41–4). The report built on a number of other inquiries and reports that had explored the relationship between local and central government (HMSO, 1986, Communities and Local Government Committee, 2009; DCLG, 2012; DBIS, 2012) and used the coalition government's localism policies, and particularly the Localism Act 2011, to accelerate the pace at which local government could be freed from the centre. A vital argument of the committee's report was that past non-statutory attempts to readjust and rebalance the relationship had failed because of the unwillingness of government departments to act within the frameworks suggested by attempts such as the European Charter of Local Self-Government (signed by Britain in 1997 and ratified in 1998), or the Central–Local Concordat of 2007. Indeed, evidence to the committee from local government stressed the failure of these approaches to fundamentally shift the relationship and to alter the status of local government and that of councillors as local politicians.

The committee's report stated that with the statutory codification of central and local relationships the 'constitutional role and the rights of local government would be clearly defined' (House of Commons Political and Constitutional Reform Committee, 2013: 33) and be brought into line with much of local government in Europe. Mindful of the need to go further than statutorily setting out how local and central government would interact, the report proposed a 'constitutional lock', which would mean that the code could only be changed by the use of an amended provision of the 1911 Parliament Act so as to devise and protect a long-term settlement. The code itself was a concise crystallisation of some core principles that, if enshrined, would produce the foundation for an independent local government (House of Commons Political and Constitutional Reform Committee, 2013: 41–4) and suggested a set of fundamental freedoms and rights for local government to which all ministers and government departments would adhere. Indeed, local government would work in an irrevocable framework of general competence where councils would be free to regulate and administer all public affairs and matters of concern within their boundaries, and with the direction of accountability for its actions being towards local citizens not central government. A vital provision of the code was the statutory duty on central government to consult with local government at the earliest stage when any policy development that impacted on local government was being considered or developed, thus allowing local government some time to marshal resources and arguments around any proposed policy change.

Vital to the independence of local government was the provision that would remove the power of central government to control the borders, boundaries and shape of individual councils or local government as a whole – thus, no more wholesale government-inspired structural reorganisations. Equally as vital to any real independence for local government are the provisions on the financial freedom of local government, and on that subject, the code had the following to say:

1. Councils shall be financially independent of central government. Equalisation arrangements will continue as now. Equalisation will be conducted through a process independent of central government and continue to be based on the principle of ensuring fairness and balance between councils.
2. Councils may raise additional sources of income in their localities in any way they wish [subject to the rule of law and human rights legislation] if they gain the consent of their electorates.
3. Local government shall have a guaranteed share of the annual yield of income tax. This share shall be renegotiated whenever service-provision responsibilities are transferred between central and local government.
4. Councils shall be able to raise any loans, bonds or other financial instruments which their credit rating allows and will be exclusively responsible for repayment. All councils shall operate 'a balanced budget' so that all outgoings, including interest repayments on borrowings, shall not exceed income.
5. Central government may not cap, or in any way limit, council's taxation powers. Central and local government may contract with each other to pursue their own policy objectives.
6. The same financial transparency standards will apply to local and central government, alike.

(House of Commons Political and Constitutional
Reform Committee, 2013: 43)

While this does not go as far as the financial model set out in the 'fantasy local government' system in the preceding chapter, it does provide a framework within which, given the suggested equalisation methods, councils could operate with greater freedom in taxation, spending and finance-raising powers. It would remove, once and for all, central government capping power. In addition, a guaranteed share of the annual yield of income tax would see central government relinquish part of its control of national taxation, handing the proceeds over to the localities.

The government produced its response to the report in May 2013 (TSO, 2013b) and while it reiterated its commitment to localism and further devolution to councils and communities, it preferred an incremental approach to improving the relationship between the centre and the localities rather than a 'rigid, constitutional blueprint through a statutory code' (TSO, 2013b: 4). Yet the door has not been fully closed, as the chair of the Political and Constitutional Reform Committee, Graham Allen, the MP for Nottingham North, engaged with myself as the academic who drafted the code and presented to Parliament in July 2014 a Local Government (Independence) Bill, which included the code. While that Bill had little chance of success, it does keep open the ongoing debate about rebalancing the constitutional status of local government and strengthening its independence from the centre. Moreover, as the parties prepared their manifestos for the 2015 general election, localists had a ready-made weapon with which to confront the centralists in all parties.

But the code and the Bill speak only of local government, so what of councillors within all the proposed changes? Under the provisions of the code, councillors would find that their political room for manoeuvre was greatly increased, and an independent local government means councillors are also independent of central constraints and restrictions on what they can do within their councils. A more powerful local government equates to a more powerful set of councillors, who would then operate within a framework that statutorily recognised them and their institutions as a central component of the overall governing system of the country and one which had a constitutionally safeguarded independence from central interference. Councillors and their communities would benefit from a localised focus on the problems they experience and an enhanced ability to solve those problems and control the future direction of their localities. But until that day occurs, councillors will still need to find ways of overcoming the limitations of their office to be able to take the political action they were elected to take, and they will need to continue to cope with the reshaping of their office by the centre. That there are still so many of our fellow citizens who are willing to commit their time and energy to governing our local communities, despite the limitations and frustrations they experience, is testament to them and their office.

A final three cheers

Attempting to defend councillors and their office may seem a task that sails against the prevailing public, media and government wind. While this book was being written, councillors across the country have been voting to reduce their own allowances, suggesting and accepting reductions in their numbers on a range of councils, and in some cases seeking or being cajoled into accepting council mergers which would further reduce their numbers. A form of self-denying ordinance is in operation. But worse, it is an ordinance where councillors must be seen to publicly flagellate themselves and their colleagues and to placate and contribute to a dangerous undermining of local government and democracy. A robust future for the government of the localities rests on the current self-denial being a temporary aberration, driven by the starvation diet of austerity and the need for councillors themselves, not just local government, to be seen to be taking a share of the pain.

While austerity may be the long-term context within which councillors will operate, it is not a permanent one. Neither is it a good enough reason to contemplate the sacrifice of local representative government or the office of councillor to the altar of financial restraint. Far from it. It is in times of crisis that communities rely more and more on their fellow citizens who are councillors to govern with sensitivity and from the knowledge they have of the area that they represent. We thus return to the question of proximity. We have seen that proximity is a unique feature of the office of councillor and is what ensures councillors have more than a passing acquaintance with the area and people that they represent and govern. Councillors may find that the functions, tasks, responsibilities and duties of their office at the end of their term may be different from those on the day they were elected. But that constancy of change is matched by the constancy of the link to local citizens that councillors provide between the council and a range of bodies operating in governance networks, and that link is maintained because councillors are citizen-politicians.

Holding the office of councillor has a powerful impact on the public and private life of those elected, but those effects are weighed by councillors against what they wish to achieve for the benefit of their localities, and thus any negative impacts are seen as 'worth it' in the long run. Councillors are human. They do not rise to a higher level of virtue, honour and integrity on hearing that they have been 'duly elected to serve'. Rather, they are subject to the weaknesses, whims and vices of all of us, as well as to the dedication, hard work, compassion that all of us can display. Do we expect too much from councillors? Probably, and on occasions most certainly, especially given that councils are not set up to ensure that councillors are automatically supported in what they do to the extent required to make them powerful local politicians. Rather, it is their own skill and imagination that makes it possible for them to accrue the resources to take local political action. But that can be a frustrating process. In many of the councils visited during the research, there was often a physical separation in the council building, with councillors' accommodation, group rooms, democratic services and even the council chamber located in one part of the building and officers in another. Such physical separation was not always the case, but where it did occur it simply made the separation between councillors and the council part of the fabric of the system.

Councillors are very much part of the fabric of local democracy and are confronted not only with linking the citizen to the council but also with linking the citizen to the wider world of interactions that is the complexity of modern-day policy- and decision-making. It is the councillor who puts the government into governance; it is the councillor who provides legitimacy to the activities and decisions of the complex and otherwise unaccountable political decision-making that takes place beyond the council. It is the councillor who is expected at one moment to deal with multi-million-pound budgets, or to make complex budget reductions, to take decisions about closing schools or commissioning public services from an outside provider, or to oversee the entry of the council into the energy market or other commercially orientated venture, and at the next moment to deal with a complex case for a constituent, the ultimate outcomes of which could be life changing for that person, and at the next moment, to make sure the council removes that dumped mattress from the end of the road or repairs that annoying flickering street light.

They may be castigated in the local press, abused at public meetings or even in the streets, subject to personal scrutiny of their private lives, treated with often barely concealed contempt by ministers, have little or no time for family, friends and relaxation or even simply watching a bit of TV – although it is amazing how many councillors interviewed were fans of *Game of Thrones*. They may be expected to keep up with new ways of working or new advances in social media which offer another intrusion into other facets of their life, but they put up with that in order to govern, represent and serve their local citizens. They do so from a sense of public service that is linked to the holding of elected public office and so, at the same time, they display a democratic spirit that is vital to the effective working of local representative democracy and government.

Now, it would be easy to be overly romantic about councillors and the office they hold, and at this stage, some may say: too late. Yet that is a danger in any defence, and there are plenty who will decry councillors, seek to undermine them or even see far fewer of them in office; so a defence must be just that: a defence. We have, however, seen in this book some critique of councillors, especially over the inability of many to come to terms with cabinet and scrutiny distinctions – an approach to local politics commonplace across Europe. However, such critique is not intended to undermine the office or its holders, and the suggestions for strengthening the governing role of the councillor are made from a position of inherent trust in those we elect locally and are intended to enhance their status and that of their office. We undermine or hold councillors with disdain at our peril, and those that do so are wittingly or unwittingly undermining local democracy.

It is safe to say that if it were not for councillors our democracy would be far less rich, our political culture far less vibrant, our system of government far less reflective of the views of the local citizenry, our democracy far more centralised, the opportunities for involvement in politics far more limited and our local papers far, far more boring. We have councillors to thank for the personal sacrifices they make in dealing with the challenges faced by local communities, for developing innovative and imaginative solutions to complex problems that impact on our localities, for bringing government closer to the people, and for recognising the special features of each locality and its population when developing a vision of its future. And, as the book has shown, we have councillors to thank for a lot more besides.

Bibliography

Aars, J., A. Offerdal and D. Rysavy (2012), 'The careers of European local councillors: A cross-national comparison', *Lex localis*, 10:1, 37–62

Ackerman, J. (2004), 'Co-governance for accountability: Beyond exit and voice', *World Development*, 32:3, 447–63

Adams, J. and L. Kenny (1989), 'The retention of state governors', *Public Choice*, 62:1, 1–13

Alkopher, T. (2005), 'The social (and religious) meanings that constitute war: The Crusades as Realpolitik vs. Socialpolitik', *International Studies Quarterly*, 49:4, 715–38

Allen, P. (2012), 'Falling off the ladder: Gendered experiences of councillor turnover', *The Political Quarterly*, 83:4, 711–13

Andrews, R., G. A. Boyne, J. Law and R. M. Walker (2003), 'Myths, measures and modernisation: The comparative performance of English and Welsh local government', *Local Government Studies*, 29:4, 54–75

Ashworth, R. (2003), 'Toothless tigers? Councillor perceptions of new scrutiny arrangements in Welsh local government', *Local Government Studies*, 29:2, 1–18

Ashworth, R. and S. Snape (2004), 'An overview of scrutiny: A triumph of context over structure', *Local Government Studies*, 30:4, 538–56

Ashworth, R., S. Aulakh and S. Snape (2007), 'Plugging the accountability gap? Evaluating the effectiveness of regional scrutiny', *Environment and Planning C: Government and Policy*, 25:2, 194–211

Atkinson, M. and W. Coleman (1992), 'Policy networks, policy communities and the problems of governance', *Governance*, 5:2, 154–80

Bäck, H. (2004), 'The partified city: Elite political culture in Sweden's two biggest cities', ECPR Joint Sessions of Workshops, Uppsala

Barber, B. (1984), *Strong Democracy: Participatory Politics for a New Age*, University of Californian Press, Berkeley, CA

Barber, J. (1965), *The Lawmakers*, Yale University Press, New Haven

Barker, B. (1983), 'The operation of Bristol Labour Party: A view from the edge', School of Advanced Urban Studies, Working Paper 27, Bristol University

Barnett, N. (2011), 'Local government at the Nexus?', *Local Government Studies*, 37:3, 275–90

Barron, J., G. Crawley and T. Wood (1989), 'Drift and resistance: Refining models of political recruitment', *Policy and Politics*, 17:3, 207–19

——(1991), *Councillors in Crisis: the Public and Private Worlds of Local Councillors*, Macmillan, London

Bealey, F., J. Blondel and W. P. McCann (1965), *Constituency Politics: A study of Newcastle-under-Lyme*, Faber & Faber, London

Bekkers, V., G. Dijkstra, A. Edwards and M. Fenger (2007), 'Governance and the democratic deficit: An evaluation', in V. Bekkers, G. Dijkstra, A. Edwards and M. Fenger (eds), *Governance and the Democratic Deficit*, Ashgate, Aldershot, pp. 295–312

Berg, R. and N. Rao (eds) (2005), *Transforming Local Political Leadership*, Palgrave, Basingstoke

Bevir, M. and R. Rhodes (2006), *Governance Stories*, Routledge, Abingdon

Birch, A. H. (1959), *Small Town Politics: A Study of Political Life in Glossop*, Oxford University Press, Oxford

Bjørnå, H. and N. Aarsæther (2009), 'Local government strategies and entrepreneurship', *International Journal of Innovation and Regional Development*, 2:1, 50–65

Bloch, A. (1992), *The Turnover of Local Councillors*, Joseph Rowntree Foundation, York

Bloch, A. and P. John (1991), *Attitudes to Local Government: A Survey of Electors*, Joseph Rowntree Foundation, York

Blunkett, D. and K. Jackson (1987), *Democracy in Crisis: The Town Halls Respond*, Hogarth Press, London

Bochel, H. and C. Bochel (2010), 'Local political leadership and the modernisation of local government', *Local Government Studies*, 36:6, 723–37

Bogdanor, B. (2009), *The New British Constitution*, Hart Publishing, Oxford

Boogers, M. and J. van Ostaaijen (2009), 'Who is the boss in Oss? Power structures in local governance networks of a small Dutch city', paper at EGPA Conference 2009, Standing Group IV Local governance and democracy, Malta

Borins, S. (2001a), 'Encouraging innovation in the public sector', *Journal of Intellectual Capital*, 2:3, 310–19

——(2001b), 'Innovation, success and failure in public management research: Some methodological reflections', *Public Management Review*, 3:1, 3–17

Borraz, O. and P. John (2004), 'The transformation of urban political leadership in Western Europe', *International Journal of Urban and Regional Research*, 28:1, 107–20

Bottom, K. and C. Copus (2011), 'Independent politics: Why seek to serve and survive as an independent councillor?', *Public Policy and Administration*, 26:3, 279–305

Bozeman, B. (2002), 'Public–value failure: When efficient markets may not do', *Public Administration Review*, 62:2, 145–61

Brady, H., K. Schlozman and S. Verba (1999), 'Prospecting for participants: Rational expectations and the recruitment of political activists', *American Political Science Review*, 93:1, 153–68

Brown, T. (2003), 'Towards an understanding of local protest: hospital closure and community resistance', *Social & Cultural Geography*, 4:4, 489–506

Brugue, Q. and J. Valles (2005), 'New-style councils, new-style councillors: From local government to local governance', *Governance*, 18:2, 197–226

Budge, I. and D. Farlie (1975), 'Political recruitment and dropout: Predictive success of background characteristics', *British Journal of Political Science*, 5:1, 33–68

Bulpitt, J. G. (1967), *Party Politics in English Local Government*, Longmans, London

Burns, D. (2000), 'Can local democracy survive governance?', *Urban Studies*, 37: 5–6, 963–74.

Byrne, T. (1994), *Local Government in Britain*, Penguin Books, London

Carvel, J. (1984), *Citizen Ken*, The Hogarth Press, London

Centre for Public Scrutiny (CfPS) (2014), *Annual Survey of Overview and Scrutiny in Local Government*, CfPS, London

Chamberlayne, P. (1978), 'The politics of participation: An enquiry into four London Boroughs 1968–74', *London Journal*, 4:1, 49–68

Chandler, J. (2007), *Explaining Local Government: Local Government in Britain Since 1800*, Manchester University Press, Manchester

——(2010), 'A Rationale for Local Government', *Local Government Studies*, 36:1, 5–20

Clark, A., K. Bottom and C. Copus (2008), 'More similar than they'd like to admit? Ideology, policy and populism in the trajectories of the British National Party and Respect', *British Politics*, 3:4, 511–34

Clark, P. and J. Wilson (1961), 'Incentive systems a theory of organisation', *Administration Quarterly*, 6:2, 129–66

Clarke, M. and J. Stewart (1998), *Community Governance, Community Leadership and the New Local Government*, Joseph Rowntree Foundation, York

Clements, R. V. (1969), *Local Notables and the City Council*, Macmillan, London

Cockburn, C. (1977), *The Local State: Management of Cities and People*, Pluto Press, London

Cole, A. and P. John (2001), *Local Governance in England and France*, Routledge, Abingdon, Oxford

Cole, M. (2002), 'The role(s) of county councillors: An evaluation', *Local Government Studies*, 28:4, 22–46

Cole, M. and G. Parston (2006), *Unlocking Public Value: a New Model for Achieving High Performance in Public Service Organisations*, John Wiley and Sons, New Jersey

Committee of Inquiry into the Conduct of Local Authority Business (1986a), *Report of the Committee into the Conduct of Local Authority Business*, Cmnd 9797, HMSO, London (Widdicombe)

Committee of Inquiry into the Conduct of Local Authority Business (1986b), *Research Vol. II: The local government councillor*, Cmnd 9799, HMSO, London

Committee on the Management of Local Government (1967a), *Vol. I, Report of the committee*, HMSO, London (Maud)

Committee on the Management of Local Government (1967b), *Research Vol. II: The local government councillor*, HMSO, London

Communities and Local Government Committee (2009), *The Balance of Power: Central and Local Government*, Sixth Report of Session 2008–09, TSO, London

Communities and Local Government Committee (2013), *Councillors on the Frontline*, Sixth Report of Session 2012–13, TSO, London

Copus, C. (1999), 'The party group: A barrier to democratic renewal', *Local Government Studies*, 25:4, 77–98

—— (2003), 'Re-engaging citizens and councils: The importance of the councillor to enhanced citizen input', *Local Government Studies*, 29:2, 32–51

—— (2004), *Party Politics and Local Government*, Manchester University Press, Manchester

—— (2007), 'Public participation in local representative democracy: Exploring a tension and evaluating practices through assessing the perspectives of the local political elite', in P. Delwit, J.-.B Pilet, H. Reynaert and K. Steyvers (eds), *Towards DIY-Politics? Participatory and Direct Democracy at the Local Level in Europe*, Vanden Broele/Nomos, Bruges/Baden-Baden, pp. 239–76

—— (2008), 'English councillors and mayoral governance: Developing a new dynamic for political accountability', *Political Quarterly*, 79:4, 590–604

—— (2010a), 'English local government: Neither local nor government', in P. Swianiewicz (ed.), *Territorial Consolidation Reforms in Europe: Local Government and Public Service Reform Initiative*, Open Society Institute, Budapest, pp. 95–126

—— (2010b), 'The councillor: Governor, governing, governance and the complexity of citizen engagement', *British Journal of Politics and International Relations*, 12:4, 569–89

——(2011), 'English local government: Reflecting a nation's past or merely an administrative convenience?', in A. Aughey and C. Berberich (eds), *These Englands*, Manchester University Press, Manchester, pp. 193–213

Copus, C. and G. Erlingsson (2013), 'Formal institutions versus informal decision-making: On parties, delegation and accountability in local government', *Scandinavian Journal of Public Administration*, 17:1, 51–69

Copus, C. and M. Wingfield (2014), 'Are independent councillors really Conservatives in disguise?', *Local Government Studies*, 40:5, 647–69

Copus, C., A. Clark, H. Reynaert and K. Steyvers (2009), 'Minor party and independent politics beyond the mainstream: Fluctuating fortunes but a permanent presence', *Parliamentary Affairs*, 62:1, 4–18

Copus, C., M. Wingfield, K. Steyvers and H. Reynaert (2012), 'Parties and nonpartisanship in cities', in K. Mossberger, S. Clarke and P. John (eds), *The Oxford Handbook of Urban Politics*, Oxford University Press, Oxford pp. 210–31

Corina, L. (1974), 'Elected representatives in a party system: A typology', *Policy and Politics*, 3:1, 69–87

Coulson, A. and P. Whiteman (2012), 'Holding politicians to account? Overview and scrutiny in English local government', *Public Money & Management*, 32:3, 185–92

Cutler, H. (1982), *The Cutler Files*, London, Weidenfeld & Nicolson

Dearlove, J. (1973), *The Politics of Policy in Local Government: The Making and Maintenance of Public Policy in the Royal Borough of Kensington and Chelsea*, Cambridge University Press, Cambridge

De Groot, M. (2009), 'Democratic effects of institutional reform in local government, The case of the Dutch local government Act 2002' (PhD thesis, Enschede)

Delwit, P., J. B. Pilet, H. Reynaert and K. Steyvers (eds) (2007), *Towards DIY-Politics? Participatory and Direct Democracy at the Local Level in Europe*, Vanden Broele/Nomos, Brugge/Baden-Baden

Denters, B. and L. Rose (2005), *Comparing Local Governance: Trends and Developments*, Palgrave Macmillan, Basingstoke

Department for Business, Innovation and Skills (DBIS) (2012), *No Stone Unturned: in Pursuit of Growth*, DBIS, London

Department for Communities and Local Government (DCLG) (2006), *Strong and Prosperous Communities*, Cm 6939-1, DCLG, London

——(2012), *Decentralisation: An Assessment of Progress*, DCLG, London

——(2008), *The Government's Response to the Councillors Commission*, CLG, London

——(2007), *Representing the Future: the Report of the Councillors Commission*, HMSO, London

Department for Environment, Transport and the Regions (DETR) (1998a), *Modernising Local Government: Local Democracy and Community Leadership*, DETR, London

——(1998b), *Modern Local Government: In Touch with the People*, Cm 4041, London

——(1999), *Local Leadership: Local Choice*, DETR, London

Department for Transport, Local Government and the Regions (DTLR) (2001), *Strong Local Leadership: Quality Public Services*, DTLR, London

Drage, J. (2008), *A Balancing Act: Decision-Making and Representation in New Zealand's Local Government*, Institute of Policy Studies, University of Wellington, Wellington

Dunleavy, P. (1991), *Democracy, Bureaucracy and Public Choice*, Harvester Wheatsheaf, Hemel Hempstead

Erlingsson, G. and R. Ohrvall (2011), 'Why do councillors quit prematurely? On the consequences of councillors leaving their seats before the end of their term', *Lex Localis*, 9:4, 297–310

Eulau, H. and J. Whalke (1978), *The Politics of Representation*, Sage, California

Eulau, H., J. Whalke, W. Buchanan and L. Ferguson (1959), 'The role of the representative: Some empirical observations on the theory of Edmund Burke', *American Political Science Review*, 53, 742–56

Fallend, F., G. Ignits and P. Swainiewicz (2006), 'Divided loyalties? Mayors between party representation and local community interests', in H. Bäck, H. Heinelt and A. Magnier (eds), *The European Mayor: Political Leaders in the Changing Context of Local Democracy*, VS Verlag für Sozialwissenschaften, Wiesbaden, pp. 245–70.

Foley, P. and S. Martin (2000), 'A new deal for the community? Public participation in regeneration and local service delivery', *Policy and Politics*, 28:4, 479–92

Frederickson, G. (1993), *Ethics and Public Administration*, M. E. Sharpe, New York

Game, C., S. Leach and G. Williams (1993), *Councillor Recruitment and Turnover: An Approaching Precipice?* Local Government Management Board, Luton

Geddes, M. (2006), 'Partnership and the limits to local governance in England: Institutionalist analysis and neoliberalism', *International Journal of Urban and Regional Research*, 30:1, 76–97

Getimis, P. (2013), 'Municipal councillors as interest mediators: Roles perceptions and enactment', in B. Egner, D. Sweeting and P.-J. Klok (eds), *Local Councillors in Europe*, Springer, Wiesbaden, pp. 139–59

Glassberg, A. (1981), *Representation and Urban Community*, Macmillan, London

Goldsmith, M. and E. Page (eds) (2010), *Changing Government Relations in Europe: From Localism to Intergovernmentalism*, Routledge / ECPR, London

Goss, S. (1988), *Local Labour and Local Government: A Study of the Changing Interests, Politics and Policy in Southwark, 1919 to 1982*, Edinburgh University Press, Edinburgh

——(2001), *Making Local Governance Work: Networks, Relationships and the Management of Change*, Palgrave, Basingstoke

Grant, W. P. (1971), 'Local parties in British local politics: A framework for empirical analysis', *Political Studies*, 19:2, 201–12

(1973), 'Non-partisanship in British local politics', *Policy and Politics*, 1:3, 241–54

Greasley, S. and G. Stoker (2009), 'Urban political leadership', in J. S. Davies and J. L. Imbroscio (eds), *Theories of Urban Politics*, Sage, London, pp. 125–36

Green, P. (1990), 'A review essay of Robert Dahl democracy and its critics', *Social Theory and Practice*, 16:2, 217–43

Gregory, R. (1969), 'Local elections and the rule of anticipated reactions', *Political Studies*, 17:1, 31–47

Gyford, J. (1976), *Local Politics in Britain*, Croom Helm, London

——(1986), 'Diversity, sectionalism and local democracy', in Committee of Inquiry into the Conduct of Local Authority Business, *Research Vol. IV, Aspects of Local Democracy*, HMSO, London, pp. 106–31

Hajer, M. and H. Wagenaar (eds) (2003), *Deliberative Policy Analysis: Understanding Governance in a Networked Society*, Cambridge University Press, Cambridge

Hampton, W. (1970), *Democracy and Community: A Study of Politics in Sheffield*, Oxford University Press, Oxford

Hatton, D. (1988), *Inside Left*, Bloomsbury, London

Haus, M. and D. Sweeting (2006), 'Local democracy and political leadership: Drawing a map', *Political Studies*, 54:2, 267–88

Haus, M., H. Heinelt and M. Stewart (eds), (2005), *Urban Governance and Democracy: Leadership and Community Involvement*, Routledge, London

Head, B. (2005), 'Participation or co-governance? Challenges for regional natural resource management', in R. Eversole and J. Martin (eds), *Participation and Governance in Regional Development: Global Trends in an Australian Context*, Ashgate, Burlington, VT, pp. 137–54

Heclo, H. (1969), 'The councillor's job', *Public Administration*, 47:2, 185–202

Heinelt, H. (2013a), 'Councillors' notions of democracy, and their role perception and behaviour in the changing context of local democracy', *Local Government Studies*, 39:5, 640–60

——(2013b), 'Introduction: The role perception and behaviour of municipal councillors in the changing context of local democracy', *Local Government Studies*, 39:5, 633–39

Hennock, E. P. (1973), *Fit and Proper Persons: Ideal and Reality in Nineteenth-Century Urban Government*, Edward Arnold, London

Hesse, J. J. and L. J. Sharpe (1991), 'Local government in International Perspective: Some comparative observations', in J. J. Hesse and L. J. Sharp (eds), *Local Government and Urban Affairs in International Perspective: Analyses of Twenty Western Industrialised Countries*, Nomos, Baden-Baden, pp. 603–21

House of Commons Political and Constitutional Reform Committee (2013), *Prospects for Codifying the Relationship Between Central and Local Government*, Third Report of Session 2012–13, TSO, London

Jennings, R. (1982), 'The changing representational roles of local councillors in England', *Local Government Studies*, 8:5, 67–86

Jessop, B. (1998), *The Rise of Governance and the Risk of Failure: The Case of Economic Development*, Basil Blackwell, Oxford

—— (2002), 'Liberalism, neoliberalism, and urban governance: A state–theoretical perspective', *Antipode*, 34:3, 452–72

John, P. (2001), *Local Governance in Western Europe*, Sage, London

John, P., S. Cotterill, L. Richardson, A. Moseley, G. Stoker, C. Wales, G. Smith, H. Liu and H. Nomura (2013), *Nudge, Nudge, Think, Think: Experimenting with Ways to Change Civic Behaviour*, Bloomsbury Academic, London

Johnson, C. and S. Osborne (2003), 'Local strategic partnerships, neighbourhood renewal, and the limits to co-governance', *Public Money and Management*, 23:3, 147–54

Jones, G.W. (1969), *Borough Politics: a Study of Wolverhampton Borough Council 1888–1964*, Macmillan, London

—— (1973), 'The functions and organisation of councillors', *Public Administration*, 51:2, 135–46

—— (1975), 'Varieties of local politics', *Local Government Studies*, 1:2, 17–32

Jones, G. W. and J. Stewart (1982), 'The value of local autonomy – A rejoinder', *Local Government Studies*, 8:5, 10–15

—— (1985), *The Case for Local Government*, Allen & Unwin, London

Jones, R., J. Pykett and M. Whitehead (2010), 'Big society's little nudges: The changing politics of health care in an age of austerity', *Political Insight*, 1:3, 85–7

Judge, D. (1999), *Representation: Theory and Practice in Britain*, Routledge, London

Karlsson, D. (2013a), 'What do the local councillors of Europe represent?', in B. Egner, D. Sweeting and P.-J. Klok (eds), *Local Councillors in Europe*, Springer, Wiesbaden, pp. 97–119

—— (2013b), 'The hidden constitutions: How informal political institutions affect the representation style of local councils', *Local Government Studies*, 39:5, 681–702

Keen, R. (2014), *Membership of UK Political Parties*, House of Commons Library, SN/SG/5125

Keith-Lucas, B. and P. Richards (1978), *A History of Local Government in the Twentieth Century*, George Allen & Unwin, London

Kelly, R. (2010), 'Political parties', in B. Jones and P. Norton (eds), *Politics UK*, 7th edn, Pearson Education, Harlow, pp. 205–24

Kersting, N. and A. Vetter (eds) (2003), *Reforming Local Government in Europe: Closing the Gap Between Democracy and Efficiency*, Leske & Budrich, Opladen

Klijn, E. and C. Skelcher (2007), 'Democracy and governance networks: compatible or not?', *Public Administration*, 85:3, 587–608

Klok, P.-J. and B. Denters (2013), 'The roles councillors play', in B. Egner, D. Sweeting and P.-J. Klok (eds), *Local Councillors in Europe*, Springer, Wiesbaden, pp. 63–83

Kooiman, J. (2003), *Governing as Governance*, Sage, Los Angeles

Kotter, J. P. and P. Lawrence (1974), *Mayors in Action: Five Approaches to Urban Governance*, John Wiley, London

Kratochwil, F. (1993), 'The embarrassment of changes: neo-realism as the science of Realpolitik without politics', *Review of International Studies*, 19:1, 63–80

Labour Party (1995), *Renewing Democracy, Rebuilding Communities*, London

——(2013), *Labour Party Rule Book*, London

Labour Party (2014), *Local Government Innovation Taskforce: Final Report: People-Powered Public Services*, London

Lansley, S., S. Goss and C. Wolmar (1989), *Councillors in Conflict: The Rise and Fall of the Municipal Left*, Macmillan, London

Lapuente, V. (2010), 'A tale of two cities: Bureaucratisation in mayor-council and council-manager municipalities', *Local Government Studies*, 36:6, 739–57

Lasswell, H. (1960), *Psychopathology and Politics*, Viking, New York

Lawson, K. and P. Merkl (eds) (1988), *When Parties Fail: Emerging Alternative Organisations*, Princeton University Press, Princeton, NJ

Le Gales, P. (1998), Regulations and governance in European cities, *International Journal of Urban and Regional Research*, 22:3, 482–506

—— (2002), *European Cities: Social Conflicts and Governance*, Oxford University Press, Oxford

Leach, S. (2006), *The Changing Role of Local Politics in Britain*, The Policy Press, Bristol

Leach, S. and C. Copus (2004), 'Scrutiny and the political party Group in UK local government: New models of behaviour', *Public Administration*, 82:2, 331–54

Leach, S. and D. Wilson (2000), *Local Political Leadership*, The Policy Press, Bristol

—— (2008), 'Diluting the role of party groups? Implications of the 2006 local government white paper', *Local Government Studies*, 34:3, 303–21

Leach, S. and M. Wingfield (1999), 'Public participation and the democratic renewal agenda: Prioritisation or marginalisation?', *Local Government Studies*, 25:4, 46–59

Lee, J. M. (1963), *Social Leaders and Public Persons: A Study of County Government in Cheshire Since 1888*, Clarendon Press, Oxford

Leighton, W. and E. López (2012), *Madmen, Intellectuals and Academic Scribblers: The Economic Engine of Political Change*, Stanford University Press, Menlo Park, CA

Lepine, E. (2009), 'Scrutiny, public participation, and democracy – making the connections', paper presented at the Political Studies Association Conference, Manchester

Lewis, B. (2012), Parliamentary Under Secretary of State for communities and local government statement on councillor pensions, 19 December 2012 www.gov. uk/government/speeches/local-government-pension-scheme (last accessed 19 March 2015)

Livingstone, K. (1987), *If Voting Changed Anything, They'd Abolish It*, Fontana, London

Loughlin, J., F. Hendricks and A. Lindstrom (2011), *The Oxford Handbook of Regional Democracy in Europe*, Oxford University Press, Oxford

Lowndes, V. and H. Sullivan (2008), 'How low can you go? Rationales and challenges for neighbourhood governance', *Public Administration*, 86:1, 53–74

Lowndes, V., L. Pratchett and G. Stoker (2001a), 'Trends in public participation: Part 1 – Local government perspectives', *Public Administration*, 79:1, 205–22

—— (2001b), 'Trends in public participation: Part 2 – citizens' perspectives', *Public Administration*, 79:2, 445–55

—— (2006), 'Local political participation: The impact of rules-in-use', *Public Administration*, 84:3, 539–61

McClymont, K. and P. O'Hare (2008), ' "We're not NIMBYs!" Contrasting local protest groups with idealised conceptions of sustainable communities', *Local Environment*, 13:4, 321–35

MacNeil, C. (2000), 'Surfacing the realpolitik: Democratic evaluation in an antidemocratic climate', *New Directions for Evaluation*, 2000:85, 51–62

Maisel, L. and S. Buckley (2005), *Parties and Elections in America*, Rowman & Littlefield, Lanham, MD

Manin, B. (1997), *The Principles of Representative Government*, Cambridge University Press, Cambridge

Marvick, D. (1972), 'Political recruitment and careers', in D. Sills (ed), *International Encyclopaedia of the Social Sciences*, Macmillan and Free Press, New York, pp. 273–82

Michels, A. and L. de Graaf (2010), 'Examining citizen participation: Local participatory policy making and democracy', *Local Government Studies*, 36:4, 477–91

Michels, R. (1915), *Political Parties: A Sociological Study of the Oligarchical Tendencies of Modern Democracy*, The Free Press, Glencoe, IL

Michio, M. (1997), *Local Power in the Japanese State*, University of California Press, Berkeley, CA

Mill, J. S. (1948), *On Liberty and Considerations on Representative Government*, ed. R. B. McCallum, Basil Blackwell, Oxford

Mossberger, K. and G. Stoker (2001), 'The evolution of urban regime theory, The challenges of conceptualisation', *Urban Affairs Review*, 36:6, 810–35

Mossberger, K., S. Clarke and P. John (2012), *The Oxford Handbook of Urban Politics*, Oxford University Press, Oxford

Mouritzen, P. E. and J. Svara (2002), *Leadership at the Apex: Politicians and Administrators in Western Local Government*, University of Pittsburgh, Pittsburgh, PA

National Foundation for Educational Research (NFER) (2007), National census of local authority councillors 2006, NFER, Slough

—— (2009), National census of local authority councillors 2008, NFER, Slough

—— (2011), National census of local authority councillors 2010, NFER, Slough

Newman, J., M. Barnes and H. Sullivan (2004a), 'Power, participation and political renewal: theoretical and empirical perspectives on public participation under New Labour', *Social Politics*, 11:2, 267–79

—— (2004b), 'Public participation and collaborative governance', *Journal of Social Policy*, 33:2, 203–23

Newman, J., J. Raine and C. Skelcher (2001), 'Transforming local government: Innovation and modernization', *Public Money and Management*, 21:2, 61–8

Newton, K. (1976), *Second City Politics: Democratic Processes and Decision-Making in Birmingham*, Clarendon Press, Oxford

Norris, P. and J. Lovenduski (1995), *Political Recruitment: Gender, Class and Race in the British Parliament*, Cambridge University Press, Cambridge

Office of the Deputy Prime Minister (ODPM), (2005), *Vibrant Local Leadership*, ODPM, London

Osborne, S. (1998), 'The innovative capacity of voluntary organisations: Managerial challenges for local government', *Local Government Studies*, 24:1, 19–40

Ostrogorski, M. (1902), *Democracy and the Organisation of Political Parties*, Vols I and II, Macmillan, New York

Owen, D. (1982), *The Government of Victorian London 1855–1889: The Metropolitan Board Of Works, the Vestries and the City Corporation*, Harvard University Press, New York

Page, E. (1982), 'The value of local autonomy', *Local Government Studies*, 8:4, 21–42

Page, E. and M. Goldsmith (eds) (1987), *Central and Local Government Relations. a Comparative Analysis of West European Unitary States*, Sage, London

Panebianco, A. (1988), *Political Parties: Organisation and Power*, Cambridge University Press, Cambridge

Parekh, B. (ed.) (1973), *Bentham's Political Thought*, Croom Helm, London

Parkinson, M. (ed.) (1987), *Reshaping Local Government*, Policy Journals, Hermitage, Berkshire

Pateman, C. (1970), *Participation and Democratic Theory*, Cambridge University Press, Cambridge

Patterson, S. and G. Caldeira (1983), 'Getting out the vote: Participation in gubernatorial elections', *The American Political Science Review*, 77:3, 675–89

Pattie, C., P. Seyd and P. Whiteley (2003), 'Citizenship and civic engagement: Attitudes and behaviour in Britain', *Political Studies*, 51:3, 443–68

Perri 6, D. Leat, K. Seltzer and G. Stoker (2002), *Towards Holistic Governance: The New Agenda in Government Reform*, Palgrave Macmillan, Basingstoke

Phillips, A. (1994), 'Local Democracy: The Terms of the Debate', Commission for local democracy, research report No. 2, CLD Limited, London

—— (1995), *The Politics of Presence*, Oxford University Press, Oxford

Phillips, S. (2010), 'You say you want an evolution? From citizens to community engagement in Canadian cities', in E. Brunet-Jailly and J. Martin (eds), *Local Government in a Global World, Australia and Canada in Comparative Perspective*, University of Toronto Press, Toronto, pp. 55–80

Pierre, J. (ed.) (2000), *Debating Governance: Authority, Steering and Democracy*, Oxford University Press, Oxford

Pitkin, H. (1972), *The Concept of Representation*, University of California Press, Berkeley, CA

Pluss, L. and D. Kubler (2013), 'Co-ordinating community governance? Local councillors in different governance network arrangements', in B. Egner, D. Sweeting and P.-J. Klok (eds), *Local Councillors in Europe*, Springer, Wiesbaden, pp. 203–19

Prewitt, K. (1969), 'From the many are chosen the few', *American Behavioural Scientist*, 13:2, 169–88

—— (1970), *The Recruitment of Political Leaders: A Study of Citizen-Politicians*, Bobbs-Merrill, Indianapolis

Rallings, C. and M. Thrasher (2013), *Local Elections in Britain*, Routledge, New York

Rao, N. (1993), *Managing Change: Councillors and the New Local Government*, Joseph Rowntree Foundation, York

—— (1994), *The Making and Unmaking of Local Self-Government*, Dartmouth Aldershot

—— (1998), 'Representation in local politics: A reconsideration and some new evidence', *Political Studies*, 46:1, 19–35

—— (2000), *Reviving Local Democracy: New Labour, New Politics?*, The Policy Press, Bristol

Redlich, J. and F. W. Hirst (1958), *The History of Local Government in England*, Macmillan, London

Reed, S. (1986), 'The changing fortunes of Japan's progressive governors', *Asian Survey*, 26:4, 452–65

Rees, A. and T. Smith (1964), *Town Councillors: a Study of Barking*, The Acton Society Trust, London

Reiser, M. and E. Holtmann (eds) (2008), *Farewell to the Party Model: Independent Local Lists in East and West European Countries*, VS Verlag, Wiesbaden

Reyneart, H. (2012), 'The social base of political recruitment: A comparative study of local councillors in Europe', *Lex Localis*, 10:1, 19–36

Reynaert, H., K. Steyvers, P. Delwit and J. B. Pilet (eds) (2005), *Revolution or Renovation? Reforming Local Politics in Europe*, Vanden Broele, Bruges

——(2009), *Local Political Leadership in Europe: Town Chief, City Boss or Loco President?* Vanden Broele, Bruges

Rhodes, R. (1996), 'The new governance: Governing without government', *Political Studies*, 44:4, 652–67

——(1997), *Understanding Governance: Policy Networks, Governance, Reflexivity and Accountability*, Open University Press, Maidenhead

Rhodes, R. and P. 't Hart (eds) (2014), *The Oxford Handbook of Political Leadership*, Oxford University Press, Oxford

Robinson Committee (1977), *Report on the remuneration of councillors*, Cmnd 7010, HMSO, London

Saward, M. (2003), *Democracy*, Polity Press, Cambridge

Schaap, L., H. Daemen and A. Ringeling (2009), 'Mayors in seven European countries, Part II: Performance and analysis', *Local Government Studies*, 35:2, 235–51

Schlesinger, J. (1991), *Political Parties and the Winning of Office*, University of Michigan, Ann Arbor, MI.

Selinger, E. and K. Whyte (2011), 'Is there a right way to nudge? The practice and ethics of choice', *Architecture Sociology Compass*, 5:10, 923–35

Sharpe, L. J. (1970), 'Theories and values of local government', *Political Studies*, 18:2, 153–74

Skelcher, C. (2005), 'Jurisdictional integrity, polycentrism, and the design of demo-cratic governance', *Governance*, 18:1, 89–110

Somerville, P. and N. Haines (2008), 'Prospects for local co-governance', *Local Government Studies*, 34:1, 61–79

Sorensen, E. (2006), 'Metagovernance: The changing role of politicians in processes of democratic governance', *The American Review of Public Administration*, 36:1, 98–114

Sorensen, E. and J. Torfing (2005), 'Network governance and post-liberal democracy', *Administrative Theory and Praxis*, 27:2, 197–237

—— (2007), 'Governance network research: Towards a second generation', in E. Sorensen and J. Torfing (eds), *Theories of Democratic Network Governance*, Palgrave Macmillan, Basingstoke, pp. 1–21

—— (2009), 'Making governance networks effective and democratic through metago-vernance', *Public Administration*, 87:2, 234–58

—— (2014), 'Assessing the democratic anchorage of governance networks', in S. Griggs, A. Norval and H. Wagenaar (eds), *Practices of Freedom: Decentred Governance, Conflict and Democratic Participation*, Cambridge University Press, Cambridge, pp. 108–36

Stewart, J. (1992), 'The internal management of local authorities in Britain: The chal-lenge of experience in other countries', *Local Government Studies*, 18:1, 5–17

Steyvers, K. and T. Verhelst (2012a), 'Between layman and professional? Political recruitment and career development of local councillors in a comparative per-spective', *Lex Localis*, 10:1, 1–17

—— (2012b), 'Path dependency: Do councillors recruitment and career development matter?', *Lex Localis*, 10:1, 85–110

Stoker, G. (2004), *Transforming Local Governance: From Thatcherism to New Labour*, Palgrave, Basingstoke

—— (2006), 'Explaining political disenchantment: Finding pathways to democratic renewal', *Political Quarterly*, 77:2, 184–94

—— (2011), 'Was local governance such a good idea? A global comparative perspec-tive', *Public Administration*, 89:1, 15–31

Stoker, G., F. Gains, P. John, N. Rao and A. Harding (2003), *Implementing the 2000 Act with respect to new council constitutions and the ethical framework*, First report of the ELG Team, ODPM, London

Stone, C. (1989), *Regime Politics: Governing Atlanta 1946–1988*, Lawrence University Press, Kansas

—— (1993), 'Urban regimes and the capacity to govern: A political economy approach', *Journal of Urban Affairs*, 15:1, 1–28

—— (1995), 'Political leadership in urban politics', in D. Judge, G. Stoker and H. Wolman (eds), *Theories of Urban Politics*, Sage, London, pp. 96–116

Stroud, N. (2008), 'Media use and political predispositions: Revisiting the concept of selective exposure', *Political Behaviour*, 30:3, 341–66

Svara, J. (1987), 'Mayoral leadership in council-manager cities: Preconditions versus preconceptions', *The Journal of Politics*, 49:1, 207–27

Sweeting, D. and C. Copus (2012), 'Whatever happened to local democracy?', *Policy and Politics*, 40:1, 21–38

—— (2013), 'Councillors, participation and local democracy', *Urban and Regional Research International*, 14:1, 121–37

Taafe, P. and T. Mulhearn (1988), *Liverpool: A City that Dared to Fight*, Fortress, London

The Stationery Office (TSO) (2008), *Communities in Control: Real People, Real Power*, TSO, London

——(2011), *Open Public Services*, Cm 8145, TSO, London

——(2013a), *Government response to the House of Commons, Communities and Local Government Select Committee Report: Councillors on the frontline*, Cm 8582, TSO, London

——(2013b), *Government response to the House of Commons Political and Constitutional Reform Committee Report: The prospects for codifying the relationship between central and local government*, Cm 8623, TSO London

Thoenig, J.-C. (2011), 'Institutional theories and public institutions: New agendas and appropriateness', in B. G. Peters and J. Pierre (eds), *The Handbook of Public Administration*, pp. 169–79, Sage, London

Torfing, J., E. Sorensen and T. Fotel (2009), 'Democratic anchorage of infrastructural governance networks: The case of the Femern Belt forum', *Planning Theory*, 8:3, 282–308

Toulmin Smith, J. (2005), *Local Self-Government and Centralisation: The Characteristics of Each; and Its Practical Tendencies, as Affecting Social, Moral and Political Welfare and Progress, Including Comprehensive Outlines of the English Constitution*, Elibron Classics Series, London

Van Liefferinge, H. and K. Steyvers (2008), 'Family matters? Degrees of family politicisation in political recruitment and career start of mayors in Belgium', *Acta Politica*, 44:2, 125–49

Verhelst, T. and E. Kerrouche (2012), 'Family, ambition, locality and party: A study of professionalisation in the activation and apprenticeship of local councillors in Europe', *Lex Localis*, 10:1, 37–62

Verhelst, T., H. Reyneart and K. Steyvers (2013), 'Political recruitment and career development of local councillors in Europe', in B. Egner, D. Sweeting and P.-J. Klok (eds), *Local Councillors in Europe*, Springer, Wiesbaden, pp. 27–49

Wayman, F. W. and P. F. Diehl (eds) (1994), *Reconstructing Realpolitik*, University of Michigan Press, Michigan

Webb, B. and S. Webb (1920), *A Constitution for the Socialist Commonwealth of Great Britain*, Longmans, Green & Co, London

Williams, M. (1989), 'Rousseau, realism and realpolitik', *Millennium - Journal of International Studies*, 18, 185–203

Wilson, D. (1999), 'Exploring the limits of public participation in local government', *Parliamentary Affairs*, 52:2, 246–59

Wilson, D. and C. Game (2011), *Local Government in the United Kingdom*, Palgrave Macmillan, Basingstoke

Wollmann, W. and K. Thurmaier (2012), 'Reforming local government institutions and the new public management', in K. Mossberger, S. Clarke and P. John (eds), *The Oxford Handbook of Urban Politics*, Oxford University Press, Oxford, pp. 179–209

Young, K. and M. Davies (1990), *The Politics of Local Government Since Widdicombe*, Joseph Rowntree Foundation, York

Young, K. and N. Rao (1994), *Coming to Terms with Change: the Local Government Councillor in 1993*, Joseph Rowntree Foundation, York

—— (1995), 'Faith in local democracy', in J. Curtice, R. Jowell, L. Brook and A. Park (eds), *British Social Attitudes: The Twelfth Report*, Dartmouth, Aldershot, pp. 91–117

—— (1997), *Local Government Since 1945*, Blackwell, Oxford

Zillmann, D. and J. Bryant (2008), *Selective Exposure to Communication*, Routledge, London

Index

EU authorised representative for GPSR:
Easy Access System Europe, Mustamäe tee 50,
10621 Tallinn, Estonia
gpsr.requests@easproject.com

www.ingramcontent.com/pod-product-compliance
Lightning Source LLC
Chambersburg PA
CBHW052006270326
41929CB00015B/2805